BOOKS BY RENATA ADLER

*A Year in the Dark: Journal of a Film Critic, 1968–69*
*Toward a Radical Middle: Fourteen Pieces*
    *of Reporting and Criticism*

# TOWARD A RADICAL MIDDLE

*Fourteen Pieces of Reporting and Criticism*

# TOWARD A RADICAL MIDDLE

*Fourteen Pieces of Reporting and Criticism*

by RENATA ADLER

RANDOM HOUSE | *New York*

First Printing

9 8 7 6 5 4 3 2

Library of Congress Catalog Card Number: 74–85574

Grateful acknowledgment is extended to the following
publishers of songs quoted in "The New Sound, Circa
1964":
pp. 79–80: Sea of Tunes Publishing Company, Inc.:
"Shut Down."
p. 81: Edward B. Marks Music Corporation: "Tell Laura
I Love Her," words and music by Jeff Barry and Ben
Raleigh. Copyright © 1960 by Edward B. Marks Music
Corporation.
p. 81: Acuff-Rose Publications, Inc.: "Teen Angel," by
Red and Jean Surrey. Copyright © 1959 by Acuff-Rose
Publications, Inc.
p. 81: Lois Music Co.: "Last Kiss."
p. 82: Favorite Music Co. Ltd.: "Terry." Copyright ©
1964 by Favorite Music Co. Ltd.
pp. 82–83: January Music Corporation: "Mecca." Copy-
right © 1963 by January Music Corporation. International Rights Reserved.
p. 83: Screen Gems-Columbia Music, Inc.: "Uptown."
p. 84: Saturday Music, Inc.: "Bye Bye Baby" (Baby
Goodbye), words and music by Bob Crewe and Bob
Gaudio. Copyright © 1964 by Saturday Music, Inc., and
Seasons' Four Music Corp.
p. 84: Leeds Music Corporation and Welbeck Music
Ltd., London: "Downtown," by Tony Hatch. Copyright
MCMLXIV by Welbeck Music Ltd., London, England,
Music Corporation of America (Leeds Music division).
p. 85: Nom Music, Inc.: "Easier Said Than Done," by
William Linton and Larry Huff.
p. 85: Trio Music Company, Inc.: "Maybe I Know."
p. 85: S. & J. Music Publishing Corp.: "Whenever a
Teenager Cries," by Ernie Maresca.

All the articles in this book appeared originally in *The New Yorker*.

Manufactured in the United States of America by H. Wolff Book Mfg. Co.

Designed by Vincent Torre

For William Shawn

# Contents

# Introduction

In May, 1969, as I was watching *Another World,* Lee Randolph died. I had bought my television set more than two years before, after going to California to do a piece about the Sunset Strip. Buying the set had nothing to do with the piece at all, or any piece. But on assignment, in the sunny upper rooms of the Chateau Marmont in Los Angeles, I had had a case of laryngitis so extreme that I couldn't speak, even whisper on the telephone, and when I was not following the flower children of the Strip about, I stayed in my room watching daytime television—the soap operas, and when they were not on, the quiz programs. I became seriously preoccupied by them. The NBC peacock, with the announcement "the following program is brought to you in living color," was frustrating, even reproachful on a hotel room's black and white. When I got home, I bought a color set, my first TV, a Zenith Space Command with remote control, which I could operate from my bed.

For two and a half years—until now, in fact—I watched *Another World, The Doctors, Love of Life, Search for Tomorrow, Days of Our Lives,* and later *Hidden Faces* (I have never cared for *Secret Storm* or *Edge of Night*) whenever I could, and nearly always when I thought I should be doing other things. They had their tired stretches. I missed some crucial episodes. But when Lee Randolph died, a suicide who had lingered on for weeks, I watched her face being covered by a sheet, and I was ridden by the event for weeks. I suppose the script for Lee had run out, or that the actress had found another part. But it was not at all like losing a character in fiction of any other kind—not just an event in a two or ten hour imaginative experience, and then in memory. The soap operas ran along beside life five days out of seven. I saw the characters in them more often than my friends, knew their relationships, the towns. It had a continuity stronger even than the news, where stories and characters submerge and reappear—or don't—depending on where the limelight is. I know of no more constant, undisjunct narrative than the soap operas. Perhaps they are what personal life was like, before the violent, flash discontinuities of media news and personal air travel came along.

I had thought of my soap hours as a total waste of time, not a joke, not camp, not for a piece, not critically, a serious waste of time. But when the loss of Lee became such an important thing, I found that those two-and-a-half-year, open-ended narrative experiences define a lot of what I am and what I think, what I would like to write, what I think America, particularly a certain age and voice group, is, and what I think the American radical and intellectual communities are not. I guess I am part of an age group that, through being skipped, through never having had a generational voice, was forced into the broadest possible America. Even now (and we are in our thirties), we have no journals we publish, no exile we share, no brawls, no anecdotes, no war, no solidarity, no mark. In college, under Eisenhower, we were known for nothing, or for our apathy. A center of action seemed to have broken down in us. Lacking precisely the generational tie (through the media, mainly, kids now know about other kids) and just after the family unit began to dissolve, we knew what there was of our alienation privately, and not yet as a claim or a group experience. We now have vertical ties, loves, friendships, loyalties to people older, younger, other than ourselves. We are unnoticed even as we spread clear across what people call, without taking account of us, the generation gap.

I think that is our special note—we cut across. Across ages, idioms, stresses, cultural values, memories. At a moment of polarization, and other clichés that drain the language of meaning, the continuity of the American story seems to rest just now in us. The first age group to experience in its youth a murderous overvalue on precocity (which leads now to an idiot generational impasse), we held back. We grew up separately, without a rhetoric, drawing our ideas from age and cultural groups already formed, as we were not. The idiom of *Another World* is no more foreign to us than *The Green Hornet,* Joseph Conrad, *The New York Review of Books,* bourbon no more or less our own than marijuana is. Unaware of each other until now, we are in it all. Some of us have dropped a generation back, to lead a student movement that belies everything we are. Others have taken their positions quietly, in society as it was before we came and as, in the years of its most annihilating smugness, it nearly killed us off. But most of us, I think, were formed and remain one by one—formed by books and by the media, but, through the accident of our span of history, formed alone. And now I think we are a force.

In a way, in culture and in politics, we are the last custodians of language—because of the books we read and because history, in our time, has wrung so many changes on the meaning of terms and we, having never generationally perpetrated anything, have no commitment to any distortion of them. Lacking slogans, we still have the private ear for distinctions, for words. I happen to know no one who regularly watches *Another World* (although millions of Americans clearly do), or who would watch it—except to do a piece on materialism, escapism, pop culture or something. But that is the point. I know of no one whose cultural and political experience I completely share. And yet there are elements of my soap hours that seem common to a particular, still unaccounted-for sort of activist in early middle years: on the set, a sense of the human condition and the rhythm of life, with endless recapitulations for those who have not been watch-

ing, going forward; in ourselves, the bouts of muteness, watching
and inertia, the sense of work one ought to do in what is going
on, the patience with continuity, even the nostalgia for a kind
of corniness. And always a characteristic quality of attention, at
a certain humorous remove from our own experience. Lacking
an idiom entirely our own, we cannot adopt any single voice
without a note of irony. (I can't write about the soap operas, or
anything that does not make specific, human claims for action
on my part, with perfect seriousness.) A suspicion of glibness or
fluency has made the generation immediately after us value the
rhetorical and inarticulate. Not us. We all seem to view the
world still in words, as writers, arguers, archivists—even, perhaps even especially, those who do not write. In strange times,
we have kept our language, energies and heads. (It is no surprise that the disturbances at San Francisco State dissolved under police called in by one—albeit aging and not very profound
—semanticist.) And we are here.

I think the historical bridge and the moral limits of our experience—mine anyway—were defined in World War II, which
most of us still remember as The War. Totalitarianism, freedom,
genocide, courage, passion, gentleness, a community of decent
men, most of my conceptions of idealism, the monstrous and the
public world date from that war, in which we were too young to
have a part. And the bland repressions and unacknowledged dis-
illusion of the succeeding years. Everyone looked alike or tried
to, every sort of maverick was cut off and lost. Art was the prov-
ince of ladies' painting and lecture clubs; intelligence was sub-
sumed in the grand idea of American know how. The schools
were levellers for the general mediocrity; unions, parodying their
origins and aims, were becoming entrenched forces for corruption and reaction. Odd cliffs were papered over. When, on his
birthday in 1956, Adam Clayton Powell announced his support
for Dwight David Eisenhower for president, the Republican
candidate sent a birthday present to the people of Harlem—
white trucks full of black cupcakes—and the present was gra-
ciously received. The dream everywhere was going flat. Teachers, who had begun in the Depression when, on the basis of their
regular salaries, they could afford maids and were considered
rich, were now poorer, embittered and threatened by any sort of
difference. In small towns, in a travesty of the New Deal dream

of education, teachers had risen above their own class to the extent that their brothers and their colleagues' brothers—contractors and factory workers—were no longer good enough for them. They seldom married. They subscribed to the Book of the Month Club and *Reader's Digest* and shared the general passion for the ordinary. Our rebellions then, in the years when the sum of hope was to be adjusted and popular, when boys still broke themselves at team sports on a military model, which would never be of use to them again (when, in fact, people still spoke of the Army for anybody as making a man of him), were separate and one by one, and threw us back, unknowing, on the past. Some of us cut school and invented juvenile delinquency, others read.

What I am trying to say is that if there is any age group that should loathe what is called the System in its bones that group is us. We had it, in spite of Korea, at its height—the years when society was going, to its own satisfaction, so extremely well; when telephones, neon signs, subways, Western Union worked, as they haven't since; and when, through and after Senator Joseph McCarthy, the spirit of the redneck, the junior college and the drum majorette had spread so deep into the land. I think the first post-war jolt the System had in its complacency, in our time, was not social or humanitarian, but technological: in 1957, when Sputnik went up. After that, there began to be a little room for change and mavericks, who, when there is not a desperate community lie at the heart of things, are the rule. But in the interim, before the general boredom had begun to lift, we, one by one, had made some beginnings, some progress on all the public and private fronts that now exist—frontiers that polarization, paradoxically, obscures and language has to be hard won and individual to approach at all.

Accessible, almost by generational default, to all the idioms of America, we also went overseas. We were the first non-military age group to travel internationally on an almost national scale. We knew, since we had been at the mercy of institutions so utterly, what institutions were like at home, and what American tourists were like, and were treated like, abroad. But there is a particular totalitarian lie at the heart of political cliché too, and the simplicities of "imperialism," "genocide," "materialism," "police brutality," "military-industrial complex," "racism," tossed about as though they were interchangeable, and as though they applied equally to anything with which one is out of temper, are not for us. Neither are the simplicities of anti-Communism, free world, "violence," and "radicalism" itself. We observed in The War the literal extreme of violence that men have done so far. Since then, bombs dropping on villages, cops beating kids on the head, kids throwing bottles at cops, the violence to the spirit of the McCarthy years, the violation of human dignity in exclusion and poverty—there is a degree of violence in them all, but a difference of degree, an extent of metaphor, and we still distinguish among literalisms, metaphors, questions of degree. Or radicalism. A radicalism that draws its terms from the System's violence in Vietnam, then claims to be driven to revolutionary violence of its own, and, as an act of revolution, turns upon the liberal universities has an inauthentic ring, a ring of sublimation, theater. If revolutionary outrage over Vietnam had had a substantive thrust of Guevara courage on the line, there would have been American brigades fighting for Hanoi—a disaster for the country, surely, but a disaster in authentic terms. (The white revolutionary movement certainly left the American South, where the physical risk was high, fast enough.) There is an authentic radicalism in this country now, but it does not abuse the metaphor of revolution. It is not the radicalism of rhetoric, theater, mannerism, psychodrama, air. And it is not paralyzed in its own unconsummated moral impulses by viewing every human problem at a single level of atrocity.

I think what has muddled terms, what has emptied vocabularies into rhetorics and made generations out of what are only persons after all, is, in the end, a major implication of The War. Ours was the first age group to experience the end of the Just War as a romantic possibility. There are no justifications for group violence in this country any more—no outlets for aggressive physical courage, irrational fervors, the fraternity of the barricades and the decent human war. And there aren't likely to be any. Technology has made the stakes too high. We knew that separately, saw the last great romantic group fight to the death, and knew we could never have one of our own. That sounds like a blessing, and perhaps historically it is, but it puts a tremendous strain on any generation of young. From now on, it is all patient effort, unsimple victories. In this, the Vietnam War was a hiatus in moral terms. The System lifted the vocabulary of the just war, in the name of the free world, to Vietnam, and found it did not work. Radicalism lifted essentially the same vocabulary and turned it, in the name of revolution, against the System, where it does not work either. The very fact that radicalism leans so comfortably, half-consciously, upon the System and its laws, goes on almost risk-free, beside *Another World*, confirms that the System's thrust is still, on an unprecedented scale, democratic and benign. No famous or privileged white revolutionaries have gone to jail for long just yet. But obscure and black radicals have, in numbers—which raises questions, I think, not so much of politics as of fame, privilege and the in-authentic revolutionary.

What these pieces, looking back, are about, if anything, is true radicalism as opposed to what I would call the mere men-tality of the apocalypse. The apocalyptic vision has never been true to the America we know. By some accident of our size, our mix, our resources and the perfectibility of our laws, brinks van-ish here and become frontiers, immense real tensions are resolved in a paradigm of the modern world, material resources make it possible to pose moral and social questions which have never been approached on such a scale before. I think that is where we are—we who have lived from The War till now—not too old or tired to give the whole thing up, not too young to remember a time when things were worse. And, through the accident of our span of years, not too simple in the quality of our experience to know that things get better (The War's end) and worse (the succeeding years) and better again (the great movement of non-violence sweeping out of the South to move the country briefly forward a bit) and, of course, worse. But when a term like vio-lence undergoes, in less than thirty years, a declension from Au-schwitz to the Democratic convention in Chicago, from A-bomb-ing even to napalm, the System has improved. Terribly and with stumbling, but improved. And there are characters in these pieces —mocked for their tokenism when they succeeded, claimed as radical martyrs when they failed or died—who burned them-selves out over an inch of that improvement. Which is how the human condition, in its historical continuity, or real radicalism, in its social framework, works at all.

But with the closing of The War option, with the loss of final and romantic victories, there is a tendency, particularly among

intellectuals and the young, and oddly accelerated by an obscene confluence of psychoanalysis and the media, to think in
terms of final solutions anyway. To use the vocabulary of total
violence, with less and less consciousness of its ingredient of
metaphor, to cultivate scorched earth madness as a form of
consciousness (of courage, even), to call history mad, and to
dismiss every growing, improving human enterprise as a form
of tokenism, an irrelevance in which one has no obligation to
take part. The System drew back from its apocalypse in Vietnam
—always draws backs from brinks so far—restrained, in spite of
everything, the full force of its technology. But the scorched
earth psychology remains, particularly on the Left. I happened
to encounter that psychology, long before Vietnam, first in the
arts, when I was reviewing books. The professional alienist in
fiction, the group polemicist in criticism, the unearned nihilist
and overeasy breakthrough artist in mixed media, the blown
mind vanguardist in the audience. Then (except for a few reviews of what I considered genuine, private innovators: "Conversations," "Instruments") I found I was doing a lot of overeasy
polemic of my own, and I gave it up—except for one last piece
on the breakthrough artists: "Selling an Enraged Bread Pudding."
  Reporting was better, but somehow the apocalyptic sensibility had moved into politics too, into every part of life. Its earmarks were clenched teeth, personal agonies, rhetoric, the single
plane of atrocity view of Western man, above all, a psychoanalytic concept of moral responsibility—based, not on conscience, which is exercised in substantive action, but on guilt,
which is appeased in confession, sublimation, symbolic purge.
Confessions were everywhere. The guilt became retroactive, vi-
carious, unappeasable: a country, incurably genocidal, and
founded on a genocide; white Western man, blood insatiable,
leaving nothing but war, exploitation and pollution in his wake.
No matter that none of us (and few of our isolated, refugee
fathers either) were here a hundred years ago to kill an Indian,
that countless nations—India, for one—were founded by inva-
sions that exterminated aborigines, that there have always been
wars, within the limits of available technology, wherever man
is (notably tribal slaughters in Africa, and in Vietnam ever since
the Annamites), that Western powers have been the first to try

to come to terms with an international responsibility for social, medical meliorism and military restraint. (With, of course, grotesque lapses. The question is whose mistakes there is time to be patient with.) Guilt, atrocity, the luxurious mystique of the everybody else, which liberates from responsibility for one's own time and place. There was a special radical infatuation with religions of the Orient, notably Hinduism and Zen—which produced, as it happens, some of the most repellent, anti-humanist, repressive and belligerent social systems in man's history. A let-them-starve-on-earth-Nirvana sensibility caught on among a Third-World-infatuated contingent of radicals.

There was nothing to show for the apocalyptic sensibility on any front—not in art, not in politics, not in mind expansion (a ghastly misnomer), not even in the apocalyptic-pornographic view of sex—no breakthroughs, only gesture, celebrity quietism, rage, symptom, backlash. Not Rimbaud and Baudelaire, child mutations of John Dewey and Freud. Symptoms do have their real effects on the status quo (even *Another World* has its impact on the world out here), but the effects were mindless, random, dumb, a non-negotiable demand to dismantle the human experiment and begin again. A view of evil as banal was distorted into a view of banality as evil, and of all meliorism as boring and banal. Intellectual cartwheels, bad art, spite politics (I gave up reporting that after "Radicalism in Debacle" at the Palmer House), and a happy collusion, by default, with the worst elements of the System: pure huckster fashion and the redneck Right. (It is not unthinkable that, except for the broader evolution of America, we should all be called one day before an investigating committee composed of Strom Thurmond, Tom Hayden and some suitable representative of pop art and café society.) And fame: the cry of alienation made good fellows and good copy. The gesture and rhetoric of revolution were well suited to that natural creator of discontinuous, lunatic constituencies, the media.

I think radicalism's flirtation with the media, its overvalue on personal image, personal sensibility, pure air, was nurtured by the spirit of the Kennedys. Their beauty, promise, absolute lack of delivery, and their power—a power which found its major application, in the end, only in controlling the image that the country was to have of them. I don't mean anything about the sincerity of the men themselves; I mean what they came to represent. The notion that you can love glamour and be concerned with grit, that you can promise in prose and never quite deliver in fact, that as long as power is wrested into the right hands (one's own) good will follow in time, the gap between image and substance, impulse and legislation—the country was simultaneously overstimulated and corrupted by these princelings of the air. Working for Senator Joseph McCarthy, silent in the censure vote, wiretapping, Mayor Daley, segregationist judges in the South, the logic of the Bay of Pigs and Vietnam (if Cuban exiles couldn't do it, American counterinsurgents could: win an easy, a "little war"), losing cufflinks simultaneously to blacks with hopes and white auto workers armed against the possibility that a black should ever live in peace beside them—none of it fit. It generated unreason and violence. All these disparities could be considered part of a personal process of education, or seem to be reconciled on some higher symbolic plane, but they were not true to the country, to the real balance and struggle of huge forces that is here. President Johnson, I think, delivered substantively on all that promise: the social legislation and, alas, the war. But Kennedyism, cut off en route, stayed in the air, style, media power, personal packaging. Suddenly there were too many stars, too many artists, too many who thought the world well lost for their own image and sensibilities. The new enemy was boredom, in the sense of lack of drama. The new currency was fame. With special implications for the intellectuals. Ours has not been a great thirty years for intellectuals. We saw, and survived, anti-intellectualism in this country, but we also saw a generation of intellectuals—Stalinist at the time of Stalin, quiescent in the McCarthy years, mesmerized by the power and beauty of the Kennedys, nerveless in the face of the radical redneck young—always weak, always somehow lifeless and wavering in the face of force and violence. But through it all, we saw something infinitely fragile and viable in the System, in its accommodations with radicals, rednecks, soldiers, blacks, thinkers, visionaries, lunatics, the ordinary, getting better.

I guess a radical middle, in age and in politics, acts out of a consciousness of how much has been gained, how far there is to go, and what there is to lose. It is content to be obscure—to measure and implement accommodations with the System: how many blacks and former poor in jobs, unions, polling booths, public office, neighborhoods, even in soap operas, how many soldiers withdrawn, how many arms unmade, how many material, aesthetic and technological advances applied to ameliorating the human condition, how to divorce liberalism from arrogance and violence. Not many advances, but some. Enough to stay aboard and to maintain distinctions on every side: to get the unpolarized student to his class without having him clubbed or teargassed by a cop—who is not too good at making distinctions either.

We have lived after all through two sunny periods of lies, and seen some of the truth in both of them: the Eisenhower lie that the noble American experiment was complete, that all was well, that there was no need to move; and the Kennedy era lie that with glamour, image and the instantaneous application of power you can gratify immediately, totally, those human concerns that are, in reality, met by inches, by years of work and suffering. I believe that the generation gap is in part an almost meteorological collision of those airs, the two lies of those years. Some have moved and see no reason why anyone else should rock the boat: others, impatient with the slowness of motion, see no reason to move at all until the coming of the Word. We are between. Our heroes, I suppose, mine anyway, are both famous and obscure: Martin Luther King, Bob Moses, Charles Evers, Alvin Poussaint of the Medical Committee on Human Rights, John Doar, others. Our thinkers—Hannah Arendt, Richard Rovere, Bayard Rustin, Harold Rosenberg, Daniel P. Moynihan, others—write from an awareness of precedent, of what has already been said and done and what can still be said and done, without mixing artistic and political metaphor. (Everything that has been said has, after all, been said many times.) In this collection, even in the dated or term-paper influenced pieces, there ought to be a sense of tendency, despite a suspicion of groups, of that emergent "we." We are not in the world for therapy. We are non-violent. Our values are corny ones, reason, decency, prosperity, human dignity, contact, the finest, broadest possible America. Some of us have despaired and, in the only indisputably sincere expression of the apocalyptic vision, immolated themselves. But somewhere there is a reconciliation of that auto worker and that black, not on a symbolic plane, but because history is irreversible and there is a real common interest in the rich, mixed quality of life. And three of us have just come back (substantively and yet with drama), from the way to perhaps other populations, outer limits, from the moon.

RENATA ADLER

July, 1969

# TOWARD A RADICAL MIDDLE

*Fourteen Pieces of Reporting and Criticism*

# The March for Non-Violence from Selma

THE THIRTY THOUSAND PEOPLE who at one point or another took part in this week's march from the Brown Chapel African Methodist Episcopal Church in Selma, Alabama, to the statehouse in Montgomery were giving highly dramatic expression to a principle that could be articulated only in the vaguest terms. They were a varied lot: local Negroes, Northern clergymen, members of labour unions, delegates from state and city governments, entertainers, mothers pushing baby carriages, members of civil-rights groups more or less at odds with one another, isolated, shaggy marchers with an air of simple vagrancy, doctors, lawyers, teachers, children, college students, and a preponderance of what one marcher described as "ordinary, garden-variety civilians from just about everywhere." They were insulated in front by soldiers and television camera crews, overhead and underfoot by helicopters and

Army demolition teams, at the sides and rear by more members of the press and military, and over all by agents of the F.B.I. Most of them were aware that protection along a route of more than fifty miles of hostile country could not be absolute (on the night before the march, a student who had come here from Boston University was slashed across the cheek with a razor blade), yet few of the thirty-two hundred marchers who set out on Sunday morning seemed to have a strong consciousness of risk. They did not have a sharply defined sense of purpose, either. President Johnson's speech about voting rights and Judge Johnson's granting of permission for the march to take place had made the march itself ceremonial—almost redundant. The immediate aims of the abortive earlier marches had been realized: the national conscience had been aroused and federal intervention had been secured. In a sense, the government of Alabama was now in rebellion, and the marchers, with the sanction and protection of the federal government, were demonstrating against a rebellious state. It was unclear what such a demonstration could hope to achieve. Few segregationists could be converted by it, the national commitment to civil rights would hardly be increased by it, there was certainly an element of danger in it, and for the local citizenry it might have a long and ugly aftermath. The marchers, who had five days and four nights in which to talk, tended for the most part to avoid discussions of principle, apparently in the hope that their good will, their sense of solidarity, and the sheer pageantry of the occasion would resolve matters at some symbolic level and yield a clear statement of practical purpose before the march came to an end.

From this point of view, the first few hours of Sunday morning in Selma were far from satisfying. Broad Street, the town's main thoroughfare, was deserted and indifferent. At the Negro First Baptist Church, on the corner of Sylvan Street and Jefferson Davis Avenue, denim-clad veterans of earlier marches stood wearily aloof from recruits, who ate watery scrambled eggs, drank watery coffee, and simply milled about. On Sylvan Street itself, an unpaved red sand road dividing identical rows of brick houses known as the George Washington Carver Development, crowds were gathering, some facing the entrance to the Brown Chapel Church, others on the steps of the church facing out. Inside the church, more people were milling, while a few tried to sleep on benches or on the floor. For several hours, nothing happened. The church service that was to begin the march was scheduled to take place at ten o'clock, but veterans advised newcomers—in the first of several bitter, self-mocking jokes that became current on the Selma-Montgomery road—that this was C.P.T., Colored People Time, and the service actually began more than an hour behind schedule.

In a field behind the housing development, the Reverend Andrew Young, executive director of Dr. Martin Luther King's Southern Christian Leadership Conference (S.C.L.C., referred to by some of the marchers as Slick), which sponsored the march, was giving marshals and night security guards last-minute instructions in the tactics of non-violence. "Keep women and children in the middle," he said. "If there's a shot, stand up and make the others kneel down. Don't be lagging around, or you're going to get hurt. Don't rely on the troopers, either. If you're beaten on, crouch and put your hands over the back of your head. Don't put up your arm to ward off a blow. If you fall, fall right down and look dead. Get to know the people in your unit, so you can tell if somebody's missing or if there's somebody there who shouldn't be there. And listen! If you can't be non-violent, let me know now." A young man in the standard denim overalls of the Student Nonviolent Coordinating Committee (S.N.C.C., otherwise known as Snick) murmured, "Man, you've got it all so *structured*. There seems to be a certain anxiety here about *structure*." Everyone laughed, a bit nervously, and the marshals went to the front of the church.

The crowd there was growing, still arrayed in two lines, one facing in, the other facing out. There were National Guardsmen and local policemen, on foot and in jeeps and cars, along the sides of Sylvan Street and around its corners, at Jefferson Davis and Alabama Avenues. The marchers themselves appeared to have dressed for all kinds of weather and occasions—in denims, cassocks, tweed coats, ponchos, boots, sneakers, Shetland sweaters, silk dresses, college sweat shirts, sports shirts, khaki slacks, fur-collared coats, pea jackets, and trenchcoats. As they waited, they sang innumerable, increasingly dispirited choruses of "We Shall Overcome," "Ain't Gonna Let Nobody Turn Me 'Round," and other songs of the movement. There was a moment of excitement when Dr. King and other speakers assembled on the steps, but a succession of long, rhetorical, and, to a certain extent (when press helicopters buzzed too low or when the microphone went dead), inaudible speeches put a damper on that too. An enthusiastic lady, of a sort that often afflicts banquets and church suppers, sang several hymns of many stanzas, with little melody and much vibrato. Exhaust fumes from a television truck parked to the right of the steps began to choke some of the marchers, and they walked away, coughing. Speakers praised one another extravagantly in monotonous political-convention cadences ("the man who . . ."). An irreverent, irritated voice with a Bronx accent shouted, "Would you mind please talking a little louder." Several members of the crowd sat down in the street, and the march assumed the first of its many moods—that of tedium.

Then Dr. King began to speak, and suddenly, for no apparent reason, several Army jeeps drove straight through the center of the crowd. ("Didn't realize we were interrupting," said one of the drivers, smiling. He had a D.D., for Dixie Division, emblem on his uniform.) The startled crowd, divided in half for a moment, became aware of its size. Dr. King's speech came to an end, and there was a last, unified, and loud rendition of "We Shall Overcome." Then the marshals quickly arranged the crowd in columns, six abreast—women and children in the middle— and the procession set out down Sylvan Street. It was about one o'clock. On Alabama Avenue, the marchers turned right, passing lines of silent white citizens on the sidewalks. On Broad Street, which is also U.S. Route 80 to Montgomery, they turned left, and as segregationist loudspeakers along the way blared "Bye, Bye, Blackbird" and the white onlookers began to jeer, the marchers approached and crossed the Edmund Pettus Bridge. And the march entered another mood—jubilation.

The day was sunny and cool. The flat road, an amalgam of asphalt and the local sand, looked pink. The people in the line linked arms, and the procession was long enough to permit the marchers to sing five different civil-rights songs simultaneously without confusion; the vanguard could not hear what the rear guard was singing. Occasionally, various leaders of the movement broke out of the line to join interviewers from the television networks, which took turns using a camera truck that preceded the line of march. For the first few miles, the highway was flanked by billboards ("Keep Selma Beautiful, Cover It with Dodge"), smaller signs (Rotary, Kiwanis, Lions, Citizens Council), diners, and gas stations. Little clusters of white onlookers appeared at various points along the road, some shouting threats and insults, others silently waving Confederate flags, and still others taking pictures of the marchers, presumably as a warning that their faces would not be forgotten when the march was over. The procession filled the two left lanes of the four-lane highway, but in the two right lanes traffic was proceeding almost normally. A black Volkswagen passed the marchers several times; on its doors and fenders were signs, lettered in whitewash: "MARTIN LUTHER KINK," "WALK, COON," "COONESVILLE, U.S.A.," and "RENT YOUR PRIEST SUIT HERE." Several small children at the roadside waved toy rifles and popguns and chanted "Nigger lover!" "White nigger!" "Half-breed!" and other epithets. A man in front of a roadside diner thumbed his nose for the entire twenty minutes it took the procession to pass him, and a well-dressed matron briefly stopped her Chrysler, got out, stuck out her tongue, climbed in again, slammed the door, and drove off.

Several times, the march came to an abrupt halt, and in the middle ranks and the rear guard there were murmurs of alarm. Then it became clear that these were only rest stops, and the marchers relaxed and resumed their singing. Rented trucks, driven by ministers of the San Francisco Theological Seminary, carried portable toilets up and down the line. When press photographers attempted to take pictures of civil-rights leaders entering the men's rooms, the Reverend Mr. Young shouted, "Can't a man even go to the john in peace?" The photographers moved away. Three tired marchers rode a short distance on the water truck, and James Forman, the executive secretary of S.N.C.C., who was being interviewed in French for Canadian television, broke off his interview to mutter as the truck passed, "Hey, man, you cats could walk." The marchers got down from the truck at once. Forman resumed his interview. "I think he's having trouble with his French," said one of the marchers. "He just said that no Negro in America is allowed to vote." "His French is all right," said another. "But he may be less concerned with the immediate truth than with stirring up the kind of chaos that makes things change."

By sunset of the first day, the caravan was more than seven miles from Selma, and most of the marchers returned by a special train to town, where some of them left for their home communities and others were put up for the night in the Negro development on Sylvan Street. Two hundred and eighty Negroes, representing Alabama counties (a hundred and forty-eight from Dallas County, eighty-nine from Perry, twenty-three from Marengo, and twenty from Wilcox), and twenty whites, from all over the country, who had been chosen to make the entire journey to Montgomery (the court permitted no more than three hundred marchers on the twenty-mile stretch of Route 80 midway between Selma and Montgomery, where it is only a two-lane highway) turned off Route 80 onto a tarred road leading to the David Hall farm—their campsite for the night. Four large tents had already been pitched in a field. As the marchers lined up for supper (three tons of spaghetti), which was served to them on paper plates, from brand-new garbage pails, night fell. Groups of National Guardsmen who surrounded the farm lighted campfires. "It looks like Camelot," said one of the younger whites.

Camelot soon became very cold and damp. By nine o'clock, most of the marchers had retired to the tents, but within an hour they had to be roused and sorted out. One tent was for men, another for women, the third for the marchers' own night security patrol, and the fourth for the press. When everyone had been assigned to his or her proper tent, it developed that there was a shortage of blankets, winter clothes, and sleeping bags. A shivering group huddled around an incinerator, the campsite's only source of heat. A few marchers made their way to the loft of a barn beside the Hall farmhouse, to profit from the heat given off by the animals in the stalls below. Five guinea hens perched in a tree outside the barn. The march's security patrol wandered about with walkie-talkies; they had labelled their outposts Able, Baker, Charlie, and Dog, using the Army's old system, to set them apart from Alpha, Bravo, Charlie, and Delta, the outposts of the National Guard along the perimeter of the field. The night grew colder, damper, and darker, and the group around the incinerator fire grew uneasy.

There was talk of the march ahead through Lowndes County, where swamps and the woods behind them might easily shelter a sniper in a tree or a canoe. Several marchers claimed to have spotted members of the American Nazi Party along the line of march. Someone mentioned the Ku Klux Klan "counter-demonstration" that had taken place in Montgomery that after-noon.

"And the snakes," a man said.

"What snakes?" said a Northern voice.

"Copperheads and cottonmouth. It takes the heat to bring them out, but a trooper told me somebody's caught five baskets full and is letting them go where we camp tomorrow night."

"How'd the trooper hear about it?"

"Spies."

"Well, I suppose there might be spies right here in camp."

"There might. And bombs and mines. They cleared a few this afternoon. Man, this isn't any Boy Scout jamboree. It's some-thing else."

By the time dawn came, the campers were a thoroughly chilled and bleary-eyed group. The oatmeal served at breakfast gave rise to a certain amount of mirth ("Tastes like fermented library paste," said one of the clergymen), and the news that the National Guardsmen had burned thirteen fence posts, two shovel handles, and an outhouse belonging to a neighboring church in order to keep warm during the night cheered everyone considerably. At a press conference held by Jack Rosenthal, the young Director of Public Information of the Justice Department, the rumors about snakes, bombs, and mines were checked out, and it was learned that none of them were true. A reporter waved several racist leaflets that had been dropped from an air-plane and asked whether anything was being done to prevent such planes from dropping bombs. "What do you want us to do?" Rosenthal replied. "Use anti-aircraft guns?"

The procession set out promptly at 8 A.M. The distance to the next campsite—Rosa Steele's farm—was seventeen miles. Again the day was sunny, and as the air grew warmer some of the more sunburned members of the group donned berets or Stetsons or tied scarves or handkerchiefs around their heads. To the white onlookers who clustered beside the road, the three hundred marchers must have seemed a faintly piratical band. At the head of the line were Dr. and Mrs. King, wearing green caps with earmuffs and reading newspapers as they walked. Not far behind them was a pale-green wagon (known to the marchers as the Green Dragon) with Mississippi license plates, in which rode doctors wearing armbands of the M.C.H.R. (the Medical Committee for Human Rights). Farther back were some of the younger civil-rights leaders: Hosea Williams, S.C.L.C. director of the march and veteran of the bitter struggle for public accommodations in Savannah, Georgia; the Reverend James Bevel, formerly of S.N.C.C, now S.C.L.C. project director for Alabama (Mr. Bevel was wearing the many-colored yarmulke that has become almost his trademark—"a link," he says, "to our Old Testament heritage"); John Lewis, chairman of S.N.C.C.; and the Reverend Andrew Young.

Behind the leaders, some of the main personae of the march had begun to emerge, among them Joe Young, a blind greenhouse worker from Atlanta, Georgia, and Jim Letherer, a one-legged settlement-house worker from Saginaw, Michigan. ("Left! Left! Left!" the segregationist onlookers chanted as Mr. Letherer moved along on crutches.) Chuck Fager, a young worker for S.C.L.C., wearing denims and a black yarmulke, was waving and shouting, "Come march with us! Why don't you come along and march with us?" ("It sets up a dialogue," he explained. "The last time I was in jail, a sheriff pulled me aside and asked me where the hell I was from. Any sort of talk like that sets up a dialogue.") Sister Mary Leoline, a nun from Christ the King parish in Kansas City, Kansas, was talking to John Bart Gerald, a young novelist from New York. "This is a great time to be alive," she said. A few members of the night security guard had somehow acquired cameras, and they were now photographing bystanders who were photographing marchers; it appeared that a sort of reciprocal Most Wanted list was being compiled. From time to time, the marchers were still singing ("Oh-h-h, Wallace, segregation's bound to fall"), and the chief of the Justice Department's Civil Rights Division, Assistant Attorney General John Doar, tall, tanned, and coatless, was striding back and forth along the line of march to see that all was going well.

Around two o'clock, as the middle ranks of marchers passed an intersection just outside Lowndes County, a female bystander apparently could stand it no longer. "They're carrying the flag upside down!" she screamed to the nearest trooper. "Isn't there a law against that? Can't you arrest them? Look at them so-called white men with church collars that they bought for fifty cents! And them de*virg*inated nuns! I'm a Catholic myself, but it turns my stomach to see them. They said there was thousands yesterday, but there wasn't near a thousand. Them niggers and them girls! I've watched the whole thing three times, and there isn't a intelligent-looking one in the bunch. I feel sorry for the black folks. If they want to vote, why don't they just go out and register? Oh, honey, look! There goes a big one. Go home, scum! Go home, scum!" The procession began to sing a not very hearty version of "A Great Camp Meeting in the Promised Land."

Not all the bystanders along the road were white. At the boundary of Lowndes County (with a population of fifteen thousand, eighty per cent of them Negroes, not one of whom had been registered to vote by March 1, 1965), John Maxwell, a Negro worker in a Lowndes County cotton-gin mill (at a salary of six dollars for a twelve-hour day), appeared at an intersection.

"Why don't you register to vote?" a reporter from the *Harvard Crimson* asked Mr. Maxwell.

"They'd put us off the place if I tried," Mr. Maxwell said.

In the town of Trickem, at the Nolan Elementary School—a small white shack on brick stilts, which had asbestos shingles, a corrugated-iron roof, six broken windows, and a broken wood floor patched with automobile license plates—a group of old people and barefoot children rushed out to embrace Dr. King. They had been waiting four hours.

"Will you march with us?" Dr. King asked an old man with a cane.

"I'll walk one step, anyway," said the man. "Because I know for every one step I'll take you'll take two."

The marchers broke into a chant. "*What* do you *want?*" they shouted encouragingly to the Negroes at the roadside. The Negroes smiled, but they did not give the expected response—"*Freedom!*" The marchers had to supply that themselves.

Late in the afternoon, as Route 80 passed through the swamps of Lowndes County, the marchers looked anxiously at the woods, covered with Spanish moss, which began a few yards back from the road. They reached Rosa Steele's farm at sunset. Many of them seemed dismayed to find that the campsite lay right beside the highway. Fresh rumors began to circulate: a young man had been seen putting a bomb under a roadside bridge; twenty white men, with pistols and shotguns, had been seen prowling through a neighboring field; testing security, a representative of the Pentagon had managed to penetrate the security lines without being asked to show his pass. Mr. Rosenthal again put these fears to rest. "The field has been combed by Army demolition teams," he said. "If anyone from the Pentagon had made it through unchecked, you can bet there would have been one hell of a fuss. And as for the man under the bridge, it was a little boy who got off his bicycle to relieve himself. The troopers found out these things. It's nice to know that they are this aware."

As darkness fell, Dr. King held a press conference. A Negro woman lifted up her three-year-old son so that he might catch a glimpse of Dr. King. She soon grew tired and had to put him down. "I'll take him," said a white man standing beside her, and he lifted the boy onto his shoulders. The boy did not glance at Dr. King; he was too busy gazing down at the white man's blond hair.

Again the night was cold and damp. At the entrance to the field, there was so much mud that boards and reeds had been scattered to provide traction for cars. Most of the marchers went to sleep in their four tents soon after supper, but at Steele's Service Station, across the highway, a crowd of Negroes from the neighborhood had gathered. Some of them were dancing to music from a jukebox, and a few of the more energetic marchers, white and black, joined them.

"This is getting to be too much like a holiday," said a veteran of one of the earlier marches. "It doesn't tell the truth of what happened."

At about ten o'clock, the last of the marchers crossed the highway back to camp. Shortly afterward, a fleet of cars drove up to the service station and a group of white boys got out. Two of the boys were from Georgia, two were from Texas, one was from Tennessee, one was from Oklahoma, one was from Monroeville, Alabama, and one was from Selma. The Reverend Arthur E. Matott, a white minister from Perth Amboy, New Jersey, who was a member of the night patrol, saw them and walked across the highway to where they were standing. "Can I help you fellows?" Mr. Matott asked.

"We're just curious," the boy from Monroeville said. "Came out to see what it was like."

"How long are you planning to stay?" said Mr. Matott.

"Until we get ready to leave," the boy said.

A Negro member of the night patrol quietly joined Mr. Matott.

"I cut classes," said the boy from Tennessee. "Sort of impulsive. You hear all these stories. I wondered why you were marching."

"Well, you might say we're marching to get to know each other and to ease a little of the hate around here," Mr. Matott said.

"You don't need to march for that," said one the boys from Texas. "You're making it worse. The hate was being lessened and lessened by itself throughout the years."

"Was it?" asked the Negro member of the guard.

"It was," the Texas boy said.

"We never had much trouble in Nashville," said the boy from Tennessee. "Where you have no conflict, it's hard to conceive . . ."

"Why don't you-all go and liberate the Indian reservations, or something?" said the boy from Monroeville. "The Negroes around here are happy."

"I don't think they are," said Mr. Matott.

"I've lived in the South all my life, and I know that they are," the boy from Georgia said.

"I'm not happy," said the Negro guard.

"Well, just wait awhile," said the boy from Monroeville.

An attractive blond girl in a black turtleneck sweater, denim pants, and boots now crossed the highway from the camp. "Do you know where I can get a ride to Jackson?" she asked the Negro guard.

"This is Casey Hayden, from S.N.C.C. She's the granddaughter of a Texas sheriff," said the minister, introducing her to the group.

A battered car drove up, and three more white boys emerged.

"I don't mean to bug you," the Negro whispered to the girl, "but did you realize we're surrounded?"

"You fellows from Selma?" Miss Hayden asked, turning to the three most recent arrivals.

"Yeah," said one, who was wearing a green zippered jacket, a black shirt, and black pants, and had a crew cut.

"What do you want?" Miss Hayden asked.

"I don't know," the boy answered.

"That's an honest answer," Miss Hayden said.

"It is," the boy said.

"What do you do?" Miss Hayden asked.

"Well, Miss, I actually *work* for a living, and I can tell you it's going to be hard on all of them when this is over," the boy said. "A lot of people in town are letting their maids go."

"Well, I don't suppose I'd want to have a maid anyway," Miss Hayden said amiably. "I guess I can do most things myself."

"That's not all, though," said another boy. "It's awfully bad down the road. Nothing's happened so far, but you can't ever tell. Selma's a peace-loving place, but that Lowndes County is something else."

"I guess some of these people feel they haven't got that much to lose," Miss Hayden said.

"I know," said the boy.

"Do you understand what they're marching about?" Miss Hayden asked.

"Yeah—fighting for freedom, something like that. That's the idea, along that line. It don't mean nothing," the boy said.

"And to make money," the third young man said. "The men are getting fifteen dollars a day for marching, and the girls are really making it big."

"Is that so?" said Miss Hayden?

"Yeah. Girl came into the Selma hospital this morning, fifteen hundred dollars in her wallet. She'd slept with forty-one."

"Forty-one what?" Miss Hayden asked.

"Niggers," the young man said.

"And what did she go to the hospital for?" Miss Hayden asked.

"Well, actually, Ma'am, she bled to death," the young man said.

"Where did you hear that?" Miss Hayden asked.

"In town," the young man said. "There's not much you can do, more than keep track of everything. It's a big mess."

"Well," Miss Hayden said, "I think it's going to get better."

"Hard to say," said one of the boys as they drifted back to their cars.

At midnight in the camp, Charles Mauldin, aged seventeen, the head of the Dallas County Student Union and a student at Selma's Hudson High School, which is Negro, was awakened in the security tent by several guards, who ushered in a rather frightened-looking Negro boy.

"What's going on?" asked Charles.

The boy replied that he was trying to found a Negro student movement in Lowndes County.

"That's fine," said Charles.

"The principal's dead set against it," the boy said.

"Then stay underground until you've got everybody organized," Charles said. "Then if he throws one out he'll have to throw you all out."

"You with Snick or S.C.L.C., or what?" the boy asked.

"I'm not with anything," Charles said. "I'm with them all. I used to just go to dances in Selma on Saturday nights and not belong to anything. Then I met John Love, who was Snick project director down here, and I felt how he just sees himself in every Negro. Then I joined the movement."

"What about your folks?" the boy asked.

"My father's a truck driver, and at first they were against it, but now they don't push me and they don't hold me back," Charles said.

"Who've you had personal run-ins with?" the boy asked.

"I haven't had personal run-ins with anybody," Charles said. "I've been in jail three times, but never more than a few hours. They needed room to put other people in. Last week, I got let out, so I just had to march and get beaten on. In January, we had a march of little kids—we called it the Tots' March—but we were afraid they might get frightened, so we joined them, and some of us got put in jail. Nothing personal about it."

"Some of us think that for the march we might be better off staying in school," the boy said.

"Well, I think if you stay in school you're saying that you're satisfied," Charles said. "We had a hundred of our teachers marching partway with us. At first, I was against the march, but then I realized that although we're probably going to get the voting bill, we still don't have a lot of other things. It's dramatic, and it's an experience, so I came. I thought of a lot of terrible things that could happen, because we're committed to non-violence, and I'm responsible for the kids from the Selma school. But then I thought, If they killed everyone on this march, it would be nothing compared to the number of people they've killed in the last three hundred years."

"You really believe in non-violence?" the boy asked Charles.

"I do," Charles said. "I used to think of it as just a tactic, but now I believe in it all the way. Now I'd just like to be tested."

"Weren't you tested enough when you were beaten on?" the boy asked.

"No, I mean an individual test, by myself," Charles said. "It's easy to talk about non-violence, but in a lot of cases you've got to be tested, and re-inspire yourself."

By 2 A.M., hardly anyone in the camp was awake except the late-shift night security patrol and a group of radio operators in a trailer truck, which served as a base for the walkie-talkies around the campsite and in the church back in Selma. The operators kept in constant touch with Selma, where prospective marchers were still arriving by the busload. Inside the trailer were Norman Talbot, a middle-aged Negro from Selma who had borrowed the trailer from his uncle and was serving as its driver ("I used to work in a junk yard, until they fired me for joining the movement. I've got a five-year-old daughter, but after that I made it my business to come out in a big way"); Pete Muilenberg, a nineteen-year-old white student on leave of absence from Dartmouth to work for C.O.F.O., the Congress of Federated Organizations, in Mississippi; and Mike Kenney, a twenty-nine-year-old white student who had quit graduate school at Iowa State to work for S.N.C.C.

"Snick isn't officially involved in this march," Mr. Kenney said to a marcher who visited him in the trailer early that morning. "Although individual Snick workers can take part if they like. They say Martin Luther King and Snick struck a bargain: Snick wouldn't boycott this march if S.C.L.C. would take part in a demonstration in Washington to challenge the Mississippi members of Congress. We didn't want to bring in all these outsiders, and we wanted to keep marching on that Tuesday when King turned back. Man, there are cats in Selma now from up North saying, 'Which demonstration are you going to? Which one is the best?' As though it were a college prom, or something. I tell them they ought to have sense enough to be scared. 'What do you think you're down here for? For publicity, to show how many of you there are, and to get a few heads bashed in. Nobody needs you to lead them. S.C.L.C. has got plenty of leaders.' People need Snick, though, for the technicians. Some of us took a two-day course in short-wave-radio repair from one of our guys, Marty Schiff, so we could set up their radios for them. Then, a lot of Snick cats have come over here from Mississippi, where the romance has worn off a bit and it's time for our experts to take over—running schools, pairing off communities with communities up North, filing legal depositions against the Mississippi congressmen and against the worst of the police.

"We're called agitators from out of state. Well, take away the connotations and agitation is what we do, but we're not outsiders. Nobody who crosses a state line is an outsider. It's the same with racial lines. I don't give a damn about the Negro race, but I don't give a damn about the white race, either. I'm interested in breaking the fetters of thought. What this march is going to do is help the Alabama Negro to break his patterns of thought. It's also going to change the marchers when they go back home. The students who went back from the Mississippi project became dynamos. It's easier to join the movement than to get out. You have this commitment. There will be Snick workers staying behind to keep things going in Selma. We were here, working, a year and a half before S.C.L.C. came in. Man, there's a cartoon in our Jackson office showing the Snick power structure, and it's just one big snarl. Some of us are in favour of more central organization, but most of us believe in the mystique of the local people. We're not running the C.O.F.O. project in Mississippi next summer, because of the black-white tensions in Snick. Some of the white cats feel they're being forced out, because of the racism. But I can understand it. The white invasion put the Negro cats in a predicament. Not even their movement was their own anymore. I'm staying with it, though. Every Snick meeting is a traumatic experience for all of us, but even the turmoil is too real, too important, for me to get out now. It's what you might call the dramatic-results mentality. Some of the leaders may be evolving some pretty far-out political philosophy, but it's the workers who get things done—black-white tensions, left-right tensions, and all."

Later that morning, Tuesday, it began to rain, and the rain continued through most of the day. When the first drops fell, whites at the roadside cheered (a Southern adage says that "a nigger won't stay out in the rain"), but it soon became apparent that, even over hilly country, the procession was going at a more spirited pace than ever. Jim Letherer, on his crutches, appeared to be flagging. John Doar walked beside him for a while, joking and imperceptibly slowing his pace. Then Mr. Doar said, "Jim, come to the car a minute. I want to show you something back down the road." Jim disappeared from the march. In twenty minutes, he was walking again.

Back in Selma, thousands of out-of-towners had arrived and had been quietly absorbed into the Negro ghetto. On the outskirts of town, a sign had appeared showing a photograph of Martin Luther King at the Highlander Folk School and captioned "Martin Luther King at Communist School." Lying soggily upon the sidewalks were leaflets reading "An unemployed agitator ceases to agitate. Operation Ban. Selective hiring, firing, buying, selling." The Selma Avenue Church of Christ, whose congregation is white, displayed a sign reading "When You Pray, Be Not As Hypocrites Are, Standing in the Street. Matt: 6:5," and the Brown Chapel Church displayed a sign reading "Forward Ever, Backward Never. Visitors Welcome." Inside the church and its parsonage, things were bustling. There were notes tacked everywhere: "If you don't have official business here, please leave," "All those who wish to take hot baths, contact Mrs. Lilly," "Don't sleep here anymore. This is an office," "Please, the person who is trying to find me to return my suit coat and trenchcoat, not having left it in my Rambler . . ."

"Everyone here in town is getting antsy," Melody Heaps, a white girl who had come in from Chicago, said to a reporter. "We're not allowed to march until Thursday, and there's nothing to do. On the other hand, we're giving the Selma Negroes a chance to take it easy. They know what they're doing, and we don't, so they can order us around a little."

"You know what just happened?" said a white clergyman from Ontario. "Some of those white segs splashed mud all over us. It was so funny and childish we just howled."

A little later, two clergymen picked up their luggage and left the church for the home of Mrs. Georgia Roberts, where, they had been told, they were to spend the night.

"I guess I can put you up," Mrs. Roberts said when they arrived. "Last night, I put up fourteen. I worked as a cook at the Selma Country Club for thirteen years, before they fired me for joining the movement. I've been friendly to all the other guests, so I guess you'll find me friendly, too. I never thought I'd see the day when we'd dare to march against the white government in the Black Belt of Alabama."

At the Tuesday-night campsite, a farm owned by the A. G. Gastons, a Birmingham Negro family who had become millionaires in various businesses, the ground was so wet that the marchers could walk through the clay-like mud only by moving their feet as though they were skating. A Negro family living in the middle of the property had received several intimidating phone calls during the day, and as a consequence, they barred their house to marchers. They held a party in their little front garden to watch the goings on.

The marchers had by then been joined by Mrs. Ann Cheatham, an English housewife from Ealing, who had flown across the Atlantic just to take part in the last two days of marching. "It seems to me an outrage," she said. "I saw it on the telly— people being battered on the head. I came to show that the English are in sympathy. I can see there are a lot of odd bods on this march, but there were a lot in the marches on Aldermaston and Washington. This appalling business of barring white facilities to Negro children! People say it's not my business, but I would deny that. It's everybody's business."

In the early evening, a clergyman became violently ill, and doctors blamed the marchers' water supply. The marchers had all along complained that the water tasted of kerosene, and, upon investigation, it turned out the water was in fact polluted, having come from a truck that was ordinarily used for draining septic tanks. (Fortunately, no other marchers seemed to suffer from the contamination.) Later, the singer Odetta appeared at the campsite, and found all the marchers, including another singer, Pete Seeger, fast asleep.

Wednesday, the fourth and last full day of marching, was sunny again, and the marchers set out in good spirits. In the morning, a minister who had rashly dropped out at a gas station to make a telephone call was punched by the owner, and a free-lance newspaper photographer was struck on the ear by a passerby. (Although he required three stitches, he was heartened by the fact that a Montgomery policeman had come, with a flying tackle, to his rescue.) There seemed, however, to be fewer segregationists by the side of the road than usual—perhaps because the Montgomery *Advertiser* had been running a two-page advertisement, prepared by the City Commissioner's Committee on Community Affairs, imploring citizens to be moderate and ignore the march. The coverage of the march in the Southern press had consistently amused the marchers. "Civil Righters Led by Communists" had been the headline in the Birmingham weekly *Independent;* the Selma *Times-Journal,* whose coverage of the march was relatively accurate, had editorialized about President Johnson, under the heading "A Modern Mussolini Speaks, 'We Shall Overcome,'" "No man in any generation . . . has ever held so much power in the palm of his hand, and that includes Caesar, Alexander, Genghis Khan, Napoleon, and Franklin D. Roosevelt"; and the Wednesday *Advertiser*'s sole front-page item concerning the march was a one-column, twenty-one-line account, lower right, of the Alabama legislature's resolution condemning the demonstrators for being "sexually promiscuous." ("It is well known that the white Southern segregationist is obsessed with fornication," said John Lewis, chairman of S.N.C.C. "And that is why there are so many shades of Negro.") At 9 A.M., Ray Robin announced over radio station WHHY, in Montgomery, that "there is now evidence that women are returning to their homes from the march as expectant unwed mothers." Several marchers commented, ironically, on the advanced state of medical science in Alabama.

By noon, most of the marchers were sunburned or just plain weather-burned. Two Negroes scrawled the word "Vote" in sunburn cream on their foreheads and were photographed planting an American flag, Iwo Jima fashion, by the side of the road.

Flags of all sorts, including state flags and church flags, had materialized in the hands of marchers. One of the few segregationists watching the procession stopped his jeering for a moment when he saw the American flag, and raised his hand in a salute. The singing had abated somewhat, and the marchers had become conversational.

"This area's a study in social psychopathology," said Henry Schwarzschild, executive secretary of L.C.D.C. (the Lawyers Constitutional Defense Committee). "In a way, they're asking for a show of force like this, to make them face reality."

"And there's the ignorance," said another civil-rights lawyer. "A relatively friendly sheriff in Sunflower County, Mississippi, warned me, confidentially, that my client was a 'blue-gum nigger.' 'Their mouths are filled with poison,' he said. 'Don't let him bite you.'"

"And what did you say?" asked a college student marching beside him.

"What could I say?" the lawyer replied. "I said I'd try to be careful."

"The way I see this march," said a young man from S.N.C.C., "is as a march from the religious to the secular—from the chapel to the statehouse. For too long now, the Southern Negro's only refuge has been the church. That's why he prefers these S.C.L.C. ministers to the Snick cats. But we're going to change all that."

"I'm worried, though, about the Maoists," said the student.

"What do you mean by that, exactly?" asked another marcher.

"A Maoist. You know. From the Mau Mau."

In the early afternoon, Dr. King and his wife, who had dropped out for a day in order for him to go to Cleveland to receive an award, rejoined the procession. The singing began again. Marching behind Dr. King was his friend the Reverend Morris H. Tynes, of Chicago, who teased Dr. King continuously. "Moses, can you let your people rest for a minute?" Mr. Tynes said. "Can you just let the homiletic smoke from your cigarette drift out of your mouth and engulf the multitude and let them rest?" Dr. King smiled. Some of the other marchers, who had tended to speak of him half in joking, half in reverent tones (most of them referred to him conversationally as "De Lawd"), laughed out loud.

A Volkswagen bus full of marchers from Chicago ran out of gas just short of the procession. "Now, we all believe in non-violence," one of the passengers said to the driver, "but if you don't get this thing moving pretty soon . . ."

"Are you members of some sort of group?" asked a reporter, looking inside the bus.

"No," said the driver. "We're just individuals."

At last, on the outskirts of Montgomery, the marchers reached their fourth campsite—the Catholic City of St. Jude, consisting of a church, a hospital, and a school built in a style that might be called Contemporary Romanesque. The four tents were pitched by the time they arrived, and they marched onto the grounds singing "We *Have* Overcome." They also added two new verses to the song—"All the way from Selma" and "Our feet are soaked." Inside the gates of St. Jude's, they were greeted by a crowd of Montgomery Negroes singing the national anthem.

"*What* do you *want?*" the marchers chanted.

This time, the response from the onlookers was immediate and loud: "*Freedom!*"

"*When* do you *want* it?"

"*Now!*"

"How *much* of it?"

"*All* of it!"

On its fourth night, the march began to look first like a football rally, then like a carnival and a hootenanny, and finally like something dangerously close to a hysterical mob. Perhaps because of a new feeling of confidence, the security check at the main gate had been practically abandoned. Thousands of marchers poured in from Selma and Montgomery, some of them carrying luggage, and no one had time to examine its contents. The campsite was cold and almost completely dark, and a bomb or a rifle shot would have left everyone helpless. Word got out that doctors on the march had treated several cases of strep throat, two of pneumonia, one of advanced pulmonary tuberculosis, and one of epilepsy, and because of the number and variety of sick and handicapped who had made the march a macabre new joke began to go the rounds: "What has five hundred and ninety-nine legs, five hundred and ninety-eight eyes, an indeterminate number of germs, and walks singing? The march from Selma."

An entertainment had been scheduled for nine o'clock that night, but it was several hours late getting started, and in the meantime the crowd of thousands churned about in the mud and chanted. A number of people climbed into trees near the platform where the entertainment was to take place. On the outskirts of St. Jude's, in a section normally set aside as a playground, a few children spun the handpowered carrousel, or climbed over the jungle gym in the dark. In the wires of the telephone poles around the field, the skeletons of old kites were just visible in the dim lights from the windows of St. Jude's Hospital.

A minister, who had been seeking for several hours to clear the platform, wept with chagrin. "Betcha old Sheriff Clark and his troopers could clear it!" someone shouted. In the darkness, there were repeated cries for doctors, and a soldier stood on top of the radio trailer and beamed a flashlight into the crowd, trying to find the sources of the cries. Thousands crowded around the platform, and several of them were pressed against it and fell. Several others, mostly members of the special group of three hundred marchers, fainted from exhaustion. A number of entertainers, each of whom had been given a dime to use for a phone call in case of an emergency, and all of whom had been instructed to stand in groups of not fewer than six, appeared on the platform. Among them were Shelley Winters, Sammy Davis, Jr., Tony Perkins, Tony Bennett, and Nina Simone. A number of girls in the crowd collapsed and, because there was no other lighted space, had to be carried onstage, where Miss Winters did her best to minister to them. Before long, twenty people, none of them seriously ill or seriously injured, were carried off to the hospital on stretchers. A large group started an agitated march within the campsite.

"I'm tired," said a white college student. "If only I could walk someplace and get a cab!"

"Man, that's not cool," said a Negro. "There are a lot of hostile people outside that gate."

"Inside it, too, for all I know," said the student. "See any white sheets?"

Finally, the entertainment got under way, and the situation improved. Tony Perkins and a few others spoke with well-considered brevity. The crowd clapped along with the singers as they sang folk songs and songs of the movement, and it laughed at the comedians, including Dick Gregory, Nipsey Russell, Mike Nichols, and Elaine May. ("I can't afford to call up the National Guard," said Mike Nichols, impersonating Governor Wallace. "Why not?" said Elaine May, impersonating a telegraph operator. "It only costs a dime.")

At 2 A.M., the entertainment and speeches were over, and the performers left for a Montgomery hotel, which was surrounded for the remainder of the night by shouting segregationists. Most of the crowd drifted off the field and headed for Montgomery, and the tents were left at last to the marchers. Suddenly security tightened up. At one point, the Reverend Andrew Young himself was asked for his credentials. The hours before dawn passed without incident.

On Thursday morning, the march expanded, pulled itself together, and turned at once serious and gay. It finally seemed that the whole nation was marching to Montgomery. Signs from every conceivable place and representing every conceivable religious denomination, philosophical viewpoint, labor union, and walk of life assembled at St. Jude's and lined up in orderly fashion. A Magic Marker pen passed from hand to hand, and new signs went up: "The Peace Corps Knows Integration Works," "So Does Canada," "American Indians" (carried by Fran Poafpybitty, a Comanche from Indiahoma, Oklahoma), "Freedom" in Greek letters (carried by a Negro girl), "Out of Vietnam into Selma" in Korean (carried by a white girl), "The Awe and Wonder of Human Dignity We Want to Maintain" (on a sandwich board worn by a succession of people), and, on two sticks tied together, with a blue silk scarf above it, a sign reading simply "Boston." A young white man in a gray flannel suit hurried back and forth among the platoons of marchers; on his attaché case was written "D. J. Bittner, Night Security."

Near the tents, Ivanhoe Donaldson and Frank Surocco (the first a Negro project director for S.N.C.C. in Atlanta, the second a white boy, also from S.N.C.C.) were distributing orange plastic jackets to the original three hundred marchers. The jackets, of the sort worn by construction workers, had been bought for eighty-nine cents apiece in Atlanta, and jackets like them had been worn throughout the march by the marshals, but for the marchers the orange jacket had become a singular status symbol.

There was some dispute about who was entitled to wear one. There was also a dispute about the order of march. Some thought that the entertainers should go first, some that the leaders should. Roy Wilkins, of the N.A.A.C.P., demurred on behalf of the leaders. Odetta said, "Man, don't let the morale crumble. The original three hundred deserve to be first." The Reverend Andrew Young was served with a summons in an action by the City of Selma and the Selma Bus Lines protesting the operation of buses in competition with the Selma company.

Finally, after another session of virtually inaudible speeches, the parade was ready to go. "Make way for the originals!" the marshals shouted, forming a cordon to hold back the other marchers and the press. Behind the three hundred came Martin Luther King, Ralph Bunche, A. Philip Randolph, the Reverend Ralph Abernathy, the Reverend Fred L. Shuttlesworth, Charles G. Gomillion, the Reverend F. D. Reese, and other civil-rights leaders; behind them came the grandfather of Jimmie Lee Jackson, the Negro boy who had been shot in nearby Perry County, and the Reverend Orloff Miller, a friend of the Reverend James Reeb's, who had been beaten with Reeb on the night of Reeb's murder; and behind them came a crowd of what turned out to be more than thirty thousand people. "We're not just down here for show," said Mr. Miller. "A lot of our people are staying here to help. But the show itself is important. When civil rights drops out of the headlines, the country forgets."

Stationed, like an advance man, hundreds of yards out in front of the procession as it made its way through the Negro section of Montgomery and, ultimately, past a hundred and four intersections was Charles Mauldin, dressed in his Hudson High sweat shirt and blue jeans and an orange jacket, and waving a little American flag and a megaphone. One pocket of his denims was split, and the fatigue in his gentle, intelligent face made him seem considerably younger than his seventeen years. "Come and march with us!" he shouted to Negro bystanders. "You can't make your witness standing on the corner. Come and march with us. We're going downtown. There's nothing to be afraid of. Come and march with us!"

"Tell 'em, baby," said Frank Surocco, who was a few yards back of Charles.

"Is everything safe up ahead?" asked the voice of Ivanhoe Donaldson through a walkie-talkie.

"We watching 'em, baby," said Surocco.

"Come and march with us!" said Charles Mauldin, to black and white bystanders alike.

In midtown Montgomery, at the Jefferson Davis Hotel, Negro maids were looking out of the windows and the white clientele was standing on the hotel marquee. Farther along, at the Whitley Hotel, Negro porters were looking out of windows on one side of the building and white customers were looking out of windows on the other. Troopers watched from the roof of the Brown Printing Company. The windows of the Montgomery Citizens Council were empty. Outside the Citizens Council building, a man stood waving a Confederate flag.

"What's your name?" a reporter asked.

"None of your goddam business," said the man.

At the intersection of Montgomery Street and Dexter Avenue (the avenue leading to the capitol), Charles Mauldin turned and looked around. "They're still coming out of St. Jude's," a reporter told him. And when the vanguard of the march reached the capitol steps, they were *still* coming out of St. Jude's. "You're only likely to see three great parades in a lifetime," said John Doar to a student who walked beside him, "and this is one of them." A brown dog had joined the crowd for the march up Dexter Avenue. On the sidewalk in front of the capitol, reporters stood on the press tables to look back. Charles and the rest of the orange-jacketed three hundred stood below. Behind them, the procession was gradually drawing together and to a halt. Ahead, a few green-clad, helmeted officers of the Alabama Game and Fish Service and some state officials blocked the capitol steps, at the top of which, covering the bronze that marks the spot where Jefferson Davis was inaugurated President of the Confederacy, was a plywood shield constructed at the order of Governor Wallace—"to keep that s.o.b. King from desecrating the Cradle of the Confederacy," according to a spokesman for the Governor. Martin Luther King had managed to draw a larger crowd than the leader of the Confederacy a hundred years before.

Onto a raised platform—erected by the marchers for the occasion—in a plaza between the crowd and the steps climbed a group of entertainers that included, at one point or another, Joan

Baez; the Chad Mitchell Trio; Peter, Paul, and Mary; and Harry Belafonte. As Alabamians peered from the statehouse windows, Negro and white performers put their arms around each other's shoulders and began to sing. Although the songs were familiar and the front rank of the three hundred mouthed a few of the words, none of the crowd really sang along. Everybody simply cheered and applauded at the end of each number. Then Len Chandler, a young Negro folk singer who had marched most of the way, appeared on the platform. He was dressed peculiarly, as he had been on the road—in a yellow helmet, a flaglike blue cape with white stars on it, and denims—and the crowd at once joined him in singing:

> *"You've got to move when the spirit say move,*
> *Move when the spirit say move.*
> *When the spirit say move, you've got to move, oh, Lord.*
> *You got to move when the spirit say move."*

In the subsequent verses, Mr. Chandler changed "move" to "walk," "march," "vote," "picket," "cool it," and "love," and the crowd kept singing. Joan Baez, wearing a purple velvet dress and a large bronze crucifix, even broke into a rather reverent Frug.

After an invocation by a rabbi and speeches by the Reverend Ralph Abernathy, the crowd turned away from the Confederate and Alabama state flags flying from the capitol, faced its own American flags, and sang the national anthem. At its close, the Reverend Theodore Gill, president of the San Francisco Theological Seminary, looked before and behind him and said a simple prayer: "Forgive us our trespasses." One marcher applauded, and was immediately hushed. Then there was the succession of speeches, most of them eloquent, some of them pacific ("Friends of freedom," said Whitney Young, of the Urban League), others militant ("Fellow Freedom Fighters," said John Lewis, of S.N.C.C.), and nearly all of them filled with taunts of Governor Wallace as the list of grievances, intimidations, and brutalities committed by the state piled up.

"This march has become a rescue operation," Charles Mauldin said quietly to a friend as the speeches continued. "Most of those Negroes along the way have joined us, and although this Wallace-baiting sounds like a little boy whose big brother has come home, standing outside a bully's window to jeer, these Negroes are never going to be so afraid of the bully again. When the bill goes through, they're going to vote, and the white men down here are going to think twice before they try to stop them. Big brothers have come down from the North and everywhere, and they've shown that they're ready and willing to come down again. I don't think they're going to have to."

"It's good that even a few of the civil-rights *talkers* have joined us," said another marcher. "When those people feel they have to climb on the bandwagon, you know you're on the way to victory."

As one speaker followed another, as Ralph Bunche, who had marched for two full days, and A. Philip Randolph spoke, the civil-rights leaders saluted one another and gave signs of patching up their differences. (Mr. Abernathy, second-in-command of S.C.L.C., slipped once and said, "Now here's James Peck, for James Farmer, to tell us whether CORE is with us." Peck ignored the implications of the "whether" and spoke as eloquently as the rest.) The crowd applauded politely throughout but gave no sign of real enthusiasm. S.C.L.C. and S.N.C.C. leaders seemed to be equally popular, but the N.A.A.C.P. and the Urban League, more active in other states than in Alabama, seemed to require a little help from Mr. Abernathy ("Now let's give a big hand to . . .") to get their applause. Some of the marchers crawled forward under the press tables and went to sleep. A Japanese reporter, who had been taking notes in his own language, seized one of the marchers as he crawled under a table, "What do you think of all this?" the reporter asked. "I think it's good," the marcher said. Some fell asleep in their places on Dexter Avenue. (Perhaps remembering the mob scenes of the night before, the crowd left its members ample breathing space in front of the capitol.) A scuffle broke out between marchers and white bystanders in front of Klein's Jewelry Store, but no one was seriously hurt. It rained a little, and Charles Mauldin said, "Wallace is seeing the clouds."

Albert Turner, of Marion, where Jimmie Lee Jackson was murdered, said from the platform, "I look worse than anybody else on this stage. That's because I marched fifty miles." Then he read the Negro voting statistics from Perry County. When he said, "We are not satisfied," the crowd gave him a rousing cheer.

He looked down at his orange jacket and smiled. Mrs. Amelia Boynton spoke; during the previous demonstrations, she had been kicked and beaten, and jailed, for what some members of the press have come to call "resisting assault." She read the petition, mentioning the "psychotic climate" of the State of Alabama, that a delegation of marchers was seeking to present to Governor Wallace, and she was roundly applauded. Near the end of the ceremony, Rosa Parks, the "Mother of the Movement," who had set off Dr. King's first demonstration when she was jailed for refusing to yield her seat to a white man on a bus in Montgomery, received the most enthusiastic cheers of all. "Tell it! Tell! Tell!" some of the marchers shouted. "Speak! Speak!" Finally, after an extravagant introduction by Mr. Abernathy, who referred to Dr. King as "conceived by God" ("This personality cult is getting out of hand," said a college student, and, to judge by the apathetic reception of Mr. Abernathy's words, the crowd agreed), Dr. King himself spoke. There were some enthusiastic yells of "Speak! Speak!" and "Yessir! Yessir!" from the older members of the audience when Dr. King's speech began, but at first the younger members were subdued. Gradually, the whole crowd began to be stirred. By the time he reached his refrains—"Let us march on the ballot boxes. . . . We're on the move now. . . . How long? Not long"—and the final ringing "Glory, glory, hallelujah!" the crowd was with him entirely.

The director of the march, Hosea Williams, of S.C.L.C., said some concluding words, remarking that there should be no lingering in Montgomery that night and exhorting the crowd to leave quietly and with dignity. There was a last rendition of "We Shall Overcome." Within ten minutes, Dexter Avenue was cleared of all but the press and the troopers.

A few hours later, the delegation and its petition were turned away by Governor Wallace. At the airport, where there had been some difficulty during the preceding days (an uncanny number of suitcases belonging to marchers were mislaid by the airlines), new flights had been scheduled to get the marchers out of Montgomery. Still, many marchers had to wait at the airport all night long. They rested on the floor, and on the lawn outside, and as often as the police cleared them away they reappeared and fell asleep again. Word came that Mrs. Viola Liuzzo had been shot. Some of the marchers went back to Selma at once. Others boarded planes for home. At the Montgomery airport exit was a permanent official sign reading "Glad You Could Come. Hurry Back."

# Salt into Old Scars

IN SATIRIZING THE CLICHÉS OF modern American life, Herbert Gold has fallen among the clichés of modern American satire. The worn, familiar targets—cynical Madison Avenue, opportunistic Wall Street, sterile suburbia, impersonal New York—are set up once again and duly reassassinated. The mode of attack has become familiar, too. For years, there has been apparent—in works as disparate as *Advertisements for Myself, Good-bye, Columbus, Naked Lunch*—a modern satirical convention: the rude ear, the jaundiced eye, and the shrill, complaining voice. The writer has a grudge against society, which he documents with accounts of unsatisfying sex, unrealized ambition, unmitigated loneliness, and a sense of local and global distress. The square, overpopulation, the bourgeois, the bomb, and the cocktail party are variously identified as sources of the grudge. There follows a little obscenity here, a dash of philosophy there, considerable whining overall, and a modern satirical novel is born. In *Salt* (Dial), Mr. Gold modifies these stereotypes of subject, tone, and sensibility with a literary formula of his own: imprecise and unmelodic prose, an angry hipster liberalism, some flashes of genuine humor, and a plot structure that has recurred, like an obsessive refrain, in nearly all his novels.

*Birth of a Hero,* his first novel, told of two men, uneasy friends—one ordinary (the hero), the other crippled and inscrutable. The hero seduced the cripple's wife, the cripple attacked the hero's wife, and the climax was a fight in which the hero wrested the cripple's knife away. *The Man Who Was Not with It* told of two men, uneasy friends—one ordinary (the hero), the other a criminal and a dope addict. The hero slept with a nymphomaniac former mistress of the addict's, the addict attacked the hero's wife, and the climax was a fist fight in which the hero nearly killed his criminal friend. *The Optimist* told of two men, uneasy friends—one ordinary (the hero), the other an ineffectual failure. The hero took a mistress, the failure took the hero's wife, and the climax was a fight in which the hero kicked his rival in the groin. These three novels were set, respectively, in Cleveland, in a travelling carnival, and in Detroit. Now we have *Salt,* set in New York, and the plot is not altogether unfamiliar. It tells of two men, uneasy friends—one ordinary (the hero), the other cynical and cold. The hero takes the cynic's former mistress, the cynic sleeps with her again, and the climax is a street fight in which the hero kicks the cynic in the groin. In each of these novels, the hero's friend has played the role of mentor and father before the exchange of women and the hero's figurative emasculation of him. As a narrator, Mr. Gold appears to have bogged down in muddled Freud.

The title *Salt* warns us that we are in for symbols: the salt of the author's wit; the salt of the hero's tears; the grain of salt with which the cynic faces life; the salt of the sea, which is Mr. Gold's favorite image for waves of sexual excitement; and the salt of the earth, which the author claims his heroine to be. The oranges that Peter, the cynically detached Don Juan of stockbrokers, juggles in the privacy of his apartment are symbolic of his way of life—risky, flighty, temporarily defiant of the laws of nature. The seed catalogues that Barbara, the heroine, studies in the privacy of her apartment are symbols of her healthy, creative disposition and her frustrated longing for marriage and motherhood. The odyssey that Dan, the divorced hero, must undertake is symbolic of the trials that the artist suffers in a symbolic Sodom that is New York. Employing the plot carried over from his earlier novels and the symbols improvised and mixed for this one, Mr. Gold proceeds to construct a series of satirical tableaux —a bitter tour of the offices, living rooms, basements, and bedrooms of his wicked city.

The author is certainly not everybody's tour leader. He describes Barbara's engagement party in Greenwich Village, at which an actress in pornographic films asks the young hostess to perform an abortion for her. ("You have like the aptitude.") At a party in suburbia, a guest in pink trousers makes love to his hostess while she plays a slot machine. At the zoo, a well-dressed little boy infuriates his mother by rolling in hippopotamus excrement. ("We can use more men like that in this country.") When Dan, a romantic at heart, attempts to make love to a girl named Goneril, she says sweetly, "Dan? Want me to do some nastiness for you? You name it."

You name it indeed. Mr. Gold does considerable nastiness for his reader, and a lot of rolling in excrement, too. The question is: Why? For the sake, of course, of the modern convention of satire. But surely there are, in any era, certain elementary requirements that true satire must fulfill. It must be inventive, attacking its subjects at a point where they did not know themselves to be vulnerable. It must be telling, with an accuracy of naturalistic observation that makes its subjects convincing and recognizable. It must be funny, with that quality in humor that causes readers to improve themselves with laughter.

On the first count, satirical inventiveness, Mr. Gold is totally deficient. His views on what is deplorable in modern life scarcely constitute a revelation. We knew before we met Dan the hero that divorce is an unsettling experience and that Madison Avenue is uncongenial to the artistic temperament. We knew before we met Peter the cynic that sex between disagreeable partners can be sordid and unsatisfactory. We knew before we met Barbara the heroine that a warm single girl in her late twenties is likely to have a rough time. We knew before reading *Salt* that New York can be a lonely place, that some cocktail parties are appalling, that contemporary global problems are staggering, and that dieting has become an American compulsion. Mr. Gold tells us these things again. And when he attempts to tell us something new, he is generally wrong or unintelligible or pseudo-profound or all three:

> We do not head for the frontier to seek proof of manliness; we find ourselves at the frontier for good reasons, not psychological ones, and because we are there.

> At first, Barbara was a target. She would have preferred to be an archer or even an arrow.

> Now, at a certain midpoint, I need to gather up what I have learned thus far. Having no power corrupts; having absolutely no power at all corrupts absolutely. In the crisis of meaning which afflicts us, in a time which avoids the prime questions of life on earth . . . I like others sought to find the meaning of life in love. . . . We toy with freedom like do-it-yourself hobbyists. Comes trouble! Comes joy! We seek to give it up. . . . The heart in this world becomes a machine, a crank, bare works burning against itself, love and feeling, smoke and hurt, nothing.

With the second requirement, accuracy of observation, the author fares better, but not much. His eye and his ear are occasionally acute, but they, too, can be unreliable. The major figures in the novel slip in and out of character until it becomes almost impossible to recognize a single speaker in two successive conversations. "Alas, I'm a bitch—that is, a borderline hysteric with a distorted sense of values and a tendency to prey on men," says the same Goneril who some pages later says, "Aw, Jeez, gosharooney. . . . You got a nursy look about you." And the author's account of what people do is hardly more dependable than his transcription of what they say. Several characters are made to laugh themselves to tears in private—a familiar device for villains in cheap melodrama but scarcely something that occurs frequently in life. When Mr. Gold wishes, as he almost constantly does, to describe realistically two characters making love, he has them smiling amiably throughout. Often the author's errors of observation seem the result not of myopia but of sheer carelessness. He describes the plot of the typical children's movie as "boy-dog got girl-dog." It simply is not so, as any child movie-goer could have told him.

With the last requirement, being funny, Mr. Gold does best. Some of his lines will probably make the reader laugh (although not to tears in private). "More spiritual doings in a moment" has, in the context of a scene with Goneril, its bitter humor, as does "Once, in the dear dead bye-and-bye, he had held her ear in his mouth. Gone, gone, it was now all gone" in the context of a superbly farcical cocktail party. But, like many windy after-dinner speakers, Mr. Gold has a tendency to ruin a little joke by overdoing it:

> And he topped his hand briefly, non-pederastically, over mine in order to indicate brotherly feeling, friendship, trust, confidence, and that at this stage in his analysis he could hold hands with a man in a restaurant without feeling queer.

"Non-pederastically" establishes the joke, and the rest of the sentence repeats it. And the passage goes on:

> I squeezed back; he squeezed; we squeezed in unison; the final squeeze clinched it that I probably wouldn't be fired, maybe not just promoted, in case my campaigns failed, and that at the very least I would someday have a weekend in Southampton to remember him by. Pensively we untangled our hands from what might have been.

The trouble with the jokes in *Salt*, however, is more serious than their tendency to be repetitious and overlong; they are burlesque masquerading as satire, low comedy pretending to be high. And in true satire the joke and the moral are inseparable; in *Salt*, when the author wants to be funny, he is (in a fairly slapstick fashion), but when he wants to moralize, he preaches. No genuine satirist would indulge in the self-pity, the nagging, and the homiletics that appear in *Salt*:

> "Let's finish what I was saying. Men used to begin their lives with love and end it [sic] with ambition. Now we begin with love and ambition and finish with ambition and love—no good order to things anymore."
> "Do you miss good order?"
> "Yes, I do. I do."

Whatever this means, Mr. Gold should not have to say it. The moral should lie in the humorous portrait, and need not be gravely, didactically tacked on.

Not the least of the author's problems is that he seems caught between the naughty-boy fantasies expressed in his inscrutable characters and the righteous indignation of his basically bourgeois heroes. "My stomach hurt," says Dan after watching the interlude at the slot machine; Mr. Gold's too. On his cynical side, he repeatedly invents crude horrors—cataloguing imaginary instances of brutality, imbecility, and perversion—and then he points to them, aghast. It is often unjust to identify an author's sensibility with that of his characters, but in his case it is almost impossible not to do so: Mr. Gold has written the very novel that his urban and suburban characters, full of the satirical stereotypes that have long been current even in bourgeois irony, would have written; the clichés are precisely those of cocktail-party conversation. And he has thrown in a few imaginary scandals that only a bourgeois, essentially puritan fantasy could contrive; most of the sordid jokes are merely those that might be told, with some embarrassment, in an office men's room. It is Babbitt, walking the streets of Manhattan, who has written *Salt*, with glee and shame at the daring of his own imagination.

> Peter felt very cruel and drew obscure satisfaction from this judgment of himself.

So does Mr. Gold. And what is unfortunate is that without his commitment to cruelty and irony he might conceivably write carefully and well. When the author writes of the "spinster tributaries" into which Barbara's life divides after her affair with Peter, or of the "telebachelor nod" that Peter and Dan exchange to communicate Dan's acceptance of her, it seems possible that there lies buried in *Salt* a literary talent that has simply smothered in its own misanthropy, a product of the modern convention which requires that writing, critical or creative, become not a work of art but a line of attack. On Grub Street, as on Madison Avenue, there can be a compulsion to conform, to obtain by the suppression of one's individual talents an assurance of having entered the right circles. *Salt* is an application for membership in the fraternity of fashionable discontents, all of whom would blush to utter an unsarcastic or an unpolemic word in an angry middle-aged Establishment that perennially and tediously pre-empts the revolution. With clichés, symbols, sordid fantasies, and outraged declamations, Mr. Gold has issued yet another in the apparently interminable series of middle-class bohemian manifestoes.

# Fly Trans-Love Airways

O<small>N A LITTLE PATCH OF LAND</small>
just outside the city limits of Los Angeles, on that portion of
Sunset Boulevard which is called Sunset Strip, there is a large
billboard that advertises a casino in Las Vegas. Set on top of the
billboard, dressed in red boots, long red gloves, and black-and-
white striped panties attached across the midriff to a red bikini
top, is an immense, pink plaster chorus girl. One of her arms is
bent, hand slightly forward and upraised, at the elbow. Her
other arm extends, fingers outstretched, behind. One of her
knees is raised. The other leg is the one she stands and slowly,
continuously rotates on. Diagonally southwest across the street
from the girl, much nearer the ground, on a little pedestal, another figure in red gloves, striped panties, and red top rotates in
a similar pose. It is Bullwinkle the Moose. Somewhere west of
the girl and east of the moose, the jurisdiction of the Los Angeles

Police Department ends and the Los Angeles County Sheriff's territory begins. Since the Strip was for a good part of its history a center of gambling and prostitution, it has always remained part of the "county island" of West Hollywood, and resisted incorporation into the City of Los Angeles. For tax reasons, and perhaps because of rumors that the gambling, at least, will be allowed to return, it resists incorporation now. Very near this border outpost, on a recent Saturday night, a small band of Dickensian characters—two tall, pale women with thin, reddish hair; one short, stout, bustling brunette; and four men, rather unsteady on their feet—set up a portable loud-speaker system on the sidewalk and began to preach. Several boys and girls who had been sitting quietly on two of the benches that line the Strip at bus stops, and several others, who had been leaning against the white picket fence that surrounds a small pink-and-yellow café called Pandora's Box—closed, like several other rock-'n'-roll and cherry-Coke establishments, by the police, on account of some recent disturbances—gathered around to watch. One of them wore a kind of harlequin cap with many floppy, green ear-like appendages, from each of which there hung a silver bell. Another wore blue jeans, a suede jacket, an undershirt, a mauve tie, and a top hat. Two wore gray Confederate jackets. Several wore wooly vests over shirts with leather laces at the collar—open to reveal striped turtleneck jerseys underneath. Nearly all wore slacks cut quite low at the hips, and one wore a lumberjacket. Although the night was quite cold, three were barefoot, and one had on apparently homemade red-and-black slippers turned up at the toes. The rest wore boots. All of them stood in a loose but attentive cluster a bit to one side of the preaching band.

"My happiest moment," a man who was missing a front tooth was saying, with a practiced homiletic quaver, into the microphone, "was when I saw myself a sinner. I traded in my sins for Jesus, and, believe me, I got the best of the deal." The teen-agers drifted a short way off, and the speaker raised his voice. "I know you young people," he said. "You talk dirty and your minds are dirty. You don't want no one to have a claim on you. You don't want to be obligated. But you're obligated, sinners, because there is a God above."

"How do you know?" asked the boy in the top hat.

"Because I love God," the man said hoarsely; and as he continued to preach, one of the tall, pale women went about nudging the teen-agers and offering them inspirational tracts—among them a green one entitled "7 Communists Go Singing Into Heaven."

A Los Angeles patrol car, containing two helmeted policemen staring straight ahead, cruised by.

"Why don't they ask these hypocrites to move along?" a barefoot girl in a shaggy sweater, slacks, and yachting cap said, in a bitter voice. "They're blocking the sidewalk. They're trying to incite us to riot. They're obviously winos. How come The Man never hassles anyone but the longhairs?"

"I want to listen to this," said a short, plump girl beside her. "I haven't had such a treat in years." Suddenly, she slung her large leather purse over her shoulder, pulled a few strands of hair over one eye, and, raising the other eyebrow, began to walk slowly and suggestively back and forth in front of the speaker, who turned sideways.

"This bearded sinner tells me he is Jewish," the speaker said, pointing to a young man wearing black slacks and a black shirt, with a pair of what appeared to be calipers hung on a string around his neck. "Well, I want to tell you about the greatest Jew that ever walked the earth. . . ."

"Yodel, Billy," the barefoot girl in the yachting cap said to the young man in black. He began to yodel. The gap-toothed man continued to preach. The tall, pale woman continued to distribute pamphlets. The short, plump girl continued to walk back and forth. A bus pulled up in front of the benches, and a gray-haired, stolid-looking couple, evidently tourists, got laboriously out.

"O Lord, O Lord, O Lord, here they are, Henry, will you look at them," the lady said, smoothing down the skirt of her dress and looking directly at the girl in the yachting cap. "I'm glad I raised mine right."

"What are you looking at, you old bag?" the short, plump girl asked, standing still for a moment.

The couple began to walk away.

"It's Sonny and Chèr," the boy in the top hat said as they passed him. "I'd know them anywhere."

The gap-toothed man had leaned away from his microphone

and was now addressing the group in a rather intimate tone about "your dirty, filthy sins and your unclean habits."

The boy in the lumberjacket, who had been looking for some time at the girl in the yachting cap, suddenly walked over and took her hand. He led her wordlessly to a point directly in front of the man who was speaking, and kissed her. When, after several minutes, they looked up, the gap-toothed man (although he watched them with apparent fascination) was still preaching, so they kissed again and remained in each other's arms until the sound of a guitar farther down the street—in front of a café called the Fifth Estate—caused the teen-age group to disperse and drift toward the music.

"Before you go to bed this very night . . ." the speaker was saying, as the young longhairs walked away. And several of them tried—with such phrases as "turn on," "freak out," and "take the pill"—to complete his sentence for him.

What seems to have brought the Strip to its present impasse —it is practically deserted but for these little evangelical bands of elderly squares and young longhairs, bent on mutual conversion—was an economic battle with, and over, teen-agers; and what apparently drew the teen-agers to the Strip in the first place was a musical development. In the late fifties and early sixties, by all accounts, the Strip was dull. The old, expensive restaurants, left over from the golden days of Hollywood, were in a steep decline. Near the middle of the Strip, there was (and still is) an attractive stretch of clothing and antique shops called Sunset Plaza, but the rest was lined (and is) with hot-dog stands, car-rental agencies, and billboards—changed with the rapidity of flash cards—advertising casinos, airlines, films, and mortuaries.

Then, in 1963, a southern California surf-rock group, the Beach Boys, acquired a national reputation, and, beginning in 1964, the Los Angeles area—with Sonny and Chèr, the Byrds, the Mama's and the Papa's, the Lovin' Spoonful, and such indigenous and locally popular groups as the Love, the Seeds, the Iron Butterfly, and the Buffalo Springfield—became a center for all kinds of rock. Phil Spector, the record producer, set up offices on the Strip; a huge teen dance hall called the Hullabaloo opened down the boulevard; and a number of night clubs on the Strip went rock. This drew—in addition to the teen-age clientele—some established, serious longhairs from the two-car bohemia in the canyons above the boulevard, more serious longhairs from the less affluent bohemias of Venice and Long Beach, and some motorcycle groups. The motorcyle groups were soon dispersed; a hint from a Sunset Plaza merchants' association caused red no-parking lines to be painted all along the curb where the motor-cyclists were accustomed to park, and a hot-dog stand called the Plush Pup put up a sign announcing that complaints from neighbors had made it impossible for the place to welcome guests on motorcycles. The serious longhairs were soon made uncomfortable, too; some of their favorite haunts, like the Trip and the Action, were closed for various reasons, and the Strip itself became a very difficult place for the marijuana, drug, or LSD users among them to make a connection.

The serious longhairs returned—temporarily, at least—to their beaches and canyons; the teen-agers, however, remained awhile. The notorious sprawl of Los Angeles—where, for example, it may take a maid two and a half hours to make her way by bus from Watts to Beverly Hills—leaves the city at night diffused and lifeless. The Strip became a kind of Main Street where the young (who drove or hitched a ride from the surrounding area) could spend their time. They soon came in such numbers that they brought traffic nearly to a halt. Restaurant proprietors on the Strip, who saw their business dwindling even further, took steps. All last summer, invoking an old city-and-county curfew law that prohibits people under eighteen from lingering on the street after 10 P.M., the sheriff's men were stopping people with long hair or wearing unusual clothes to demand identification (draft cards, driver's licenses), as proof of age. In addition, a number of ad-hoc ordinances were put into effect. Twenty-one is the legal drinking age in California, but people eighteen and over had for years been welcome to dance at rock establishments with liquor licenses, where the minors got Cokes, while drinks were served to their elders; under a new ordinance, no one under twenty-one was permitted to dance in a place where liquor was served.

The Whisky a Go Go, once an important center for West Coast rock and one of the few places on the Strip to survive this legal maneuver, tried several solutions, in series. First, it continued serving liquor and put minors on benches in the balcony, but the young customers, who wanted to dance, went elsewhere. Then it stopped serving liquor and raised its admission price from two dollars to three; the minors came back, but the attractive liquor profits were lost. A few weeks ago, the Whisky enlarged its stage to occupy the entire dance floor, which means that there is no room to dance while a live performance is on. It also raised the price of admission to three-fifty, started serving liquor again, and required guests between eighteen and twenty-one to have their hands marked with an ultraviolet stamp, so that they would be easily identifiable as below drinking and dancing age. At the same time, the Whisky's entertainment went *Motown*—a change that the teen-agers, for complicated reasons of their own, associate with the return of the Mafia and Las Vegas interests to the Strip. (Young longhairs are almost unanimous in their conviction that they were cleared off the Strip to make room for more serious, less conspicuous forms of vice than lingering after curfew.) In any case, the Whisky's action could only make teen-agers feel less welcome there. Throughout the spring and summer, licenses permitting minors to be served anything at all were revoked at one place after another; several of these places reluctantly went adult and topless—a change that seemed to cause the authorities no distress. Gradually, the campaign worked. Few but the hardiest or most lost teen-agers cared to risk the "hassle" that awaited them on the Strip.

Then, just before Halloween, two high-school students mimeographed a hundred leaflets announcing a "demonstration" for the evening of November 12, 1966, in front of Pandora's Box, to protest "Police Mistreatment of Youth," and Al Mitchell, a former seaman in the merchant marine who runs the Fifth Estate, gave them the money to print a few thousand more. Mitchell, a moderate-looking man in his middle forties, had shot a film about the striking grape pickers of California, and he was preparing *Blue Fascism*, a documentary about the Los Angeles Police Department, at the time the leaflets were put out. On November 12, a crowd of thousands—high-school students, dropouts, New Left university students, parolees from a nearby reform school, serious longhairs, squares, runaways, sympathizers, passersby, and the merely curious—gathered in front of Pandora's Box, and Mitchell got more footage than he had anticipated. The crowd, through its sheer size, stopped traffic for a considerable period, and a few of its members caused a total of a hundred and fifty-eight dollars' worth of damage to a bus and a liquor store. (In a demonstration some weeks before, several U.C.L.A. football fans—disappointed that U.S.C. rather than their own team had been invited to the Rose Bowl—stopped every single car on the San Diego Freeway, ostensibly to see whether there were any U.S.C. students inside; the U.C.L.A. fans probably caused more damage, and certainly caused less outrage, than the crowd outside Pandora's Box.)

The Los Angeles police began to attack the crowd with billy clubs from the eastern side, driving them westward along the Strip. The sheriff's men, standing across the county line, saw what they thought was a hostile crowd of longhairs advancing on them and took action. Several people were hurt, others arrested. Later that night, when a group of teen-agers were gathered in Pandora's Box listening to a shy and talented group called the World War III, the police surrounded the building and ordered the management to close in seven minutes. A police bus pulled up and policemen pounded on the walls of Pandora's Box and ordered the occupants out—to arrest them for loitering after 10 P.M. William Tilden, a soft-spoken man in his thirties, who has managed Pandora's Box for seven years, let the teen-agers telephone their homes for permission to stay overnight. They finally left when the police were called off, about three in the morning. In the following weeks, Tilden was arrested on a felony charge—alleged assault on two police officers—for which he has yet to stand trial, Pandora's Box was closed and condemned, and a highway project that was to have demolished the place in 1969 was accelerated.

Since a teen-age establishment under suspension of license may legally open on holidays, Tilden opened his place on New Year's Eve. There was not room enough inside to dance, but the World War III played for several hours to a colorful, quiet audience. Tilden himself stood rather sadly outside, replying to a question posed by several young longhairs—whether he might open the place one day as a private club. He did not know; it depended on the outcome of his trial. There was an elegiac air to the occasion, and something incongruous: like a scene from *A Midsummer Night's Dream* taking place in a bomb shelter. On other evenings, there had been some demonstrations with which Al Mitchell was not involved, and two (on November 26th and on December 10th) with which he was. (He had asked Tilden to join him, but Tilden declined.) By this time, however, Mitchell had founded RAMCOM (the Rights of Assembly and Movement Committee), and he had been joined by an organization called CAFF (Community Action for Facts and Freedom), which included, among others, Lance Reventlow and the managers of the Beach Boys and the Byrds; by various unaffiliated parents, clergymen, and concerned adults in the community at large; and, indirectly, by the Provos, an anonymous anarchical group (whose original branch was formed in Holland), who complicated matters delightfully by singing Christmas carols on the Strip before Christmas, and on several occasions after. In mid-December, RAMCOM and CAFF negotiated a truce with the police—a truce that despite RAMCOM posters reading "Police Capitulate," has so far consisted only of a ban on demonstrations from the teen-age side.

All this profusion of issues and organizations seems to have bred a special California variety of cause-dilettante—hobby-activists who spend their leisure hours no longer even picketing but simply milling about on behalf of something until the police arrive and hit someone. The Strip demonstrations brought together yet again, under the general heading of Protest, those familiar adult co-demonstators—New Radicals, Zen mystics, aesthetic avant-gardists, and drug proselytizers—already so strangely easy in each other's company. They also brought police, wielding clubs on behalf of specific economic interests. The teenagers (whom the police harassed, and on whose account the demonstrations were held) saw two life styles not so much in conflict as freezing each other into attitudes: on the one hand, the constellation that is longhair, bohemia, the New Left, individualism, sexual freedom, the East, drugs, the arts; on the other, arms, uniforms, conformity, the Right, convention, Red-baiting, authority, the System.

Some middle-hairs who were previously uncommitted made their choice—and thereby made more acute a division that had already existed between them. At Palisades High School, in a high-income suburb of Los Angeles, members of the football team shaved their heads by way of counter-protest to the incursions of the longhairs. The longhairs, meanwhile, withdrew from the competitive life of what they refer to as the Yahoos—sports, grades, class elections, popularity contests—to devote themselves to music, poetry, and contemplation. It is not unlikely that a prosperous, more automated economy will make it possible for this split to persist into adult life: the Yahoos, on an essentially military model, occupying jobs; the longhairs, on an artistic model, devising ways of spending leisure time. At the moment, however, there is a growing fringe of waifs, vaguely committed to a moral drift that emerged for them from the confrontations on the Strip and from the general climate of events. The drift is Love; and the word, as it is now used among the teen-agers of California (and as it appears in the lyrics of their songs), embodies dreams of sexual liberation, sweetness, peace on earth, equality—and, strangely, drugs.

The way the drugs came into Love seems to be this: As the waifs abandoned the social mystique of their elders (work, repression, the power struggle), they looked for new magic and new mysteries. And the prophets of chemical insight, who claimed the same devotion to Love and the same lack of interest in the power struggle as the waifs, were only too glad to supply them. Allen Ginsberg, in an article entitled "Renaissance or Die," which appeared in the *Los Angeles Free Press* (a local New Left newspaper) last December, urged that ". . . everybody who hears my voice, directly or indirectly, try the chemical LSD at least once, every man, woman, and child American in good health over the age of fourteen," and Richard Alpert (the former psychedelic teammate of Timothy Leary), in an article in *Oracle* (a newspaper of the hallucinogenic set), promised, "In about seven or eight years the psychedelic population of the United States will be able to vote anybody into office they want to, right? Through purely legal channels, right?" The new waifs, who, like many others in an age of ambiguities, are drawn to any expression of certainty or confidence, any semblance of vitality or inner happiness, have, under pressure and on the strength of such promises, gradually dropped out, in the Leary sense, to the point where they are economically unfit, devoutly bent on powerlessness, and where they can be used. They are used by the Left and the drug cultists to swell their ranks. They are used by politicians of the Right to attack the Left. And they are used by their more conventional peers just to brighten the landscape and slow down the race a little. The waifs drift about the centers of longhair activism, proselytizing for LSD and Methedrine (with arguments only slightly more extreme than the ones liberals use on behalf of fluoridation), and there is a strong possibility that although they speak of ruling the world with Love, they will simply vanish, like the children of the Children's Crusade, leaving just a trace of color and gentleness in their wake.

The Fifth Estate, a white stucco structure, managed by Mitchell and, until three weeks ago, owned by a publishing house that puts out *Teen, Hot Rod,* and *Guns and Ammo* magazines (and whose head, Robert E. Petersen, was, until recently, a city commissioner appointed by Mayor Samuel Yorty), used to be entered through a patio enclosed on two sides by one white and one yellow wall. The white wall, which faces the sidewalk, has been painted with black letters that spell out "WELCOME TO LOS ANGELES: CITY OF BLUE FASCISM." The yellow wall has become little more than a tilted arch over an immense hole and a complicated pile of debris. One Monday morning in January, a motorist veered from the westbound lane of the Strip, crossed the eastbound lane, and drove through the yellow wall, across the patio, through a large picture window, and into a room at the Fifth Estate in which films used to be shown. Since the accident happened at 4:30 A.M., no films were being shown at the time. Police who investigated claim that the driver had fallen asleep at the wheel. But a boy who was sitting in the room on a folding chair when the car drove in believes the man was merely drunk.

The Fifth Estate serves coffee, hot chocolate, Cokes, and sandwiches, but its customers do not normally eat or drink much. They play cards or chess at large, round tables, or they talk. Some of them, who earn their keep by looking after the place, sleep there. (The coffeehouse is, in any case, open until 6 A.M.) Because the Fifth Estate has no entertainment license, no one is permitted to sing or to play the guitar inside, and among writings and sketches covering the walls there is a warning to this effect. (The sheriff's men, equipped with glaring flashlights, run frequent checks in search of addicts and runaways, and to see that no one inside is playing or singing.) What playing or singing there is occurs outside, in the alleyway or near the painted wall in front.

On the patio of the Fifth Estate, on a recent Thursday night (Al Mitchell, the manager, was in a back room discussing with a young lawyer from the American Civil Liberties Union the possibility of deluging the Los Angeles Police Department with lawsuits, not in any hope of winning them but for nuisance value), a few young longhairs were gathered, more or less waiting around. One of the curious things about the young longhairs on the Strip these days is the special air with which they wait around: they seem already to inhabit some sort of leisure-time frontier, where all social problems have been solved and there remain no injustices but the ones in nature, where there is nothing to do but to wait in some small café for the coming of the Word. On this occasion, the waiting young longhairs (who will be presented here under fictional first names to protect their privacy) were Zak, a twenty-two-year-old, with sideburns, from Chicago; Marie, eighteen, Zak's girl, who lives more or less with her parents in Los Angeles; Dot, another eighteen-year-old girl (wearing a dress made of white lace over burgundy satin, pale burgundy tights, and black ballet slippers, and, around her neck, a string of Indian bells), who lives with the family of another girl, "because my mother and I don't get along"; and Len, a seventeen-year-old waiter and boarder at the Fifth Estate, who had left his home in New Jersey early in October with a friend (who got homesick and hitchhiked back after a week). There was also another longhair, obviously much older than the rest, whose vest was covered with buttons reading "Jesus Pleases," "Come to Middle Earth," and "At Least George Murphy Could Dance," among other things, and who was reading a copy of the *Free Press*.

Len, who said he planned to return home "as soon as they don't need my help out here anymore," expressed sorrow that he had forgotten to write to his eleven-year-old sister on her birthday.

"I never know what to write home," Zak said, scuffing one of his boots on the stones. "What am I going to write? Hello, I'm here, you're there, hello? What else is there to say? It's always a hassle."

Dot said she would be returning to her own house for a few days, to babysit with her younger brother and sister while her parents went on a holiday to Las Vegas. (The frequency with which California teen-agers are asked to care for their younger siblings, or their friends' siblings, creates a thriving nomad-baby-sitter economy.) She asked Zak and Marie whether they would pick her up the following evening—to go first to the studio of a sculptor named Vito, and later on (from 2 to 6 A.M.) to a rock session called the After Hours at the Hullabaloo.

Zak said he couldn't afford it. He had invested all his money in applying for a license to open a coffeehouse—which, since the name "The Trip" was already taken, he hoped to call The Travel Agency. His application had made no progress at all, and he was waiting for Al Mitchell, who had promised to let him call his coffeehouse, for a time, the Fifth Estate Annex. Marie said she would hitch a ride to Dot's place, without Zak, and she and Dot could hitch a ride to Vito's place together.

A young man, fairly conventionally dressed and coiffed, crossed the patio toward the group. "Has the Man been here tonight?" he asked, speaking low and rapidly.

"No," Zak said.

The young man immediately removed his jacket and tie, and brushed what proved to be an astonishing amount of hair forward from behind his ears. "Out there, I have to think of my job," he said, and slouched against a wall to wait around with the rest.

The *Free Press* recently opened a bookstore on Fairfax Avenue, which intersects Sunset Boulevard a few yards from the eastern end of the Strip. The store is right across the street from Canter's Restaurant, a large delicatessen, inside and in front of which, for some months now, the longhairs—old and young, and of every persuasion—have been gathering at two every morning. The reaction of the restaurant's manager to the types who now frequent his place is less than hospitable; he comments, as they pass to their tables, "What a sight!" and "Why don't they wash?" and he stands, vigilant, at the cash register to block the entrance of anyone who is not wearing shoes. (A policeman outside tries to keep the crowd there from blocking the sidewalk and from engaging in traffic in marijuana or drugs.) The *Free Press* bookstore, called the Kazoo, is open from ten in the morning until 2

A.M. In addition to a very wide and good selection of paper-backs, it sells many books and pamphlets about the assassination of President Kennedy, innumerable little magazines and obscure works (including a six-page poem, "The Love Book," by Lenore Kandel, which was recently confiscated on grounds of obscenity in San Francisco), many works on drugs and hallucinogens, and some works on religions of the East (including one called *Practical Mysticism*). There is also a counter at which the shop sells objets d'art, buttons ("Ronald Reagan for Fuehrer," "Be Creative, Invent a Sexual Perversion," "Visit Your Mother Today. Maybe She Hasn't Had Any Problems Lately"), posters of movie stars, psychedelic (systematically distorted and ballooning) posters for rock groups, pastel cigarette papers, and holders, called "roach clips," for conserving the last drag on marijuana butts.

At 1 A.M. on the Friday when Marie and Dot were to hitch a ride to Vito's, John Hammond, a bearded clerk at the Kazoo, was consoling a teen-age girl who had walked into the store in tears. "A little LSD therapy is O.K., but nothing with needles," he was saying. "You want to open yourself up, not close yourself down. Find the easiest way to go, and if it's functional, that's beautiful." Some of the other clerks were knocking down walls to make room for a bookshelf, and Mrs. Art Kunkin, wife of the editor and publisher of the *Free Press,* was talking with two young entrepreneurs who were earning part of their way through college by distributing—to order—posters, bumper stickers, decals for sweat shirts, flutes, and buttons. It turned out they could supply, in particular, some highly coveted Lenny Bruce posters, and Mrs. Kunkin asked whether they could deliver a few dozen right away. She sighed as they went out the door. "It's always nice to have a brush with the ultimate success," she said.

That same morning, farther up Fairfax Avenue, in front of a coffeehouse called the Blue Grotto, whose customers generally sit about in semi-darkness in a kind of gentle half sleep, the police arrested two young longhairs on suspicion of armed robbery.

At eleven-thirty that Friday night, when Dot (still wearing the dress of white lace over burgundy satin and the string of Indian bells, but now with white net stockings and black buckled shoes) and Marie (wearing a pale-green dress, white

net stockings, and brown buckled shoes) entered the home and sculpture school of Vito Paulekas—a storefront and three floors, known to all simply as Vito's place—the entryway was dark, but the pale bare feet of a young man slouched on a chair against the wall were visible. Vito called to the girls from the top of a flight of stairs to go down and see the sculptures in the basement. They went down. The sculpture class for the evening was over, but several people were still at work on red clay nudes, supported by dowels and wire armatures. The basement walls were covered with signs, among them a thinly lettered one reading, "Dear President Johnson. Being spring, I would prefer more flowers."

A woman in a canvas shirt, burlap slacks, and boots, who was modelling a large bust of a man, asked Dot to come over and look. "What does he look like to you?" she asked. "I mean, what sort of person?"

"He looks like a groovy guy," Dot said.

"I mean, what sort of impression does he make? Does he attract you physically?" the woman asked.

Before Dot could answer, a tall, slender girl in a polo shirt and blue jeans—looking about sixteen, and wearing a scalloped horn from an old phonograph on her head—drew Dot away to look at a small erotic sculpture, on a shelf full of small erotic sculptures, all of which (like the lettering on the psychedelic posters at the Kazoo) were distorted, like reflections in a hall of mirrors. "I just made this new one tonight," she said. "What do you think of it? It's Vito and Sue. Isn't it groovy?" (Sue is Vito's wife.)

Dot said that the little sculpture was groovy, and the girl led the way upstairs. It turned out that her name was Meg, that her parents brought her to stay at Vito's house every weekend, and that she was twelve.

The second floor of Vito's house is a kind of lair, with Oriental decor, Oriental music piped in from below, and walls hung with tapestries, bits of colored glass, feather dusters, beads, dolls, a dart board, a bamboo screen, a violin, and an armadillo shell. Between two sofas set against opposite walls is a coffee table supported by cinder blocks. On the table that night were a copy of *Time*, several delicately painted tongue depressors, some assorted photographs, a piece of velvet, a branch of pussy willow, a copy of *Playboy,* a copy of *Torrid Cinema* (with an article about Vito in it), a half-completed pair of red-and-black leather sandals turned up at the toes, and pot of glue. The young man whose bare feet had been visible in the entryway had followed Dot, Marie, and Meg up the stairs. He immediately picked up the pot of glue and began to sniff.

"Hey, that's for the sandals," Meg said. "You know nobody gets high in Vito's house."

The boy put the gluepot down.

Vito, a man in his early fifties, with a sandy mustache and pale-blue eyes, entered the room and said hello to everyone. He was wearing velvet slacks and a pale embroidered cape. Sue, who was pregnant, followed him in. She was wearing a short dress, tights, and a crocheted poncho, and on her fingers she had eight rings. Vito announced that they were both going to take a nap in preparation for the After Hours at the Hullabaloo. Meg suddenly became very tense, and raced out of the room. "What shall I wear?" she shouted several times to Sue from an adjoining room. "Same thing we wear to the freakouts?" When she reappeared, she had drawn fine interlacing green lines around her eyes and across the bridge of her nose. She was wearing a poncho, completely open at the sides, apparently made out of a fluffy white bedspread, and a pair of slacks, which the poncho did not quite reach, made of the same material, bell-bottomed, and cut low at the hips. Vito and Sue retired for their nap, requesting Meg to wake them at 1 A.M.

Meg sat down next to Dot and Marie, and explained that Vito had arranged for them all to dance at the Hullabaloo as performers, because of a complicated licensing regulation. "They're wiping out the dancing, so everybody's getting zonked out, right?" she said. "As soon as everybody's on one thing, they make it illegal. Some of those kids they arrest on the Strip, you know, they call up the parents and say, 'We've got your kid on suspicion of narcotics.' 'Suspicion of narcotics.' They just don't like the kids and the dancing. They could arrest you on suspicion of being a Martian. They could arrest you for using the wrong deodorant."

"People don't think," Dot said. "It was dead on the Strip without the kids there."

"They're going to be locked in their own houses sooner or

later without us, and they don't even know it," Meg said. "But a whole lot of people are strange. I'm not even sure they're well—are you ready for that? Everybody should dance, and love, and go about their business, right? But those poor cops, those poor screwed-up cops, they don't have the words to yell, so they just scream, you know—they just came down the Strip screaming. They're frightened, right?"

"Nobody had guns," Marie said, referring to the night of November 12th.

"They didn't have guns," Meg said. "They were afraid they'd use them, they were that screwed up."

"They were afraid if they brought guns, the guns would get broken," Marie said. "We would have broken them."

"Man, if you have this hostility, you learn to take it out in loving ways," Meg said. "If you love somebody, you really groove with them, right? I'm writing things down in a book for myself, because my parents—well, they're very beautiful for their own thing, but they just don't know."

"My parents just can't stand it," Marie said. "They can't stand my bare feet. They can't stand to see me sleep all day. They say, 'You ought to find a job. You ought to be self-supporting.' I say, 'Why? All I do is sleep here once in a while. Why can't I have a free life?' My mother worries about the people I hang out with. I can't explain—people aren't what they look like or what they wear. . . ."

"You're judged by the people you run with, right?" Meg said. "I'm adopted, and my parents really love me. And that's too bad, because my real mother was probably some unwed mother that I could have grooved with." She picked up the pussy willow and waved it thoughtfully. "Sometimes I'm so messed up you don't even know," she said. "I'm not even sure if I'm really here."

"I worry about that, too," Marie said. "Sometimes I think I'm dead and I'm hallucinating the whole thing."

Three girls, all dressed in dark-blue skirts and jackets, with dark-blue hats, and with lace handkerchiefs in their jacket pockets, came up the staircase, looked around, and silently went down the stairs again.

Meg, whose slacks were splitting slightly at the seams, took them off, went to get a needle and some thread, and sat down to sew.

"Have you ever had the idea you might be in somebody else's dream?" Dot asked.

"Well, if you're hallucinating the whole thing, you can change it, right?" Meg said, biting off the thread. "It's like when you're having a bad trip—you see what's real, or what you think is real, and you get upset. You've got to say to yourself, 'You're on a drug, it's only a drug.' Sometimes it takes awhile to change it. But can you imagine how creative your mind must be if you're dreaming the whole thing?"

The conversation stayed on metaphysics for another hour, during which the girls in the dark suits appeared twice more and the boy with bare feet never uttered a word. At one point, Dot and Meg began to reminisce about how they had become acquainted—in a juvenile home, where Meg had been sent as a "habitual runaway," and Dot for the vaguer offense of what she described as being "in danger of leading an idle and desolate life." They spoke of a ghost story the Mexican inmates used to tell—about "La Harona," a woman who, crazed by syphilis, killed her children.

"They said if you shouted 'La Harona!' five times, she would come to you," Meg said, "and a lot of kids in my unit wanted to test it."

"I was so terrified I cried all night," Dot said. "They said she comes through mirrors." Both girls still seemed terrified at this thought.

"Wouldn't it be funny if you could look at yourself without looking in a mirror?" Meg said. Then she began talking about a boy friend who had first brought her to Vito's. "I was completely freaked out at the time," she said. "Pete just brought me here, and I grooved on the place. He used to wear two belts and wild flowers. Now he plays in a jazz group and wears a suit, but I still love him. The chick he married loves me, too, but I think two's company."

One of the three girls in blue suits now appeared at the top of the stairs again, wearing gold-rimmed glasses and carrying a piece of the red clay. She began to dance by herself.

Dot and Meg spoke of their last day at the juvenile home. They had sculpted a large eye together in an art class, and they had asked for permission to take it with them when they left.

"But the teacher at juvey said, 'You have to finish it,'" Meg said. "And, of course, we told her it was finished. But she said, 'No, that isn't finished, you have to paint it.' " "So we didn't get to take it," Dot said.

By this time, Vito and Sue were getting up from their nap, and a crowd gradually assembled at the top of the stairs. A fourth girl in dark blue now joined the three others. An Oriental boy in a paisley shirt and suede pants appeared, and then a girl in a scarlet pants suit, and one in a purple pants suit (both wore matching derbies and ties), and a man in what looked like a matador outfit, a man with chaps and a ten-gallon hat, a girl in a piece of silk bordered and tufted with fur, a girl in a fringed deerslayer jacket and orange bell-bottom trousers, a bearded man in a kind of bishop's mantle, and several others in puff hats or floppy hats or with red bows tied all over their hair. The entire group departed in four carloads for Sunset Boulevard, to dance onstage in the After Hours at the Hullabaloo.

At 2 A.M. on Saturday, January 14th, the Hullabaloo, which holds about two thousand people, and which lies directly across the boulevard from the Hollywood Palladium (where, earlier that evening, Lawrence Welk had played for the National Smooth Dancer's Association Ball), was so full that the longhairs waiting outside occupied the entire block, not in any sort of line but extending radially over the area. A parking lot beside the Hullabaloo was full of cars, nearly all with their radios on, so a kind of concert of Donovan, the Beach Boys, Sonny and Chèr, and the Buffalo Springfield ("Fly trans-love airways/Getcha there on time. . . . Gotta keep those a'lovin' vibrations a'happenin' with her. . . . The best goes on. . . . Paranoia strikes deep/Into your life it will creep") was rising from the asphalt. Vito led his group in among the cars and around to the back of the building, where, after being questioned only briefly at the entrance, he smuggled them as "performers" up a ramp, and onto the back of the stage. Since the hours before morning had been Friday the thirteenth, thirteen groups were scheduled to play: the Sound Machine, the Mandala, the Peanut Butter Conspiracy, the Smokestack Lightning, the Factory, the Electric Prune, the Yellow Payges, the Sons of Adam, the Coloring Book, the Wild Ones, the Iron Butterfly, the Seeds, and the Love. The stage floor was a rotating platform divided in two by a backdrop curtain, so that while one group was playing the next could be warming up. (This arrangement created a sound backstage not unlike the one intentionally produced by some of the groups in the course of their normal engagements. The Love, for example, often plays with someone else's record of another song as background music.) The area backstage was full of people in costumes of one sort or another—denims, satins, burlaps, suedes, and one tutu. A lonely troubadour wearing knickers and a ruffled shirt walked around throughout the performances strumming a guitar. No one seemed to know him, and he was not a member of any group.

When the Sound Machine started to play, with a beat so deeply resonant that many members of the audience began to cough, Vito sent some of his group onstage. These included Meg, Dot, the barefoot boy, Vito's pregnant wife, and six others, and from the reaction of the audience—a polite but unsurprised attentiveness—it was obvious that they had seen the group before. Meg raised her arms and began to run quite gracefully about the stage, Dot began to bend at the waist and straighten up with regularity, as though she were keening, Sue began to wave her arms about in the air, pivot, and droop from side to side, and the barefoot boy began to sway quietly in place. The others frugged or improvised. The members of Vito's troupe who had remained backstage soon grew restless, and Vito kept promising them that they could go on at any moment. But the girl in the tutu could bear it no longer; she ran out onstage. A few seconds later, Meg's pants began to split again, and some of the audience started to laugh—though not unkindly—and applaud. Meg, looking rather frantic about the eyes, arrived backstage.

"Fix your pants, baby," Vito said quite calmly, producing what he called a "fraternity button," designed by him. "Just relax." Meg took the button, pinned her pants, and returned onstage.

By 5 A.M., six groups had played, and the Monkees, the Miracles, and the Mama's and the Papa's had joined the audience. Vito's group had been taken offstage earlier when it was announced that all further dancing would be done by two union dancers, in red spangles, on the balconies of the dance hall. Within moments, however, the two union dancers had been supplemented by a dancer in a silver costume and silver boots, who materialized onstage, and since no one seemed to know whether she was union or not, Vito took this as a cue to send his group back onstage, where they remained. The size of the audience had not diminished in the slightest, nor had the volume of the radio concert in the parking lot. At five, there was a pause, and both the audience and Vito's group seemed tense; everyone was quite sure that it was the Love's turn to play. By five-twenty, when there was still no sign of the Love, the management was trying to divert the crowd with jukebox music. The audience, however, appeared quite accustomed to delays of this sort; the pause seemed to bear out their expectation that the Love would be the next group to go on.

It was. A record was cut off abruptly, the front curtain rose, a group of four whites and three Negroes was revealed, and the lead singer, dressed in a black stocking cap and brown pants and vest, leaned slightly sideways, yawned briefly, and began to sing. The group, with what seemed a kind of driving, electronic desperation, played a song called "I Flash on You." When the song was over, the audience cheered a kind of desperation cheer, as one might cheer an acquittal verdict for a defendant against whom the case looked bad. The group played two more numbers, and then, in the middle of a song called "She Comes in Colors," the lead singer walked off. He did not return for several minutes, but the group played on. Then, when he did return, he ignored the microphone and sat down abruptly on a crate amid the electronic equipment. Several times, as the group still played, he seemed on the point of rising but sat down again. Finally, he rose, walked carefully forward, and, grasping the microphone, leaned forward a few moments, with teeth bared, and began to sing. He sang a long time, then stopped and let the group play several minutes more. Suddenly, in a calm speaking voice, he wished the audience a Merry Christmas and reminded them that Halloween might soon return. The front curtain dropped. The audience cheered again.

There was another extended pause, and then the Seeds appeared. They were greeted with an affection almost as obvious and ardent as the reception given the Love. Shortly after the Seeds had finished, the Peanut Butter Conspiracy began to play. And shortly after that (since the Hullabaloo is permitted to stay open only until 6 A.M.) the police, by unplugging the Conspiracy's electronic equipment and rounding up Vito's obviously exhausted but still enthusiastic dancers, induced the audience to leave. Only eight groups out of the scheduled thirteen had played, but the After Hours at the Hullabaloo was over.

In the early hours of the morning, posters had appeared at the Fifth Estate and the Kazoo and outside the Hullabaloo and Pandora's Box announcing "A Gathering of All Tribes, a Human Be-In," for noon on Saturday, in Los Angeles' Griffith Park—in sympathy with a similar event, with Allen Ginsberg, Timothy Leary, and Dick Gregory, to be held at the same hour in San Francisco. By 1:30 P.M. on Saturday, the park, which is in the canyons above Sunset Boulevard, had the air of a small-town picnic ground, with, instead of friendly interlocking groups from the Lions, Kiwanis, and Rotary, friendly interlocking groups from the drug, New Left, and teen-rock establishments. The Sound Machine was playing once again. Someone was distributing olive branches. Someone else was selling *Oracle*. Someone else was selling colored paper flowers. A fourth person was giving paper flowers away. Several people had brought their children, their dogs, and, in paper bags, their lunch. One young man was lying barefoot on the grass (it was a sunny day) with an Army helmet, painted gold, over his face; he kept running his fingers softly across the top of a lunchbox at his side. A St. Bernard with a paper flower in its collar was licking the young man's toes. Several transistor radios were playing softly. Vito and Meg were there, and so were Marie and Dot, the bearded clerk from the Kazoo and the girl he had consoled, and the boy who had not written to his eleven-year-old sister in New Jersey. A photographer for a fashion-trade publication was unobtrusively taking pictures. There was no police around at all.

# Sartre, Saint Genet
# and the Bureaucrat

Anti-Social violence can take either of two forms—crime or revolution—and the distinction between them is not always clear. The explosion of a bomb in the public square of an occupied city can be criminal or revolutionary, or both, depending on its motive and its result. The more democratic the government, however, the sharper the distinction becomes, until, in a truly free society, an idealist cannot be a man of violence at all. The conscience that impelled yesterday's revolutionary already finds peaceable expression in the social worker, Peace Corpsman, Freedom Rider, or president of the World Bank; his destructiveness is embodied only in the delinquent, the thief, and the murderer. When a society becomes so benevolent that there can be no legitimate confusion between personal insufficiencies and social grievances, the armed rebel has simply lost his cause to the good citizen, and his arms to the sick man of violence, in exile or in crime.

Jean Genet is a rebel in a society free and benign enough to embrace most good causes; since just wars are out of date, he cannot even vent his destructiveness abroad, as a soldier. He is, however, for apparent personal reasons (his illegitimacy, his ugliness, his sexual preferences) a violently angry man, and, in the absence of a moral outlet for physical hostility, he is left with crime itself as the ideal of his rebellion. Since philosophers from Socrates to Kant have argued fairly successfully, that one cannot consistently know the Good and promote Evil, Genet, as a philosopher-criminal, deliberately begins and ends in paradox. He desires what is, by definition, undesirable: failure; unhappiness; crime. It is the paradox of perfect masochism. A classic refuge of the mind from ignorance or paradox is mysticism, and Genet has founded a private cult, "the mystery of the nothing and the no," in which thieves are saints, murderers are gods, homosexuals are communicants, and "it is precisely sin which puts [one] in a state of Grace."

As a philosopher, Genet cannot be taken seriously. His position is simple, old, and untenable, and since he has no gift for abstractions, he is an unworthy heir to Protagoras, Raskolnikov, Faust, Iago, even the serpent in Eden, all of whom advanced powerful arguments against conventional morality before subsiding into or being defeated by it. As an artist, he does not bear comparison with Villon, de Sade, Huysmans, Baudelaire, or Gide either.

> The taste for singularity, the attraction of the forbidden, conspired to deliver me to evil. . . . Certainly this betrayal causes me infinite suffering, making me aware at once of my friendliness toward my victim and my still lively love of man. But, in the midst of this suffering, shame having burned me all over, it seems to me that there exists, amid the fires or rather the vapors of my shame, something invulnerable, formed of sharp, severe lines, a Diamond of the sort precisely called the Solitaire.

What is curious about this passage from his "Pompes Funebres" is that Genet should choose—in preference to the romantic metaphor of *fleurs du mal*—the image of a diamond purified within the flames of Hell. There is no flowering image of fertility, mortality, rather purity and permanence. And Genet is more akin to the Christian ascetics (the Jesuit Gerard Manley Hopkins' "immortal diamond") than to the French decadents to whom he has been compared. He seems to have a consistent repugnance for the notion of fertility. Whatever the reasons, Genet's art requires of him a puritanic abstinence from the temptations of the Good.

Genet falls short philosophically as a nihilist and aesthetically as a decadent, but there is a respect in which he is remarkable. From Lucifer to Zarathustra, for nihilists and decadents alike, the justification for radical rebellion against the moral law has been an aristocratic boredom of the superman in any order, however good. Modern psychology has, by implication, undercut this argument-from-superiority, and claimed to find its origins in sexual pathology. Rebellion has been reduced for Genet to Oedipal terms, and the detached intellectual or aesthetic princeling, theorizing and overturning forms at his leisure, becomes a wayward child, striking out against an essentially paternal authority. As a post-Freudian writer, Genet begins at the post-Freudian beginning, not with a proud statement of principle but with a whimpered confession of fact, with abject confidences. There is an old trick, Genet remarks at one point, "the trick of partial confession. Spontaneously I confess a little, the better to keep more serious things hidden." Sex, as a "more serious thing hidden," has since Freud lost its force in the arts. By making his confession overt, Genet leaves room for a still unanalyzed, unknowable "serious thing" beneath the surface of the obvious. Unlike de Sade, for example, Genet begins his radical rebellion in every sense from below; he arrives at his faulted theories only laboriously, through acts. He did not decide to become a criminal; he awoke one morning to find that he already was one, and felt obliged to explain himself. He is therefore qualified to articulate, as no genuine intellectual could, the rationale of that new and surprising phenomenon—the pure delinquent, the causeless rebel, the natural criminal who indulges in anti-social violence not out of principle or for material gain but for no discernible reason other than the sheer romance of crime. Genet has been described as a Cartesian philosopher meditating upon first principles and arriving at total negation. Nothing could be sillier: Genet is less a Cartesian in cerebral contact with the Devil than a conscious betrayer of the underworld, a stool pigeon, trying to render unto society an intelligible account of that dark underside of the social system which the French call "le Milieu."

What makes Genet's testimony particularly elusive is not only that it results, philosophically, in paradox—or that it assumes, aesthetically, an abstinence on behalf of decadence, or even that, by pure confession, it wards off Freudian analysis— but that it rests in fact upon a deception, a pose. "I love imposture," says Genet, and, even in his sexual role he is in every sense a man of the theatre. His novel *Our Lady of the Flowers* (Grove), an erotic fantasy jotted down on pieces of brown paper during one of his many terms in prison, is full of ruses, masquerades, and (a combination of mysticism and theatricality) rituals. "Our Lady" himself is a homosexual thief and strangler, assigned, in the author's fantasy, a Christlike role; Divine, another homosexual (who ultimately murders a child), becomes a kind of invert madonna; his consort, Darling, is a footloose pimp who embodies, one is led to suppose, the intervention of an elusive Holy Spirit.

Genet, lying in his prison cell, directs these imaginary characters through a series of disconnected scenes, alternately voluptuous and mystical. His book is a combination catechism and pornography, designed to titillate the author. On the wall facing his cot, Genet has hung for inspiration twenty photographs of infamous murderers and thieves, clipped from tabloids and popular magazines. He becomes sentimental about these heroes, like an adolescent girl with clippings from *Modern Screen*. Genet follows his characters through trials and orgies derived—he admits, with irony—from pulp fiction. And when, like many sentimental heroines, Divine dies, Genet renders lyric homage:

> Here is how our Great Divine died. Having looked for her little gold watch, she found it between her thighs and, with her fist closed over it, handed it to Ernestine, who was sitting at her bedside. . . . A vast physical peace relaxed Divine. Filth . . . spread out beneath her like a warm little lake, into which she gently, very gently . . . was engulfed, and with this relief she heaved another sigh, which rose to her mouth with blood, then another sigh, the last. Thus did she pass away, one might also say drowned.

Like many movie heroes, Our Lady arrives at a courtroom scene and a moment of glory—in Our Lady's case, the gratuitous confession of his crime, and an arrogant refusal to throw himself upon the sympathies of his accusers. He strangled his victim, he says, "because I was fabulously broke," and in the juxtaposition of "fabulous" and "broke" Genet finds yet another paradox—this time the Christian ethic of spiritual wealth in material poverty—to his argument, which finds in perfect sin an invert "sanctitude."

Paradox of any kind is quite congenial to Jean Paul Sartre, author of *Being and Nothingness,* who begins by stealing Genet's joke (calling the avowed arch-sinner "Saint Genet") and proceeds to write what is perhaps the longest work of criticism ever to be devoted to a minor author in his lifetime. Or perhaps *Saint Genet: Actor and Martyr* cannot properly be called a work of "criticism" at all. It is more like a skillful job of taxidermy. Sartre announces that Genet in his negativism is "dead." Then he empties the alleged corpse of its antinomies one by one: the Christian ("The summit of pride is the abyss of humility"), the Freudian ("The instant of the most intense pleasure is the end of pleasure"), the Kantian ("Theft, crime, and falsehood do not warrant being raised to the Universal"), the personal ("Jean Genet, the weakest of all and the strongest"), and, finally, the purely Sartrian ("There is only one [motive], the absence of motives"). Then, after warning us "not to regard as psychosis what is freedom working out its own salvation," he disregards his own warning and props Genet up again, full of the axioms of Existential psychology.

It is apparent from the first that Sartre is impatient with the unappetizing realities of his subject, and eager to turn to the ontological questions that have preoccupied Jean Wahl, Merleau-Ponty, and, of course, Sartre for years. Most of *Saint Genet* has little to do with Jean Genet, who becomes an almost embarrassing irrelevancy, an excuse for a textbook on Existentialism and phenomenology in which Sartre speaks, familiarly, of "doing for the sake of being" and in which he remarks typically, apropos of a girl who killed a rapist, that "she did not kill because she was raped; she was raped because she had to kill."

These remarks are not very illuminating for the character of Genet. At one rather surprising point, however, the philosophy of Sartre and the confessions of Genet do converge, in an implicit, almost Heraclitean idea of substance: the notion that while forms remain constant, personalities can flow in and out of them. In Genet's play *The Balcony,* when the real occupant of the royal household is killed by rebels, the madam of a bordello becomes queen in her stead. The forms are unaltered; only the personalities that occupy them are passing through. Or, as Our Lady says in court, "The public prosecutor has asked for my head and he will probably get it. But if he had lived my life he might be where I am now, and if I had lived his I might be prosecuting him." Or again, in a scene in *Our Lady of the Flowers,* when the homosexuals of Paris are called upon to testify, and are stripped on the witness stand of the mystery of their names (First Communion, Divine, Our Lady, and Mimosa become ordinary Antoine Berthollet, Louis Culafroy, Adrien Baillon, and René Hirsch), the banality of substance is exposed beneath the poetry of forms. "The faggots . . . lost their loveliest adornment, their names. . . . [and] showed the framework which Darling discerned behind the silk and velvet of every armchair." Even Genet's idea of Sanctitude-in-Evil is based upon traditional notions of substance and attribute: he objects that Saint Vincent de Paul, who served as a galley slave so that a prisoner might go free, was not a genuine saint (or Jesus, by implication, a true Saviour) because he adopted only the appearance of suffering, punishment, rather than the essence of suffering, the crime itself. To take on the burden of a sinner, a saint must take on not only the formal punishment but the substantial crime.

Sartre adapts Genet's idea of substance to Existential purposes. He claims that although Genet's birth was a "blunder," Genet himself was "inevitable" and "began as any child whatever." In other words, there existed substantially or statistically a Genet Position, a void that someone must occupy, but it was a historical accident that this particular Genet should grow to fill it. Sartre argues that from the moment when the child Genet was caught in his first act of theft, he was forced by his discoverer to fill the position of the Thief Genet, that the very act of discovery was a kind of rape which created the Homosexual Genet, and that the Murderer Genet was such a foregone conclusion of these premises that "Genet need not murder because he is a murderer already." (There is some question-begging here, but Sartre seems content.) Sartre claims further that the Genet Position fills a larger void, the position of *advocatus diaboli*, which must be occupied in every generation so that Evil, which is self-defeating, may continually defeat itself on behalf of the Good. Society requires wicked men, as virtuous women require prostitutes—"as objective manifestations of man's propensity for doing wrong." And Genet, who in sinning spares the virtuous man the necessity to sin, thereby acquires Sanctitude. Genet is ostracized, sin is exorcised in his person, and the Good triumphs.

One trouble with this argument is that the Grand Inquisitor phrased it better. Another is that in its fatalism it allows Genet only the leap of accepting his destiny, of willing what is in fact the case. And to will what is the case is the essence of a staid Conservative position, so that Genet, when Sartre gets through with him, is not a rebel but a bureaucrat, doing the job Fate has assigned him. And the final difficulty, the one that does the greatest violence to Genet, is that it accepts him as a philosopher, whereas philosophy is his weakest point, and acceptance undermines everything he is trying to achieve. "Witnesses are almost always for the prosecution," says Genet at one point, and Sartre, by giving warm testimony on behalf of Genet the Cartesian, becomes an inadvertent witness for the prosecution. While Sartre, for example, is at great pains to demonstrate Existentially that criminality begins at the moment the thief is caught, Genet tells us that in fact "crime begins with a carelessly worn beret." The superficial gesture of contempt for society leads easily to petty theft, which leads in turn to the reformatory, and the discovery that reformatory uniforms have only one pocket. The loss of the second pocket sets the incipient criminal one step farther away from society, intensifies his quarantine, unites him with those who share it, and gives rise eventually to the whole mystic brotherhood of crime. "One starts with a little superstition and then falls into the arms of God."

In the underworld, according to Genet, the careless wearer of berets becomes obsessed, like the meticulous wearer of them, with a desire "not to disappoint." He enters a group whose customs are as rigid as those of good society, except that every act must be performed at the level of pure exception. The criminal must free himself of every venal motive for theft and murder and deliver himself to crime in its dispassionate, exacting purity. As a good man is ultimately accountable not to his peers but to his God, a wicked man owes his ultimate fidelity to his curse. The redness of a tie can inspire him to strangle. Only afterward does he permit himself to think of personal gain: "Nothing is so hard to find as money after a premeditated murder." The criminal in his venality and gregariousness is the offside of the businessman; in his pure accountability to evil, he is the churchman in reverse.

Genet is at his best when he is at his worst, speaking as a criminal in a free society. The argot of thieves, the mannerisms of queens, the ambience of prisons, the milieu itself. His style is an unlikely but powerful combination of classical French (derived, perhaps, from the library volumes of the orphanage in which he spent years of his childhood) and the rich slang of Paris and Marseille. At times his prose is controlled, almost austere:

> Poetry . . . is not an abandonment, a free and gratuitous entry by the senses; it is not to be confused with sensuality, but rather, opposing it, was born, for example, on Saturdays, when, to clean the rooms, housewives put the red velvet chairs, gilded mirrors, and mahogany tables outside, in the nearby meadow.

But at other times, like Divine, Genet "started making up fatal tales, or stories that seemed flat and trivial, but in which certain explosive words ripped the canvas, showing through these gashes a bit of what went on." And the general fascination of "what goes on" is undeniable: the burgher reads his tabloids as avidly as the artist or intellectual reads his Genet. The rock of convention is lifted and a few lizards appear. Immediately (or almost immediately; for a time, Genet was banned even in France), society makes house pets of them. This is Genet's defeat and his triumph: society seems now to need its enemies. Genet has become an ornament of salons and cocktail parties, as well as a subject for an elaborate Sartrian discourse on the history of philosophy. Genet, the stylist, and Sartre, the Methodologist, are, of course, at polar extremes, and Genet's last refuge from Sartre's efforts, and society's, to reclaim him would be to argue that he has not been completely understood:

I now confess that I have never felt anything but the appearance of warm caresses, something like a look full of a deep tenderness which, directed to some handsome young creature standing behind me, passed through and overwhelmed me.

Sartre, by simply using the Man of Crime for essentially irrelevant purposes, simply falsifies him at every turn, and seems to direct just that "look full of a deep tenderness . . . to some handsome young creature standing behind" the real Genet.

# The New Sound, Circa 1964

Oₙₑ OF THE MANY THINGS TO accelerate in our time is the progress of the generations. It used to be that any given generation was separated from the generations that immediately preceded and followed it by between twenty and thirty years. Now the interval has diminished, not only because people marry and have children at an earlier age but also because the common attitudes and experiences by which a generation tends to define itself have come to vary so widely in so short a span of time. A few simple questions (Who came from the planet Krypton? What is the Breakfast of Champions? What position did Phil Rizzuto play?) quickly identify a generation and set it apart not only from its parents and its children but from its brothers and sisters as well. My generation, for example, is the last to remember the Second World War, and was the first to be subject to the draft in peacetime. We remember the war as something we collected silver paper, scrap iron, and milkweed pods for. (These last, we were told, were used in making parachutes; we became, in collecting them, the most virulently poison-ivy generation.) The war was also something that pervaded our nightmares and our comic books, in which one enemy conveniently identified himself by periodic exclamations of "*Jawohl!*" and "*Achtung!*" the other by cries of "*Banzai!*" and a habit of disembowelling himself in lurid colors. The end of the war consisted for us of two nights on which we were permitted to stay up late and roam the streets, a morning on which bubble gum again became available, and a succession of weeks in which uniformed relatives came home. For people older than we, the war must have more solid associations, but for people two years younger it is only an episode recounted somewhere near the end of their history textbooks.

Since we were, in childhood, also the last pre-television generation, our tastes in certain respects were formed by comics and the radio. In comics—aside from the war kind—we were the last pre-horror, pre-space, and pre-true-romance generation; in radio, we were the last fans of the Lone Ranger, the Shadow, the Green Hornet (and, when we were sick at home, Helen Trent, Young Widder Brown, and Our Gal Sunday); we were also the last owners of Captain Midnight Code-a-graphs, for which we sent away labels from jars of Ovaltine. Ask anyone five years younger than we about the shortage of bubble gum, the military importance of milkweed pods, or the meaning of "SHAZAM," and the gap between the generations opens up. And that chasm yawns even in the classroom; immediately after my generation learned to read, the command to "sound it out" became meaningless in most parts of the country. (Now that phonetic reading has come back, we can talk to the very young again.) Unhomogenized milk, fillings without Novocain, avoiding beaches for fear of infantile paralysis—these experiences separate us from our immediate juniors. High-school dances without the Twist, college years without political enthusiasms, and a youthful vocabulary based on images of heat and extravagance (as opposed to "cool" and "neat")—how are we to communicate with those only a few years younger than we? In one thing only, the generation now between twenty-five and thirty seems closer to the succeeding generations than to the middle-aged: we initiated the present era in disc jockeys and the music that they play. This is no trifling matter.

For some reason, lyrics set to music commit themselves to memory more easily and permanently than any other verbal form. The number of songs any given person knows by heart probably exceeds by far all the other verbatim sequences he knows, and the size of a shared musical repertory is probably as good a measure as any of how much the members of a group have temperamentally and socially in common. The jingles and commercials with which everyone's mind is ridden make it clear that minds can be programmed involuntarily for life with messages of the most extreme banality and ugliness. Slogans, hit tunes of the moment, oldies, classics, 78 r.p.m.'s, 45's, and album cuts are summoned to the mind by strangers, as though memory were a smoky bar with an enormous jukebox, where anyone can play thoughts and moods at will by choosing among song titles. There is probably no other set of responses so automatically accessible to strangers as the mental turntable, except perhaps the involuntary mechanism for transmitting and receiving yawns.

Let's assume that a former radio addict who kicked the habit in 1954 now switches to WABC, 770 on the AM dial. If he is under thirty and has tuned in during news time, he may think for a moment that nothing has changed: Fred Foy, one of the newscasters, used to be the announcer for "The Lone Ranger," and another, George Ansboro, used to be the announcer for "Young Widder Brown." In a few minutes, however, he will hear one of the disc jockeys—Herb Oscar Anderson, Bob Dayton, Dan Ingram, Bruce Morrow, Charlie Greer, or Bob Lewis—and then, the chances are, his mood and Weltanschauung will change entirely. To begin with, he is likely to be addressed at once, familiarly, as "cousin," for it is customary, on jukebox-music stations, to enlist disc jockeys and fans in some sort of group or family. At WABC, listeners are "cousins" and disc jockeys are "All Americans"; at WMCA, listeners are simply listeners, but disc jockeys are "Good Guys"; and at WINS, where disc jockeys are simply disc jockeys and listeners are simply listeners, the disc jockeys show their solidarity by playing basketball as a team and challenging all comers.

However that may be, in any given quarter hour, our hypothetical WABC listener will be joining a chronologically mixed but aesthetically unified new generation of about a quarter of a million child cousins, teenage cousins, and perennially young adult cousins who are listening to the new music—the New Sound—over what has become, according to The Pulse Inc., a rating service, the most popular radio station in New York. (WOR, its nearest competitor, is a relatively non-generational "talk" station.) Our listener can hear WABC in most of New England and at least as far south as the United States Naval Base at Guantanamo. (Late at night, according to Station KOB, which is bringing suit, he can also hear it as far west as Albuquerque, New Mexico, where it allegedly interferes with local stations.)

Our listener will probably begin by turning the volume down, for, depending on the hour, he may be greeted by astral screams of "*Swing*, Charlie, *swing!*" "All the *way* with HOA!" "*More* music and *much* more *excitement, here* at *Day*ton *Place!*" "Bo*baloo,* the big fat *Da*ddy *Poo!*" or "*Cousin Brucie! Cou*sin Bru*cie! Cou*sin Bru*cie! Cou*sin Bru*cie! Cousin Brucie!*" There may also be voices—apparently submerged in several feet of water—gurgling "Your music authority, seventy-seven, WA-BeatleC!" and conversation thereafter always proceeds at fever pitch. The listener may be urgently invited to vote in the "Principal of the Year Contest" (sixteen million handwritten votes were received last year), to send in for a "Kissin' Cousin Card" or a "Kemosabe Card" (a hundred and fifty thousand requests have been filled in a single week), to participate in a "Beatle Drawing Contest" (seventy-five thousand entries have been received, the winning entries to be exhibited in Huntington Hartford's Gallery of Modern Art), or to send in a box top—any old box top—"just as a whim!" (A few days later, he may be asked whether he knows anyone who can use a warehouseful of box tops.)

If he has tuned in during the early morning, our listener will hear Herb Oscar Anderson crooning his theme song, "Hello Again," and reading notices about dogs and persons who have disappeared during the night. ("Dear Nancy, eighteen years old. We're sorry you left. Please come back and we'll forget all about it. Love, Mom and Dad." Nancy usually hears it and comes back; the lost dogs are usually found and returned, also.) In the late morning, he will hear Bob Dayton welcoming his listeners to

"Dayton Place" and wishing a happy birthday to many of them. In the early afternoon, there is Dan Ingram, on "Your Ingram Singram" or "Your Ingram Flingram," announcing that he is there "laughing and biting, and scratching." Now and then, Dan will shout "Charge!" or announce a weather report as having come to him from "Peter the Meter Reader and our weather girl Fat Pontoon and her Soggy Stockings." In the evening, there is Bruce Morrow announcing, with terrific intensity, that it is or will soon be "Date Night," and giving all his girl listeners a big kiss (pronounced "mmmwa") as he asks all fans in cars to blow their horns at once. (If our listener has his window open, he will doubtless hear horns blowing all up and down the street.) Bruce Morrow may recount some recent escapade, like a breakdown of his car that forced him to buy a horse from the owner of an applecart and to ride it at full gallop through the Lincoln Tunnel on his way to a record hop in Palisades Park.

Then it is time for Bob Lewis, "the big fat Daddy Poo," making weird choking noises to introduce a commercial for an exam cram book ("Kids, have exams got you by the throat?") and announcing record hops as far away as Galesburg, Michigan ("I don't think many of you will be able to attend this one, but . . ."). Finally, there is Charlie Greer, on "Your All Night Office Party," who repeatedly warns the listener, "Don't be a dial twister or I'll give you a Charlie Greer blister," until it is morning and time for Herb Oscar Anderson to sing "Hello Again" again. All the disc jockeys will keep up this continuous stream of chatter, singing with or answering back to records, relaying personal messages to fans, reading traffic reports phoned in by regular "cousins" (like Eddie Schmeltz, a construction worker in Passaic, and Joe Firmata, a hearse driver in Brooklyn), coughing, sneezing, groaning, chortling, or laughing wildly, until our listener is more than likely to be stunned into becoming a non-generational cousin himself.

These twenty-four hours of frenetic, high-pressure, high-volume sound emanate from Studio Three in the WABC radio offices at Broadway and Sixty-fourth Street. The studio is illuminated by fluorescent lights, and around its walls are four clocks —no one of which is quite synchronized with any other. The microphone into which the disc jockey of the hour speaks or sings has a tin horn, of the type used by New Year's Eve celebrants, protruding from its non-functional end. On the disc jockey's left is a five-foot high, rotating cylindrical cartridge tree, containing small, transparent, rectangular tape cartridges of all the songs that will be played in the course of the hour. On his right are a telephone and a large glass-panelled cabinet, which contains a great pile of sugar cubes for his coffee. In front of him is a panel with red lights that flash when he is on the air, and beyond the panel is a radio engineer, who, as he manipulates tape cartridges and constantly alternates songs and commercials with station breaks, resembles an extremely dexterous short-order cook. Among the main jobs of the sound engineer is that of interrupting whatever may be going on with zany, irrelevant "wild tracks"—phrases clipped from old radio dramas or movie sound tracks or concocted expressly for the occasion. "See the *zom*bie, see the *mum*my, see the *zom*bie's mummy!"; "*Coach*, will I *make* the *Hall* of *Fame?*"; "He*llo*, Edgar"; "Hi*ho*, Edgar!"; "You put in some carbolic *acid*, some *sour cream*, a little *broken glass* . . ."; "He's got that idealistic type head"; "We can use him in our outfit"; "I'm sorry I *asked*"; "That's a real knee-slapper"; "Stand clear, everybody"; "Oh, how can I ever thank you"; "It's *too* much to *take*. It's *horrible!*"; "It's best that we part. [pause] *You* have another *wife*. [pause] And *I* have another *husband*. [pause] And *he* has another *wife*. [pause] And *she* has another husband. [long pause] Not the *least* complicated sort of situation, is it?"—these are among the hundreds of interruptions that occur during the programs, whenever the disc jockeys choose to fling the "wild" tapes to the engineers and the engineers are able to insert them. They not only keep the broadcasts at a high pitch but also protect everybody against the possibility that there will be a moment of unnecessary silence while any of the disc jockeys are on the air.

And underneath it all, of course, is the disc jockey's raw material, the jukebox music itself—approximately eighteen hours of it a day on WABC alone—and it is by this music, the New Sound, that the modern generation of cousins seems to be more or less clearly defined. The New Sound is indeed new—new rhythms, new chord progressions, new timbres, new subject matter for the lyrics. It is a lively, aggressive, often funny, seldom sentimental sound, and though much of it is downright ugly (suggesting to some the epithet "kallikakbox"), much of it is very good. The Sound can be traced back, historically, to 1954, when the late Alan Freed, a disc jockey for WINS, introduced Negro rhythm-and-blues numbers (like "Sincerely," by the Moonglows, and "Rock Around the Clock," by Bill Haley and his Comets) to his predominantly white audience, which had been accustomed, until that time, to popular music of the traditional sort—either straight big-band music or a vocalist backed by a big band—as played, for example, on Martin Block's "Make-Believe Ballroom" (the most popular disc-jockey show of the late forties and early fifties). Freed, who kept time by pounding on a telephone directory, selected music with an ever more pronounced beat. The rhythm section—drums, steel drums, guitars, electric guitars—began to dominate the instrumental groups in all the records Freed would consent to play. Within a short time (and until he was ruined by the payola scandals of 1960), Freed had become the most popular disc jockey on the air; to describe his music, he had adopted the expression "rock 'n' roll"; Elvis Presley had come upon the scene and become the country's leading performer; and the Make-Believe Ballroom sound had been superseded by the Age of Rock 'n' Roll.

On the business end, meanwhile, the spread of rock 'n' roll was accelerated by the fantastic growth of B.M.I., a songwriters' and song publishers' society organized by the broadcasting companies themselves, in 1940, as a rival to A.S.C.A.P. From 1914, when it was founded, until 1940, A.S.C.A.P. had been, for all practical purposes, the only performance-rights society for composers of popular music. In 1939, A.S.C.A.P. was receiving a fee from broadcasters equal to approximately five per cent of the industry's income, in return for a blanket license to play A.S.C.A.P. music. In 1940, when it was rumored among broadcasters that A.S.C.A.P. was about to raise its fee to between seven and a half per cent and fifteen per cent, six hundred stations quickly banded together to form B.M.I., which began to enlist non-A.S.C.A.P. composers—many of them unknown and some of them high-school students or dropouts—to produce songs at a blanket license fee that the stations felt they could afford. In early 1941, when the new A.S.C.A.P. rates were offered to the broadcasters, some seventy-five per cent of them chose not to renew their A.S.C.A.P. contracts. The result was that these stations were unable to play A.S.C.A.P. music and turned to B.M.I. as their principal source of musical material. Although A.S.C.A.P. made peace with the industry later that year, B.M.I. was firmly established in the performance-rights business and served thereafter as the way to financial success for the young, unknown composers—exactly the ones who later produced rock 'n' roll. The impact on the popular-music industry was profound: In 1939, there were a thousand composers and a hundred and thirty-seven publishers (all of whom were represented by A.S.C.A.P.) entitled to fees for performance rights; in 1964, there were eighteen thousand songwriters and ten thousand publishers (some half of them members of B.M.I.) entitled to fees. The price of blanket licenses, meanwhile, had dropped, in the case of A.S.C.A.P. to slightly over two per cent, while that of B.M.I. was established at an average of one per cent. One consequence of all this was the development of a new breed—the hugely successful teenage composers and performers, some of whom rose only briefly out of the professional heap and then sank into anonymity again.

Once rock 'n' roll had swept the nation, there was a pause between the generations, and a standoff: the 78-r.p.m. set stuck loyally by its traditional pop tunes and show tunes; the teenagers bought their Elvis Presley 45s. Then, in 1958, came an important extra-musical development, the hula hoop, and, in the early sixties, the Twist, cutting across generational lines and setting the country, from nursery to geriatrics ward, into agitated, rhythmic motion. (The same hip movements that were considered outrageous when Elvis Presley made his first appearance suddenly acquired respectability.) By 1964, the Beatles had arrived, consolidated the New Sound, and demonstrated once and for all the new affluence of the generation between six and eighteen and its power to take over the airwaves, where the Sound now reigns supreme.

The New Sound, as it has evolved, manages to accommodate a wide variety of old sounds, and what you are likely to hear on WABC now is a musical amalgam—a product of African influences, folk influences, jazz influences, blues influences, West Indian influences, Latin-American influences, Country Western influences, Gospel influences, boudoir influences, nursery influences, and political influences, as well as tape and echo-chambers—but if you have trouble describing a new song to your own satisfaction, let a record review in the magazine *Cash Box* suggest a vocabulary. You may have heard a "pulsating shuffle-wobble ballad," or a "plaintively harmonic, rhythmic warmhearted romancer with a contagious repeating melody riff," or even an "infectious shuffle-beat rock-a-cha-cha that's, loaded with commercial ingredients." If one is in a nostalgic state of mind, he must buy a record and turn it over to the "underlid . . . a re-release of the pretty, soft-beat cha-cha weeper click of a while back" ("a while back," in current New Sound usage, is one or two years), or find "on the flip . . . a lilting reworking of the tender folk chestnut." Pulsating shuffle-wobble ballads, contagious repeating melody riffs, shuffle-beat rock-a-cha-chas, soft-beat cha-cha weeper clicks, and lilting reworkings of tender chestnuts will not come as any surprise to members of the "Cry" and "Hounddog" generation, but to the pre-45-r.p.m. generation they may present problems.

The first line of access to the New Sound consists in holding still for a few minutes and catching the words of the songs themselves. This is not easy. The practice of "dubbing over" (superimposing several recordings by a single voice to produce the effect of several voices) and the strongly articulated rhythm of the (predominantly percussion) instruments guarantee that the new songs cannot be understood within their first five hearings. By the sixth, however, a determined listener begins to make progress. It is important at the outset to listen for and filter out nonsense syllables. "Tra la la" has vanished, for the most part, but "sha la la" is in, and there are many other equivalents. "Weem a Waffa," "shoop shoop," "do wah diddy," "do lang ooh lang ooh lang," "da do ron ron," "pa pa oom mow mow," "pa pa doo ron de ron," "rama lama ding dong," "she ba," and "yeh yeh yeh yeh" are the current markers of time, or indicators of inexpressible emotion. Sometimes the words that do mean something present problems of their own. Intensive study of a musically splendid recording, "Shut Down," by the Beach Boys, yields, for the first twenty hearings, nothing intelligible. Five hearings more yields the following:

> *Tak it up, tak it up, buddy, gonna shut you down.*
> *It happened on the strip where the road is wide,*
> *Two cool shorts standin' side by side.*

*Yea, my fuel-injected Stingray and a Four Thirteen*
*Revvin' up our engines, and it sounds real mean.*
*Tak it up, etc.*
*Declinin' numbers at an even rate,*
*At the count of one, we accelerate.*
*My Stingray is light, the slicks are startin' to spin,*
*But the Four Thirteen's wheels are diggin' in.*
*Gotta be cool now. Powershift, here we go.*
*The Superstock Dodge is windin' out in low,*
*But my fuel-injected Stingray's really startin' to go.*
*To get the traction, I'm a-ridin' the clutch.*
*My pressure plate's burnin', that machine's too much.*
*Pedal's to the floor, hear his dual quads drink.*
*And now the Four Thirteen's lead is startin' to shrink.*
*He's hot with ram induction, but it's understood.*
*There's a fuel-injected engine sittin' under my hood.*
*Shut if off, shut it off, buddy, now shut you down.*

This song, which dominated the record charts for a number of weeks in 1963, and which is still played on many radio stations as an "oldie but goodie" or a "solid-gold hit from out of the past," clearly represents a change in spirit and an advance in knowledgeability from its nearest old-style analogue, "In My Merry Oldsmobile." The older generation, however, is by no means barred from the highways of the New Sound. There is, for example, "The Little Old Lady from Pasadena," than whom, at the wheel, "there's nobody meaner"; she finds it impossible to withdraw her foot from the accelerator until she is separated by a full car's length from every motorized rival. Or, on the same general subject, there is the ageless lyric simplicity of "Wipe Out," by the Surfaris; the song consists of surf noises and the words "Wipe out," uttered only once and followed by some maniacal laughter and some agitated, though melodic, strumming.

Where there is speed there are hazards, and the New Sound takes ample account of them. The automotive casualties are legion. They began in the fifties with "The Death of Hank Williams," a relatively low-key account of the demise, by heart attack, of a famous folk singer in the back seat of his chauffeured car. In 1960 came Ray Peterson with "Tell Laura," the story of a young man who tried to earn in a stock-car race the price of a wedding ring for his fiancée. From his deathbed, and later from his grave, his ghostly voice sang the refrain

> *Tell Laura I love her.*
> *Tell Laura I need her.*
> *Tell Laura not to cry.*
> *My love for her*
> *Will never die.*

Within months, there was the young man who tried to persuade his girl to leave a car that was stuck on the railroad tracks. She remained loyal to the car, and the result was "Teen Angel":

> *Teen angel, can you hear me?*
> *Teen angel, can you see-ee me?*
> *Are you somewhere up above?*
> *And am I still your own true love?*

More recently, there have been "Dead Man's Curve" and "Last Kiss"—in which a young driver, blood streaming into his eyes, asks the question

> *Where, oh where can my baby be?*
> *The Lord took her away from me.*
> *She's up in heaven so I've got to be good. . . .*

There are also motorcycle fatalities, one of the most recent being "The Leader of the Pack." In this one, the girl's parents disapprove of her association with a motorcyclist. She breaks off with him, reminding him in parting to drive carefully. Roar, screech, crunch:

> *I'll never forget him, the leader of the pack.*

Although the verbal content of these songs may be far from sunny, they are by no means musically morose. The New Sound, with a beat so distinct and regular that even the most arhythmically inclined teenager cannot fail to catch it and adjust his steps to it, is an eminently danceable sound, and it is not at all rare to find a roomful of couples shuffle-wobbling to songs with overtones of widowhood, like the Beatles' "Baby's in Black [And I'm Feelin' Blue]," or, more recently, of suicide, like "Terry," by Twinkle:

*He said to me he wanted to be near to me.*
*He said he never wanted to be out of my sight.*
*But it's too late to give this boy my love tonight.*
*Please wait at the gate of Heaven for me, Terry.*
*He said to me he wanted to be close by my side.*
*We had a quarrel, I was untrue on the night that he died.*
*But it's too late to tell this boy how great he was.*
*Please wait at the gate of Heaven for me, Terry.*
*He rode in to the night.*
*Accelerated his motorbike.*
*I cried to him in fright,*
*Don't do it, don't do it, don't do it. . . .*
*One day he'll know how much I prayed for him to live.*
*Please wait at the gate of Heaven for me, Terry.*

With a total incongruity of musical style and verbal subject matter (radio fans can remember from the fifties the musical dirge "Oh Happy Day [Oh Lucky Me]"), any number of harsh and serious realities can be lightheartedly accommodated in the New Sound. Sociological themes, for example, can be treated with a certain subtlety and depth, and social geography, in particular, has lately received much earnest commentary. In the fifties, there was the relatively unthinking treatment of urban neighborhoods in "Penthouse Number Three":

> *Uptown, in Penthouse Number Three.*
> *Uptown, that's where I want to be.*

Then, a few years later (in a kind of pulsating weeper click with Casbah undertones), the urban East-West axis came under consideration, with Gene Pitney's "Mecca":

> *I live on the West side,*
> *She lives on the East side*
> *Of the street.*
> *And though they say that East is East,*
> *And West is West,*
> *And never the twain shall meet,*
> *Each morning I face her window,*
> *And pray that our love can be,*
> *'Cause that brownstone house*

> *Where my baby lives*
> *Is Mecca, Mecca*
> *To me.*

In 1962, a fine record called "Uptown," by the Crystals, re-flected a serious change, and "uptown" acquired the meaning it must have for a large proportion of both the audience and the creators of the New Sound:

> *He gets up every morning and he goes Downtown,*
> *Where everyone's his boss, and he's lost in an angry land.*
> *He's a little man.*
> *But when he comes Uptown each evening*
> *To my tenement,*
> *Uptown, where folks don't have to pay much rent,*
> *And when he's there with me, he can see*
> *That he's everything.*
> *Then he's tall, he's so tall he's a king.*
> *Downtown, he's one of a million guys,*
> *He don't get no breaks and he takes all they've got to give,*
> *'Cause he's got to live.*
> *But then he comes Uptown, where he can hold his head up*
>     *high,*
> *Uptown he knows that I'll be standing by.*
> *And when I take his hand, there's no man*
> *Who can put him down.*
> *The world is sweet, it's at his feet,*
> *When he's Uptown.*

In 1963, the Drifters reintroduced a vertical dimension to the flight from sociological realities in "Up on the Roof," and in 1964 they amplified this notion with "Under the Boardwalk." (Such continuity in songs by a single group, or by different groups, is not uncommon. When the Drifters' "Saturday Night at the Movies" sold a million copies, they made "[Friday Night] At the Club." When Lesley Gore's "It's My Party and I'll Cry If I Want To" sold a million copies, she made "Now It's Judy's Turn to Cry." Ferlin Husky's "Dear John" was answered in "Dear Anne," and Jim Reeve's "He'll Have to Go" was followed by "He'll Have to Stay." The melody usually, but not necessarily, varies from original to sequel.)

Most recently, however, an English singer named Petula Clark took note of changes in the social climate with what is almost certainly the best, and what promises to be the most popular, demographic statement of them all, "Downtown":

> When you're alone, when life is making you lonely,
> You can always go Downtown.
> When you've got no worries, all the noise and the hurry
> Seems to help, I know. Downtown.
> Just listen to the music of the traffic in the city,
> Linger on the sidewalks where the neon signs are pretty.
> How can you lose?
> The lights are much brighter there.
> You can forget all your troubles, forget all your cares.
> So go Downtown.
> Things will be great when you're Downtown.
> You'll find a place for sure Downtown.
> Everything's waiting for you. . . .

When social consciousness infiltrated the New Sound, a certain personal worldliness crept in as well, and nowhere is this trend more clearly evident than in the new treatment of that old theme unfaithfulness in love. Perhaps under the influence of the "Frankie and Johnnie" folk tradition, or perhaps because the modern teenager is so frequently a married man himself, the old-fashioned love triangle no longer afflicts only couples going, simply and trustingly, steady; it afflicts married couples as well. No fewer than eight recent, more or less danceable hits—"Devil Woman," "Go On Home," "Walk On By [Wait on the Corner]," "If a Woman Answers [Hang Up the Phone]," "Smoky Places," "Walk Away," "Bye Bye Baby," and "My Love Forgive Me"—are explicitly concerned with adultery, as the couples contemplate, arrange, renounce, or terminate a rendezvous. Here, for example is the awkward situation in "Bye Bye Baby":

> If you hate me after what I say . . .
> I've just got to tell you anyway. . . .
> Should've told you that I can't linger,
> There's a weddin' band on my finger. . . .
> Bye bye, baby; baby, goodbye.

This sort of wavering on the matrimonial front seems to have engendered a certain detachment, even heartlessness, in males who are involved in merely non-adulterous triangles. The lover in a song called "She Cried," for example, recounts how he told his old girl that he no longer loved her, and takes a certain satisfaction in the result. She cried. Encouraged, he made matters a little worse by telling her of his new love. She cried again. Finally, he kissed her ("a kiss that only meant goodbye"), and a full chorus announces triumphantly that, once again "She cried." (He sings about this scene of rejection with a certain clinical interest, as though breaking the news had been a laboratory experiment with a gratifyingly lachrymose result.)

The girls have not taken such blows to love and marriage lightly. The woman's voice on the jukebox is the voice of society still, and in the face of male inconstancy that voice is taking on an increasingly hysterical ring. On the one hand, there is a kind of ostrich attitude—"Don't Say Nothin' Bad About My Baby," "People Say [But I Don't Care What the People May Say]," and "Maybe I Know":

> *Maybe I know that he's been a-cheatin'*
> *Maybe I know that he's been untrue-ooh,*
> *But what can I do?*

Some girls are running in desperation to their mothers, who deliver grave warnings of the possible consequences of boy's inhumanity to girl, notably in "Whenever a Teenager Cries":

> *Rain falling from the skies,*
> *Bluebirds they don't fly,*
> *The stars, they're not so bright,*
> *The moon stays in at night.*
> *It seems the whole world dies*
> *Whenever a teenager cries.*
> *. . . tears will fill my eyes, etc.*

The tears filling the maternal eye, however, are nothing compared to the new glint in the eye of the daughter, for far more common than the ostrich or run-to-mother attitude toward infidelity is the development of a truly formidable female aggressiveness. It began slowly, with some tentative statements of policy in regard to the opposite sex—a girl's shaky resolve, for example, to accost an admired stranger, in "Easier Said Than Done":

> *My friends all tell me Go for him, Run to him,*
> *Say sweet lovely things to him,*
> *My friends all tell me Sing to him, Swing with him,*
> *Just do anything for him . . .*
> *Now, I know that I love him so,*
> *But I'm afraid that he'll never know. . . .*
> *Tell him he's the one. . . .*
> *But it's easier, easier said than done.*

And the leisurely advance of the Shirelles, in "I Met Him on Sunday":

> *Well, I met him on Sunday,*
> *And I missed him on Monday,*
> *Well, I found him on Tuesday,*
> *Well, I dated him Wednesday,*
> *And I kissed him on Thursday. . . .*

Then came the swift and brutally forthright proclamations of open season—"Today I Met the Boy I'm Going to Marry" (a clearly unilateral decision) and "I Want to Be Bobby's Girl," in which the vocalist, having been informed by a male chorus that she's "not a kid anymore," succinctly states her life's ambition:

> *When people ask of me,*
> *What would you like to be?*
> *Now that you're not a kid anymore. . . .*
> *I know just what to say,*
> *I answer right away,*
> *There's just one thing I've been wishing for:*
> *I want to be Bobby's girl,*
> *I want to be Bobby's girl,*
> *That's the most important thing to me.*
> *I want to be Bobby's girl,*
> Etc.

Another female vocalist announces not just an ambition but a fait accompli: "I *Have* a Boyfriend!"—and any girl who does not already possess, or who breaks ranks in the pursuit of, this valuable commodity is likely to incur the wrath of a whole female chorus (choruses in the New Sound tend to perform as did the chorus in Greek tragedy; they comment on the action, and they speak for Fate), notably the Shirelles, in "Foolish Little Girl":

> *Foolish little girl, fickle little girl,*
> *You didn't want him when he wanted you.*
> *Well, he's found another love,*
> . . . *It's her he's dreaming of*
> *And there's not a single thing that you can do.*

When the foolish little girl in question keeps protesting softly, "But I love him, I still love him," the implacable chorus simply shouts her down with a shrill "Nyah, nyah, nyah, nyah, nyah, nyah!" "Nyah" is itself, of course, an unmistakably little-girl sound, and the fact that the hunting age is diminishing yearly is evidenced in many lyrics besides this one—for example, the predatory nursery song "My Boy Lollipop."

Confronted by all this (increasingly precocious) female ferocity, masculine confidence seems to have ebbed a bit. Men are demurring that their mothers told them to "Shop Around," or are consulting "Father Sebastian," or are entreating friends to "Tell Her No," or holding interior pep rallies ("Talk Back Trembling Lips"), or devoting themselves entirely to drag racing, or threatening to leave for "Surf City." Others are becoming solicitous ("What's the Matter with You, Baby?" "What in the World's Come Over You?") or conciliating ("Daddy's Home," which, reassuring as it is meant to be, has the subdued but ominous refrain "rata-tat-tat"). Some are regressing to boyhood fantasies that yield readily to psychoanalysis:

> *Puff, the Magic Dragon lived by the sea,*
> *And frolicked in the autumn mist in a land called Honah*
> *Lee.*
> *Little Jackie Paper loved that rascal Puff,*
> *And brought him strings and sealing wax and other fancy*
> *stuff. . . .*
> *Together they would travel on a boat with billowed sail.*
> *Jackie kept a lookout perched on Puff's gigantic tail. . . .*

And others are resorting, in desperation, to medicinal expedients:

> *I took my troubles down to Madame Ruth,*
> *You know, that gypsy with the gold capped tooth.*
> *She's got a pad down at 34th and Vine,*
> *Sellin' little bottles of Love Potion Number Nine.*

*I told her that I was a flop with chicks.*
*(I've been this way since 1956.)*
*She looked at my palm and she made a magic sign.*
*She said: "What you need is Love Potion Number Nine"* . . .
*I didn't know if it was day or night,*
*I started kissin' ev'rything in sight.*
*But when I kissed the cop down on 34th and Vine,*
*He broke my little bottle of Love Potion Number Nine.* . . .

Unless the kissing of cops (and their subsequent breaking of bottles) can be interpreted as symbolizing a distrust of authority figures, there seems to be little overt rebelliousness in the lyrics of the New Sound. Elders (parents, prelates) are constantly being consulted for advice in new songs, and "Abigail Beecher Classroom Teacher" is as swinging a character as "The Little Old Lady from Pasadena." There is one mild and minor revolutionary with the name—made famous in a quite different context—"Charlie Brown" ("He called the English teacher 'Daddy-o'"). And there is a couple terrified of parents in "Wake Up Little Susie" (they fell asleep at the movies, and no one at home will ever believe that). There are many couples who are fleeing and hiding for one reason or another. But, by and large, the New Sound is, at least on the surface, a law-abiding, civic-minded, elder-respecting sound.

Under the surface, however, a kind of half-conscious, half-articulate revolution-by-ellipsis seems to be going on. It is expressed through lyrics that can be interpreted as hinting at forbidden practices (prostitution in "The House of the Rising Sun," drug addiction in "Walk Right In," and marijuana smoking in "Puff, the Magic Dragon"), which are never directly referred to in the songs themselves; through song titles that are suggestive and lyrics that contain double-entendres; through the theme of self-destruction in songs in which lovers meet sudden death; and through the primitive tempo and the high noise level of some of the music. Transgressions against authority are seldom frankly acknowledged. (In a song called "Give Him a Great Big Kiss," when a chorus suggests to the soloist that her boyfriend is "bad," she feels called upon to explain that "he's good-bad, but he's not evil.") What direct violence there is is done to the laws of grammar, and there seems to be a trend toward superficial obedience even in this realm: a current song is called, magnificently, "It Was I."

Some of the New Sound—exemplified in such records as "Rhythm of the Rain," by the Cascades; "Little Children," by Billy J. Kramer; "Keep Searchin'," by Del Shannon; "Dawn," by the Four Seasons; "Fun, Fun, Fun," by the Beach Boys; "Pretty Woman," by Roy Orbison; "Don't Think Twice," by Peter, Paul, and Mary; "Hello Stranger," by Barbara Lewis; "Needles and Pins," by the Searchers; and almost anything by Petula Clark, Elvis Presley, Ricky Nelson, the Beatles, Peter and Gordon, or the Everly Brothers—has already acquired musical standing among musicians who are not themselves connected with the New Sound. And the names of some of the other performers— the Zombies, the Kinks, the Gestures, the Righteous Brothers, the Soul Sisters, Solomon Burke, Adam Faith, Marianne Faithfull, the Miracles, Major Lance, Travis Wammack, the Contours, the Orlons, the Chiffons, Bent Fabric, the Jelly Beans, Reparata and the Delrons, Ronnie Dove, Bobby Bare, Bobby Bland, the Honeycombs, the Dixie Cups, the Butterflys, Ronny and the Daytonas, Gladys Knight and the Pips, Martha and the Vandellas, Brian Poole and the Tremeloes, Alvin Cash and the Crawlers, Patty and the Emblems, the Tokens, the Supremes, the Temptations, the Quotations, the Vibrations, the Serendipity Singers, the Exciters, the Wailers, the Reflections, the Beau Brummels, the Radiants, the Cookies, the Murmaids, the Sapphires, the Pyramids, the Shangri-Las, the Rivieras, the Chariots, and the Spaniels—seem to entitle them to a hearing on the ground of poetry alone. Finally, the sheer eclecticism of the New Sound—the incorporation of various musical strains, the unlikely combinations of instruments (for example, guitar with steel drums and trumpet), the persistent phenomenon of white performers trying to sound like Negroes and (through dubbing over) of a single performer sounding like many, the occurrence of English groups with names like the Nashville Teens (and with Negro-American accents), and the generally wide range of the subject matter of the lyrics—makes for a creative ferment and may lead anywhere.

WABC is not, of course, the only station to propagate the New Sound. Stations all over the country thrive upon it. In New York, there is still WINS, where rock 'n' roll first gained its wide acceptance, but in 1961 WINS staged a Sinatra Marathon, which, for the first two days, enjoyed a huge success but which, in the weeks thereafter, caused fans under thirty to desert the station in such numbers that its ratings have never quite recovered; and a few weeks ago, Murray the K, its most popular disc jockey (famous for his convention of putting "iaz" after the first letters of words, and for introducing the expression "It's what's happenin', baby" into the modern disc-jockey idiom), announced his intention of leaving the station and touring England with the Biazeatles (who have designated him honorary Beatle Number Five). WMGM used to be a popular New Sound station, but in 1962 it changed its name to WHN and began to play a soft, Muzak-like sound, from which its ratings have never fully recovered, either. WMCA is now WABC's nearest New Sound rival, and seems to be broadening its New Sound listenership. There is also WWRL, a highly successful Negro-oriented radio station, which plays Gospel and rhythm-and-blues numbers under the general heading "Soul Music."

But WABC has one advantage over every other New Sound station in New York. It belongs to the A.B.C. network, and thus has access to facilities that the non-network, independent stations do not enjoy. This advantage was apparent, for example, on the Beatles' last visit to New York, when WABC alone had the facilities to broadcast directly from Delmonico's, where the Beatles were staying. Outside the hotel, on the night of the Beatles' arrival, there was the usual crowd of shrieking teen-agers. As the Beatles entered the lobby, one of the girls tore off Ringo's St. Christopher medal. Ringo was upset, and appealed to the WABC staff members at the hotel to help find the medal. They in turn began to broadcast appeals to their listeners, and two of the WABC disc jockeys emerged from the hotel, in the hope of finding the over-avid teenager in the crowd that still pressed against the barricades in front of the hotel. Sure enough, she was still out there, screaming. The disc jockeys quickly captured the girl, and, on an inspiration of the moment, and with her cooperation and her mother's permission (given on the telephone), took her to a suite in the hotel. Then, for the rest of the night, the station broadcast moving appeals for the return of the medal, and frantic telephone interviews with fans who claimed to know its whereabouts. Within hours, the other New Sound stations had unsuspectingly cribbed the appeal. In the morning, WABC produced the medal and the girl, who was more than compensated for her night away from home by a joyful reunion with Ringo (and ample coverage in the press). With such facilities, such ingenuity, and such presence of mind, it is not surprising that WABC should be New York's most popular radio station.

One curious aspect of the New Sound is the process whereby the radio stations choose the songs they will play for the public. At WABC, whose procedure is fairly typical, the disc jockeys meet every Tuesday morning at ten o'clock in the office of Rick Sklar, the station's program director, to select the numbers for the following week. Mr. Sklar is a brown-haired, green-eyed man of thirty-five, who worked for WMGM in its heyday, and WINS in *its* heyday. His office is a comfortable place, full of chairs, a desk, a sofa, and some hi-fi equipment. Behind the desk hangs a large reproduction of the Mona Lisa (a leftover from a Mona Lisa painting contest that WABC held some years ago), and in the Mona Lisa's hand is a transistor radio. On top of the desk lies a paperweight in the shape of a football helmet, and on the walls of the office are various framed awards from Chambers of Commerce, Army and Air Force recruiters, youth groups, and Mayor Wagner, the last for WABC's cooperation in the city's Stay-in-School campaign. By the time the disc jockeys enter the office, however, all the frames have been turned askew by Dan Ingram, who performs this prank every Tuesday morning, knowing that the program director cannot bear to see a picture that is not hanging straight. Mr. Sklar carefully and rather resignedly rights the frames, and the morning's session begins. The meetings are top secret, but a log is kept for future reference by Ellie Lewis, Mr. Sklar's young secretary, and Jim Maher, the young man who is the station's record librarian.

The group has before it a variety of national and local record surveys, and piled up on a cabinet that contains the hi-fi equipment are about fifty new releases, which were brought in on the previous Friday by salesmen for the record companies. (These salesmen, being under terrific pressure from the companies they represent, often put substantial pressure on the station to play a song. Since the payola scandals, however, this pressure is mainly of an emotional sort, and tears at sales interviews are not uncommon.) What the local surveys show to be the top twenty records will be played automatically, and certain other records, ranging back, usually, to about 1960, will be played as "solid gold hits from out of the past." It remains for the meeting to choose a few new records to play—only a few, for a large number of unfamiliar records played in rapid succession provokes, in WABC's experience, instant tuneoff—and, from these, to choose a record to be played hourly, as the station's "Pick Hit of the Week."

Once Herb Oscar Anderson, Bob Dayton, Dan Ingram, Bruce Morrow, and Bob Lewis (who range in age from twenty-seven to thirty-five) are on the scene, Rick Sklar puts a record on the turntable. (Charlie Greer, having been up all night at the Office Party, rarely attends these sessions.) At a recent session, it was "Thou Shalt Not Steal," by Dick and Deedee, No. 23 on Record World's "100 Top Pops" for the week.

"I don't hear it," said Dan Ingram.

"I dig it," said Bob Dayton. "That's always the kiss of death."

Rick Sklar's secretary put on another record—"Breakaway," by the Turtlenecks.

"What's he saying—'Break a leg'?" asked Bob Dayton.

"Well, you see, Bob, it's this theatrical thing," said Dan Ingram.

"Very funny," said Rick Sklar. "What's next, Ellie?"

" 'Moody Blues,' " she said.

"Don't talk baby talk, Ellie," said Bob Lewis.

"I can't help it. That's what it's called," she said.

"Sounds like the epitome of abomination and putrefaction," said Dan Ingram.

"Speaking of 'Moody Blues,' did you know octopuses turn blue when they get excited?" asked Bob Lewis.

"Yes," said Dan Ingram. "And some dinosaurs are no larger than a chicken."

"Must we have this, fellows?" asked Rick Sklar. "After all, this involves people's careers. Put on the Wayne Newton record, Ellie."

"Has his voice changed yet?" asked Dan Ingram, seriously.

"No, but they've put the Beach Boys behind him," said Rick Sklar.

"Where's Newton himself?" asked Bob Dayton after the record had been playing for a while. "They must have buried him."

"He the guy singing 'ooh-ah,' or what?" asked Herb Oscar Anderson. Rick Sklar shook his head, and called for another record.

"I don't hear it," said Herb Oscar Anderson.

"It's on the Barf label," said Bob Dayton.

"More fun than an open grave," said Dan Ingram.

"Fooh pooh," said Bruce Morrow, and laughed.

"Forget it," said Rick Sklar. "The year is 1947. It's not going to happen."

"I certainly don't fall out over it," said Dan Ingram. He walked over to the window. "New York is a rumpled Cadillac fender," he said.

Rick Sklar tried a new record—"The Boy from New York City," by the Ad Libs:

> *Tell you about the boy from New York City.*
> *You ought to see how he walks. . . .*
> *He has the finest penthouse I've ever seen in town. . . .*

"Sounds to me like a thousand mules' bowels," said Dan Ingram.

"You've got to hear it as you hear it on a transistor," said Rick Sklar, and he turned the treble up and the volume down.

"It's going to be a mother," said Dan Ingram.

"Yeah, it has the Dan Ingram Seal of Upheaval," said Bruce Morrow.

They agreed to play "The Boy from New York City" the following week.

Rick Sklar later dismissed a song called "Jolly Green Giant" (on the ground that it sounded like a disguised commercial for canned vegetables), a song called "Twine Time" (on the ground that its lyrics contained lines that were in questionable taste), and a song called "Letter from Vietnam" (on the ground that it was just plain terrible). Everyone had coffee, and Bruce Morrow put five sugar cubes in his cup.

"I've got a song for you by Jerry Lewis's son Gary," said Rick Sklar, and put "This Diamond Ring" on the turntable.

Ellie and Jim got up and began to dance.

"It's a wild one," said Dan Ingram. "Scares away the old folk. I like it."

"How old is Jerry's boy now?" asked Bruce Morrow.

"Ninety-two," said Herb Oscar Anderson.

By the end of the session, the disc jockeys had dropped eight records that had been played during the preceding week, and had picked up eight new ones. They had also decided to ask Shirley Ellis, singer of a hit song called "The Name Game" ("Shirley, Shirley, Bo Birley, Banana Fanna, Fo Firley, Fee Fi, Mo Mirley, Shirley"), to do a "Name Game" record based on the names of the WABC disc jockeys. As "Pick Hit of the Week," they had selected a folksy, danceable re-release of an old weeper click about nuclear fallout—"What Have They Done to the Rain?", by the Searchers.

With that, the meeting broke up.

"Don't talk too much on the air, boys," said Rick Sklar. "The audience may want to hear the music."

Everyone laughed.

From Studio Three, over radios scattered through the WABC offices, everyone could now hear the current "Pick Hit of the Week"—"The 'In' Crowd," by Dobie Gray, rather cheerfully truculent in tone:

*I'm In with the In crowd. I go where the In crowd goes.*
*I'm In with the In crowd, and I know what the In crowd knows.*
*How to have fun any time of the year. Don't you hear.*
*How to have fun dressin' fine, makin' time,*
*We breeze up and down the street.*
*We get respect from the people we meet.*
*They make way, day or night.*
*They know the In crowd is out of sight.*
*I'm In with the In crowd. I know every latest dance.*
*When you're In with the In crowd, it's easy to find romance.*
*And we work out at a spot where the beat's really hot.*
*Yeah, we work out. If it's square, we ain't there.*
*We make every minute count.*
*Our share is always the biggest amount.*
*Other guys imitate us, but the original's still the greatest.*
*We got our own way of walkin'.*
*Got our own way of talkin'.*
*Gotta have fun any time of the year. Don't you hear?*
*Gotta have fun, spendin' cash, talkin' trash.*
*Girl, I'll show you a real good time.*
*Come on with me and leave your troubles behind.*

*I don't care where you've been.*
*You ain't been nowhere till you've been In*
*With the In crowd.*
*We gotta a whole way of walkin', a whole way of talkin', yeh.*
*In the In crowd.*

The In crowd seems to be a young crowd, with a distinct sense of urgency, affluence, hostility, solidarity, and power, and whatever "the In crowd knows," and whatever is being said in the whole new "way of talkin'," the In crowd seems to be making its own highly individual adjustment to the shuffle-wobble realities of its time.

# Polemic and the New Reviewers

IN LITERARY CRITICISM, POLEMIC is short-lived, and no other essay form becomes as quickly obsolete as an unfavorable review. If the work under attack is valuable, it survives adverse comment. If it is not, the polemic dies with its target. A critic is therefore measured not by the books he prosecutes but by the ones he praises (we turn to Edmund Wilson for Proust, Joyce, Eliot, and Hemingway, not for Kafka), and it is surprising that among a younger generation of critics polemic should be so widely regarded as the most viable and rewarding kind of criticism. Three recent works—*The Sense of Life in the Modern Novel,* by Arthur Mizener (Riverside); *A World More Attractive,* by Irving Howe (Horizon); and *Doings and Undoings,* by Norman Podhoretz (Farrar, Straus)—may provide an explanation.

Arthur Mizener is the most affirmative critic of the three, the least polemical, and the least interesting. His book is little more than a splicing together of enthusiasms. He recounts plots (from Trollope to Updike), lists dates, quotes and compares passages (good ones, from many sources); he seems tempted to pick up the novels whole and deliver them to the reader. His critical sympathies, in short, are strong; his critical intelligence, however, is weak or self-effacing. Mr. Mizener seldom explains or analyzes, and whenever he does, his prose neatly strangles whatever his thought may have been:

> The problem for writers like Dreiser is apparently how to release from deep beneath the viscous and muddy surface of their conscious minds their imaginative apprehension of their experience, and the only way they seem to be able to do so is, paradoxically, by a slow roiling of the muddy surface.

> What criticism of the novel needs is a theory that will put at the center of our attention the world envisioned by the novel, which will then serve to limit and discipline the exercise of our metaphysics upon it. Our lot would very much like to circumambulate the novel's charms for the nearly exclusive purpose of keeping our metaphysics warm. The only valid source of discipline for this corrupting impulse to metaphysical speculation is the unique object that is the novel itself.

What the second of these paragraphs seems to recommend is that the critic leave theories alone and let literature speak for itself. And Mr. Mizener, for one, seems clearly well advised to do so. The effect, however, of his constant citing of excerpts from the works themselves is to make his book almost a scrap album. Or a whirlwind tour of the sights. ("And on your left, ladies and gentlemen, the beautiful opening passage of *Across the River and into the Trees*. . . . And, on your right, the historic scene from E. M. Forster. . . . Notice, in particular, the portico . . .") The effect is also, on a slightly higher plane, that of a benign, unanalytic book column in a reviewing section of the Sunday newspapers, to which Mr. Mizener is a frequent contributor.

While Mr. Mizener subordinates himself so completely to the works he admires that his intelligence becomes invisible, Irving Howe does the reverse; he dominates a book and wrenches it to suit his concern of the moment. And his concern is nearly always extra-literary—sociological or political. The title of his new book,

*A World More Attractive,* suggests a utopian outlook, and even in his literary essays he is primarily concerned with social action —"images of war and revolution, experiment and disaster, apocalypse and skepticism; images of rebellion, disenchantment, and nothingness." When a writer—Wallace Stevens, for example— seems less preoccupied with these "images" than Mr. Howe himself, Mr. Howe discerns them as a "premise," or a "background," or a "pressure upon all subjects":

> Stevens does not examine society closely or even notice it directly for any length of time; he simply absorbs "the idea" of it. . . . A perspective upon history is brilliantly maintained; history as it filters through his consciousness of living and writing at a given time.

This line of argument can, of course, be used to demonstrate that anyone is really writing about anything whatever—"as it filters through his consciousness of living and writing at a given time"—and the author of *A World More Attractive* makes frequent and imaginative use of what we might call the ascribed, or foisted, premise: "Dostoevsky had not read Max Weber. But the anticipation is there." For Mr. Howe seeks, above all, to establish a position, and he uses his intelligence to force that position upon the literary work. (If the work resists, so much the worse for it; Mr. Howe will find it lacking in "moral style.") Yet it need not be supposed that this exercise of intelligence gives Mr. Howe an advantage in clarity over Mr. Mizener:

> The ideal of socialism has become a problematic one, but the problem of socialism remains an abiding ideal.
> But if one turns from the immediate political struggle to a kind of socio-cultural speculation by means of which certain trends are projected into an indefinite future, there may be some reason for anticipating a society ruled by benevolent Grand Inquisitors, a society of non-terroristic and bureaucratic authoritarianism, on top of which will flourish an efficient political-technical elite—a society, in short, that makes Huxley's prophecy seem more accurate than Orwell's, except insofar, perhaps, as Orwell's passion and eloquence helped invalidate his own prophecy.

Whatever these two sentences may mean, their vocabulary, at least, suggests that we are in the presence of an intellectual—a radical intellectual, of the sort that was identified in the thirties with such "little journals" as *Partisan Review*. And as an intellectual of the thirties Irving Howe has become, if not an interesting critic, at least an interesting criticism of the predicament of letters in the sixties—particularly in the little journals, to which he is a frequent contributor. Most of these journals were born of the depression and defended underdogs, who seemed at the time to fall into two broad categories—the artists and the poor. After the Second World War, old issues began to cloud, old protégés made good, and expository writers with a low tolerance for complexities were at a loss. A good part of the thirties' poor had become the fifties' bourgeoisie; most genuine depression artists had become the culture heroes of an age of affluence. Whom to defend? A stalwart revolutionary, Mr. Howe seemed to find himself without a cause, a comrade, or an enemy. He soon started a magazine of vaguely Socialist persuasion, called *Dissent*, and the dissenting position he has taken is a paradoxical one. He has turned upon old protégés to begrudge them the successes that time has brought. He now assails the former underdog, part of the post-depression middle class, for everything—its new comforts, its tastes, and its morals. He now wishes to bar from "the raids of mass culture," and from the "contamination" of the "middle-brow," the "serious culture" that the radicals sought in the thirties to bring to the people. At the same time, he wants to bar to the artists and intellectuals the success—"this rise in social status"—that he sought in the thirties to help them achieve. If only, he seems to be saying, the middle class and the artists might become befriendably poor again:

> Today, in a sense, the danger is that the serious artists are not scorned enough.
>
> Suppose, then, that the goal of moderate material satisfaction is reached. . . . What would the intellectuals say? . . . [They] would be like Christ, facing the Grand Inquisitor.] He has nothing to say. . . . [His] kiss is a kiss of despair, and He retreats, forever, in silence.

In short, now that the revolution of the thirties has begun to bear fruit, Mr. Howe has come to distrust the notion of progress, and he seeks in literature ( or imposes upon literature) that aversion to the modern which he himself feels. Lacking a new direction for his liberalism, he dissents; he seems to bear his banner proudly backward toward the thirties and the "world more attractive" those years represent for him.

An editor of *Commentary* and a regular reviewer for *Show*, Norman Podhoretz inhabits a middle ground between the tame Sunday newspapers of Arthur Mizener and the radical little journals of Irving Howe. He is, in fact, one of those writers for little journals who have of late been assimilated almost en bloc into the magazines of broader circulation, and his adjustment, as a thirties liberal, to the sixties is a highly pragmatic, even a classic one. The rebel whose cause has succeeded traditionally develops a concern with personal power, and the title of Mr. Podhoretz's collection of critical essays, *Doings and Undoings*, implies a faith in the power of the critic to affect, or even determine, the fate of authors and literary works—"to correct," in Mr. Podhoretz's phrase, "what he considers to be an egregious error in the prevailing estimate of a book or a literary reputation."

*Doings and Undoings* is not, Mr. Podhoretz points out, a unified collection. "How many people wrote it, then? Two, I think, or possibly three." The first estimate seems accurate; there are two distinct personalities at work in this book—one a literary critic far more canny than Mr. Mizener, the other a post-revolutionary, extra-literary polemicist far more effective than Mr. Howe. Essays on Faulkner, Edmund Wilson, and Nathanael West seem to reflect the first personality; essays on Norman Mailer, Mary McCarthy, Hannah Arendt, and John Updike, among others, seem to reflect the second. Since the second personality—the author, one supposes, of *Undoings*—is the more recent chronologically, and since his work clearly dominates the collection, it might be well to begin with his position, as Mr. Podhoretz defines it in the piece entitled "Book Reviewing and Everyone I Know." In praise of contributors to a new periodical, *The New York Review of Books*, Mr. Podhoretz remarks:

> All these reviewers inhabit much the same intellectual milieu, and what they have in common, apart from talent and intelligence, is an attitude toward books and an idea about the proper way to discuss them. This attitude might be characterized as one of great suspiciousness: a book is assumed to be guilty until it proves itself innocent—and not many do. . . . The major premise be-

hind such suspiciousness is that books are enormously important events, far too important to be confronted lightly, and certainly too important to permit of charitable indulgence.

The argument that a sign of a book's importance is that it should be "assumed to be guilty until it proves itself innocent" is a curious one, since our whole legal system rests upon the opposite premise—that the sign of an individual's importance is that he should be assumed innocent until he is proved guilty. But Mr. Podhoretz conceives of this position of "great suspiciousness" as an antidote to the "bland and uncritical" reviewing columns of the Sunday newspapers (so much for Mr. Mizener) and as a solution (here he agrees with Mr. Howe) to the "problems of mass culture . . . and . . . the need for an embattled struggle against the deterioration of literary and intellectual standards." Finally, he pinpoints what he considers the salient quality of *The New York Review* reviewers: "A book for them is, quite simply, an occasion to do some writing of their own." And he adds that if only *The New York Review* were to succeed in establishing itself on a permanent footing . . . everyone I know would certainly be happy."

There are several remarkable things about this essay and the point of view it represents. First, "everyone I know" occurs fourteen times (aside from its appearance in the title), and "someone I know," "no one I know," "someone I don't know," and "everyone they know" make one appearance each. Although it must be admitted that ironic repetition is a rhetorical device of which, in any case, Mr. Podhoretz has always been inordinately fond ("what really happened in the thirties" occurs nine times in another essay, and "tells us nothing about the nature of totalitarianism" several times in a third), it seems quite safe to say that "Book Reviewing and Everyone I Know" is pervaded by a sense of comradeship and solidarity; Mr. Podhoretz clearly does not consider himself a speaker in isolation. On the other hand, such terms as "embattled," "struggle," and "suspiciousness" seem to indicate, on behalf of the group, a feeling of beleaguered hostility. Moreover, such unembarrassed statements as "Among our most talented literary intellectuals (including just about everyone I know) reviewing is regarded as a job for young men on the make" and "A book for them is, quite simply, an occasion to do some writing of their own" imply that the New Reviewers regard criticism less as a sympathetic response to literature than as an opportunity for an assertion of personality. (One conclusion is inescapable here: A book is going to have an exceedingly difficult time "proving itself innocent" if the reviewer "assumes" it "guilty" and then uses it, "quite simply," as "an occasion to do some writing of [his] own.")

Finally, a glowing nostalgic reference to "the back files of magazines like *Partisan Review* and *Commentary*," combined with an expression of despair over the present ("But except for Dwight Macdonald and one or two others, everyone I know—indeed, everyone who writes—is often afflicted with the feeling that all he is doing is dropping stone after stone down the bottomless well of American culture. Who listens? Who cares?"), seems to complete a picture, a philosophical adjustment, an answer to the predicament of Mr. Howe. The radical child of the thirties, the contributor to the back files of little journals, finding himself at present directionless, embattled, and perhaps even unheeded, achieves a solidarity in numbers in the security of "everyone I know." The political fervor of the ex-revolutionary is not lost; it is simply redirected into literary channels, where it appears as a certain hostility toward books ("assumed guilty"), a pronounced defensiveness toward presumptive readers ("the bottomless well of American culture"), and an attitude toward the job at hand—reviewing—as an opportunity to assert personal ambition ("young men on the make . . . do some writing of their own"). In short, the rebellion has succeeded, the junta is in power, and it is now the era of the purge.

To interpret a whole collection on the basis of a single essay would be, of course, to oversimplify, and Mr. Podhoretz is a more complicated and interesting writer than this single essay might suggest. But "Book Reviewing and Everyone I Know" does announce a group, a program, and perhaps even the emergence of a new critical school, and since Mr. Podhoretz is a singularly articulate spokesman for that school, it might be well to explore his program as it recurs in some of the other essays in *Doings and Undoings*, and in the work of other New Reviewers —those who share what Mr. Podhoretz calls "the same intellectual milieu."

Mr. Podhoretz, to begin with, clearly regards reviewing as a continuous dialogue, and he devotes, in his reviews, considerable attention to the opinions of previous reviewers. In the essay "In Defense of James Baldwin" he writes:

> With few exceptions, the major reviewing media were very hard on *Another Country*. It was patronized by Paul Goodman in *The New York Times Book Review*, ridiculed by Stanley Edgar Hyman in *The New Leader*, worried over . . . by Elizabeth Hardwick in *Harper's*, summarily dismissed by *Time's* anonymous critic, loftily pitied by Whitney Balliett in *The New Yorker*, and indignantly attacked by Saul Maloff in *The Nation*.

And in "A Dissent on Updike" he cites not only written opinions but spoken ones as well:

> When his first novel, *The Poorhouse Fair*, came out in 1958, I remember arguing about it at great length with Mary Mc-Carthy. . . .
> I cannot for the life of me understand what there is about him that so impresses people like Mary McCarthy, Arthur Mizener, and Stanley Edgar Hyman—to mention only three critics who . . .

The "Defense" in one case and the "Dissent" in the other might seem to require such a roll call, but it is Mr. Podhoretz's method throughout the collection to orient his point of view in terms of what he calls "the prevailing estimate of a book or a literary reputation." And he is not the only one to do so. There is a kind of reciprocity along the reviewing circuit that, while it occasionally imparts a pleasing continuity to critical discussion (the reader who suspects that the reviewer does not do justice to the book under consideration may be consoled by the knowledge that the reviewer has read at least all previous reviews of it), more often resembles nothing so much as a ticker-tape compendium or a caucus in an airless convention hall. "Irving Howe and I discussed this tendency some time ago, and wrote . . ." says Lewis Coser in *Partisan Review*. "The last time I remember talking about the novel was a year ago last June or July," Norman Mailer writes in *Esquire*, "and it was in a conversation with Gore Vidal." "Even Norman Mailer," Alfred Chester writes in a review of William Burroughs' *Naked Lunch*, "unpredictably mislaid himself long enough to write: 'Burroughs is the only American novelist living today who may conceivably be possessed by

genius.'" "It was from Sartre that I first heard of Jean Genet,"
Lionel Abel writes in *The New York Review;* and "These have
been duly underscored by her critics," says another contributor
to the same periodical, "notably Lionel Abel, in a long and
trenchant essay in . . ." "I have only once had the privilege of
meeting Paul Goodman," George Steiner remarks in *Commentary.* "I stress 'privilege.' There is no one whose encounter flatters
in a more exacting way."

This elaborate system of cross-references is one to which Mr.
Podhoretz—at least in *Undoings*—subscribes, and when he feels
he must disagree with what he frequently calls "the serious
critics," he does so warily. His essay on James Baldwin continues:

> Three of these reviewers—Goodman, Hardwick, and Hyman—
> are first-rate critics, and I therefore find it hard to believe that
> their wrongheaded appraisals of *Another Country* can be ascribed
> to a simple lapse of literary judgment. How could anyone as sensi-
> tive and knowledgeable as Elizabeth Hardwick have been so led
> astray . . . ? How could a man of Stanley Edgar Hyman's sophis-
> tication have been so fooled . . . ? How could Paul Goodman,
> who most assuredly knows better, have taken . . .

Mr. Podhoretz is not, of course, the only reviewer to feel so
bewildered by his own divergence from the mainstream of critical opinion that he must temper his remarks with "sensitive,"
"sophistication," and "knows better." Occasionally, such differences are bridged with the elaborate courtesy of a junior executive introducing his immediate superior at a Rotary banquet.
"This collection of essays . . . reflects the amazing catholicity of
Mr. Schlesinger's tastes and interests," Lewis Coser begins his
attack on Arthur Schlesinger, Jr. "His range is wide indeed." And
Frank Kermode, concluding an ambivalent review of Mary Mc-
Carthy's essays, concedes himself "aware that one is incompar-
ably less honest, as well as less clever, than she," and adds, "I can
think of no writer whose silence would be more damaging to our
moral and intellectual hygiene."

A more relaxed approach, along the reviewing circuit, to the
moment of painful dissent is manifest in the use of first names:
Norman Mailer, in attacking Nelson Algren, calls him "Nelson";
Alfred Chester, in disparaging Henry Miller, calls him "Henry";

Paul Goodman, in disagreeing with Harold Rosenberg, calls him "Harold"; and Lionel Abel, in discussing the misdeeds of the ghetto leader Chaim Rumkowski, refers to him familiarly as "Chaim." Mr. Podhoretz is more formal. "On the other hand, Macdonald, Rahv, and Kazin," he concludes his summary dismissal of their essays, "even in their perfunctory moments, have more to say than most of us when we are trying hard." The apparent source of such affectionate concern with the opinions of other reviewers is a conviction that the value of an opinion can be defined by the admiration one feels for the holder of that opinion. "Not which idea but whose?" the reviewer seems to ask himself. The original judgments of respected critics quickly acquire an aura not only of self-evidence but of finality (they, at least, are assumed innocent until they are proved guilty): "I admire [Edmund] Wilson greatly," Lionel Abel writes, in an essay on Alfred Kazin, "from which it will be seen that I do not . . ." And, says another reviewer, "As a conscious artist, O'Neill was stiff and crude, as Mary McCarthy has established." The New Reviewers hastily stand up to be counted, and reviewing becomes not merely a circuit but a cartel.

Apart from the group orientation of *Doings and Undoings*, the book is interesting primarily for its arguments. In his introduction, Mr. Podhoretz establishes the premises on which his critical arguments are based:

> Most often the event [that produced these essays] was the appearance of a new book that seemed to me to raise important issues . . . and almost always it was the issues rather than the book itself that I really cared about. Is that a damaging admission for a literary critic to make? . . . We may be looking in the wrong place for the achievements of the creative literary imagination when we look for them only where they were last seen—in novels and poems and plays. . . . These may all be of great interest to me as a student of literature, and they may be of some interest to me as an habitual reader. But they are of no interest to me as a man living in a particular place at a particular time and beset by problems of a particular kind.

This position is a consistent and audacious one, and Mr. Podhoretz adopts it with full awareness of its implications. But again, particularly in his lapse of faith in pure fiction, he does not speak entirely in isolation. "I wonder, who reads short stories?" writes John Thompson in *Partisan Review*. "When you pick up a magazine, do you turn to the short story? What is it doing there, anyway? It looks as boring as a poem, and probably it is. Maybe if you yourself write short stories, yes, you take a quick slice at it, to see who's doing it now, is he one up on you or not, what's he copying . . ." "The novel is having a hard time," Alfred Chester remarks in *Commentary;* and in *Show* Kenneth Lamott observes, "People who care about such things have agreed for as long as I can remember that the novel is in a bad way." "Her book is memorable to me," Julian Moynahan writes of Brigid Brophy in *The New York Review*, "only because halfway through reading it I was seized by a cramping suspicion that the novel as a viable literary form might after three hundred years of life be ready for burial." And, referring to a statement made by Paul Goodman, a reviewer writes, "Such an observation calls into question the validity of fiction itself."

Mr. Podhoretz, however, does not go quite so far; he does not discount fiction altogether. He has simply, in his words, "lost my piety toward the form in its own right, which means that I do not feel an automatic sympathy for the enterprise of novel-writing," and he continues:

> A large class of readers . . . has found itself responding more enthusiastically to . . . non-fiction (and especially to magazine articles and even book reviews) than to current fiction. . . . And what the novel has abdicated has been taken over by discursive writers. Imagination has not died (how could it?) but it has gone into other channels. . . . What I have in mind—and I cheerfully admit that the suggestion sounds preposterous—is magazine articles.

The suggestion does not sound preposterous at all, particularly in a passage pointing out the literary take-over by "discursive writers." (It explains, for one thing, why reviewers pay so much attention to other reviewers.) One result, however, of a conviction that imagination has been diverted from fiction into expository writing is that the expository writer, particularly the reviewer, is often tempted to press his own imagination upon the work of fiction, to prescribe for the novelist the kind of work that the reviewer thinks he ought to have written. Thus, Mr. Podhoretz berates John Updike for having written about old age, and not having written a reminiscence of childhood, in *The Poorhouse Fair:*

> . . . In any case there was something that gave me the creeps about the way he had deliberately set out to reverse the usual portrait-of-the-artist-as-a-young-man pattern of the first novel.

And he further instructs the novelist (as though Mr. Podhoretz's pains necessarily resembled Updike's, and as though Mr. Podhoretz himself were writing a novel including a description of them):

> Severe pain in one part of the body does not travel through the system, either on wet wings or dry; on the contrary, after the first flash of burning sensation, its effect is actually to focus one's entire consciousness on the hurt spot. . . . Consequently the appropriate images for rendering such an experience . . . would be . . .

He reproaches Saul Bellow for the ending of a novel ("If, however, Bellow had been ruthless in following out the emotional logic of *Seize the Day*, it would almost certainly have been murder—and *Seize the Day* would almost certainly have been a great book"), and he suggests his own ending for Joseph Heller's *Catch-22*. He even rebukes Harry Truman for not "admitting" in his autobiography that he was the "ambitious, perhaps lonely boy who dreamed of greatness" that Mr. Podhoretz thinks he must have been. In his conviction that it is the business of criticism to prescribe for literature, Mr. Podhoretz is again not quite alone: "It is the Orestes-Iphigenia story, we see here, that Salinger all along had been trying to rewrite," Leslie Fiedler (himself much occupied with myth) prescribes for Salinger, "the account of a Fury-haunted brother redeemed by his priestess-sister." "He could become the best of our literary novelists," Norman Mailer prescribes for another author (as opposed, one wonders, to our non-literary novelists?), "if he could forget about style and go deeper into the literature of sex." (A "forgetting" and a "going deeper" that, *bien entendu*, Mailer himself has managed to achieve.)

A difficulty, however, in pitting the reviewer's imagination against the author's, in assuming that critics have an obligation to correct not merely, in Mr. Podhoretz's words, "the prevailing estimate of a book or a literary reputation" but the book itself, is that the relationship between writer and reviewer soon becomes a contest—and a contest, occasionally, of a highly personal sort. The book under review is not written as the reviewer would have written it; he begins to speculate as to what personal deficiency in the author could possibly account for this lapse. If the author has received widespread public recognition, the line of personal attack is clear: he has been corrupted by success in the mass media—and New Reviewers will go to enormous lengths to ferret out references to the author in *Life, Time, Newsweek*, bestseller lists, and so on, in order to establish some kind of guilt by non-obscurity.

More commonly, however, the reviewer's attack upon an author is quite direct—an allegation that his personality, particularly in its sexual and moral attitudes, must be somehow diseased. Alfred Chester, for example, confidently impugns Henry Miller's sexual prowess: "Miller, in fact, never makes his reader raise more than a blush and, more often than not, the blush is for Henry's delusions of grandeur," Leslie Fielder, on the other hand, attempts psychoanalysis: "Finally, like his characters, Salinger is reconciled with everything but sex. . . ." And another *Partisan* reviewer impugns the personal competence not of the author but of previous critics: "Except for Middleton Murry, who for reasons all too transparent found *Aaron's Rod* 'the greatest of Lawrence's novels,' and F. R. Leavis, who for reasons almost as transparent is extremely indulgent toward the novel, no one has ever considered either *Aaron's Rod* or *Kangaroo* successful." The reviewer hastens, however, to assure the reader that his own house is sexually and morally in order. "I just don't want to give up my skin," Alfred Chester informs us, in a rather tangential comment on a book under review. "It feels so good, especially in the sun or in the woods or in the sea or against another." And Mr. Podhoretz himself, in the essay "My Negro Problem— And Ours," while he admits that his own moral stand is not irreproachable, excludes the possibility that most other right-thinking people can be better off. Having outlined the violent and unhappy childhood that left him, to his dismay, with a residual fear and envy of Negroes, he begins to claim for his feelings a certain universality:

This, then, is where I am; it is not exactly where I think all other white liberals are, but it cannot be so very far away either.

The pervasiveness, assurance, and self-congratulation of that "I" in *Doings and Undoings* and in the works of other New Reviewers lead occasionally to a highhandedness that is almost grotesque. Alfred Chester writes:

> I think I am precisely the man for whom serious modern novels are written, since I am one of the men they are written about. Look at four of the most influential novelists of the last twenty years. . . . By influential I mean, of course, that which has impact on the thinking of those capable of thinking, and this, at least in France, is without reference to sales or to the behavior patterns of beatniks and college students.

Having excluded "sales" (i.e., the buyers of books) and "college students" (i.e., some of the most avid readers of them) from the category of "those capable of thinking," Mr. Chester is naturally left with himself, the reviewer, as the man for and about whom "serious modern novels" are written. But one danger in the assumption that it is the reviewer who occupies the center of the literary universe is that he begins to regard everything about himself, however tangential to the book under review, as of universal interest and importance. "Nearly everyone I know would rather see a movie than read a book . . ." Mr. Chester writes. "And I count among my friends . . ." (And he counts among his friends, we may safely assume, Leslie Fiedler, whom Podhoretz notes as having said that "the sight of a group of new novels stimulates in him 'a desperate desire to sneak out to a movie.'")

Despite this tendency to express in criticism all the reviewer's little feelings and preferences—his delight in movies, the predilections of his friends, the situations in which his skin feels good—New Reviewing personalities are not, in general, so idiosyncratic that a reader cannot find one quality they have in common:

> Yet the truth is that the great national "debates" that the *New York Times* daily calls upon us to consider are invariably puerile from an intellectual point of view and far beneath the consideration of any sophisticated mind.

Showing up their weaknesses is child's play for a sophisticated critic.

Granted that painters and actors need not—indeed should not
—be capable of discussing their respective arts with genuine
sophistication, is it really necessary . . .

He is in the presence of a writer who is very sophisticated
indeed and who therefore cannot possibly be as callow and sentimental . . .

Now, this black-and-white account, with the traditional sym-
bolisms reversed, is not the kind of picture that seems persuasive
to the sophisticated modern sensibility—the sensibility that has
been trained by Dostoyevski and Freud, by Nietzsche and Kierkegaard, by Eliot and Yeats, to see moral ambiguity everywhere, to
be bored by melodrama, to distrust the idea of innocence.

On the other hand, of course, there are equally sophisticated
critics like Robert Brustein and Kenneth Tynan who have arrived
at opposite conclusions, finding [Lenny] Bruce not . . .

Those who find Bergman profound and sophisticated (as if
the artist who could move them deeply had to be a deep thinker)
are very likely to find Satyajit Ray rather too simple.

Apart from its truths, I find this very refreshing indeed, because most of us are too sophisticated to have written it or
thought it. . . . We all believe and know these things, but we
fear that to say them out loud would be to evoke the superior
smile.

What these passages (the first five by Mr. Podhoretz, the remaining three by assorted contributors to *Partisan Review* and
*Commentary*) have in common is a keynote of sophistication—
or, at any rate, the mention of the word. Sophistication, one
gathers, is a quality lacking in *Times* editorial writers, illusory in
Bergman films, absent in artists and actors talking about their
work, present in Robert Brustein and Kenneth Tynan, and con-
ditioned by Dostoevski, Freud, Nietzsche, Kierkegaard, Eliot,
and Yeats (although in what sense Dostoevski can be said to
train the modern sensibility to be bored by melodrama, or
Nietzsche to see moral ambiguity everywhere, or Yeats to distrust the idea of innocence, is something that Mr. Podhoretz is
too sophisticated to explain). Richard Chase points out the so-
phisticate's fear of evoking "the superior smile." The definite article is puzzling. The smile? Whose smile? Why, the communal

smile of Norman Podhoretz, Alfred Chester, Lionel Abel, and the rest—the collective smile of the New Reviewing school.

And the stimulus for that sophisticated, perhaps not altogether winning smile is, when it is not the author of a literary work, none other than the reader, who is allowed occasionally to believe that he is in on an exclusive circuit secret but more often is reminded that he is hopelessly out—a child permitted to eavesdrop on the nocturnal conversation of his elders. No opportunity is lost to cast aspersions on the mind and the behavior of that child. "Who listens? Who cares?" Mr. Podhoretz inquires rhetorically, and he deplores the dwindling of "a reading public literate enough to understand a complicated exposition."

Concern, in fact, about the mental calibre of a hypothetical reader slurred as middle-class, middle-brow—indeed, middle-everything—is so widespread that Fiedler professes himself disappointed because he cannot find a novel "which might have caught once and for all the pathos and silliness of middle-class, middle-brow intellectual aspiration"; and even the publisher of *Esquire* feels impelled to announce in his column that "'The mindless dictatorship of the audience' was the most provocative single sentence uttered at Princeton during the entire Response Weekend." (Calling "the mindless dictatorship of the audience" a "sentence" is but one indication of the publisher's concern.) "Is it really so difficult to tell a good action from a bad one?" Frank Kermode inquires in *Partisan Review*, and he answers with a ringing New Reviewing anti-Everyman cliché: "It would seem so, since most people appear to be wrong most of the time." "People like to think Eichmann mediocre," says Lionel Abel. "I think they also like the idea of Miss Arendt, implied by her subtitle, that evil can be banal. Perhaps they are flattered to believe that in the ordinary and dulling conduct of their lives they are at the very least doing something wrong." Here Mr. Abel delivers a threefold vote of no confidence in readers: with his grammar ("Miss Arendt" for "Miss Arendt's"); with his assumption (that the reader's conduct is any more "ordinary and dulling" than Mr. Abel's own); and with the insinuation (that the reader would accept the invalid-conversion fallacy—evil is banal, therefore banality is evil, as one might say all dogs are animals, therefore all animals are dogs—which Mr. Abel permits himself).

Not merely readers, however—everything is on the wane. A

New Reviewing Cassandra seems to have issued an encyclical announcing that the sky is falling—a conclusion that has travelled ever since, in slightly diluted form (as in the childhood game of "Whisper"), around the whole reviewing circle. "Is 'the sickness of our time' a literary hoax?" Benjamin DeMott inquires in *Harper's*. "Are the writers who call the present age a cesspool mistaking personal whiffiness for objective truth?" The questions are purely rhetorical; Mr. DeMott's answer, needless to say, is No.

> The multiplication of commodities and the false standard of living, on the one hand, the complication of the economic and technical structure in which one can work at a job, on the other hand, and the lack of direct relationship between the two have by now made a great part of external life morally meaningless.

Thus, knotting together a few strands of defeatist cliché, another reviewer exemplifies both a prose style and a world view: Everything is bad, science and technology advance, moral values are in eclipse, and there is no hope. (There is no syntax, either— only jargon to express the futility of it all.) "I . . . suppose, they talk about plot and character, style and setting," John Thompson speculates mournfully of the universities. "Maybe it is just too late."

This generalized cultural alarmism has created among the New Reviewers a forensic device that we might call not name- but catastrophe-dropping. Whenever a reviewer's exposition is in danger of disintegration, he simply mentions a calamity to distract the reader's attention (much as a member of a debating society might cry "Fire!" in a crowded auditorium when his argument is going badly). In his discussion of his Negro problem Mr. Podhoretz makes repeated reference to the violence of his feelings, as if in evidence of their universality. And Norman Mailer, inveighing querulously against modern architecture, has a comparable inspiration:

> That rough beast is a shapeless force, an obdurate emptiness, an annihilation of possibilities. It is totalitarianism: that totalitarianism which has haunted the twentieth century, haunted the efforts of intellectuals to define it, of politicians to withstand it, and of rebels to find a field of war where it could be given battle.

Totalitarianism. Haunted. Annihilation. Beast. The reader gasps. What has the analogy to do with modern architecture? But Mr. Mailer is ready with another gambit: "Our modern architecture reminds me a little of cancer cells. Because the healthy cells of the lung have one appearance and those in the liver another. But if both are cancerous they tend to look a little more alike." The reader is meant, in a state of typographical shock, to agree.

"I write the sentence, six million innocent people were slaughtered," Irving Howe writes in *Commentary*, "and for a person of adequate sensibilities may it not be as affecting as an embodiment in a conventional narrative?" Well, no, but it may give the illusion of shoring up a sickly argument. "It is dead. It is evil, like racial prejudice," Alfred Chester writes of the comedy of Vladimir Nabokov. "Less evil . . . were the Eichmann jokes making the rounds last year which mocked and trivialized the death of six million Jews—and which, nonetheless, even I and other Jews could laugh at." Racial prejudice. Dead. Evil. Eichmann. What relevance have they to the comedy of Vladimir Nabokov? They are simply a reviewer's form of literary demagoguery. Other devices on the same order are the frequent use of obscenity and a kind of strident excremental prose that masquerades as a perpetual assertion of manliness. Norman Mailer, for example, writes in a review, "A bad maggoty novel. Four or five half-great short stories were buried like pullulating organs in a corpse of fecal matter"; and Alfred Chester, addressing the author of a book on homosexuality, barks, "Better cut out all that ceaseless groping, Jack, and get down to work!"

Mr. Podhoretz, however, is seldom coarse or shrill. On the contrary, he seeks, by his own account, "a language in which it is possible to talk sensibly and with due proportion about new books." Here is Mr. Podhoretz arguing "sensibly and with due proportion" about the works of John Updike:

> His short stories—which I usually find myself throwing away in disgust before I can get to the end—strike me as all windup and no delivery.

How Mr. Podhoretz can detect the "delivery" if he throws stories away "before I can get to the end" is a problem that he seems not to have posed himself. Nor need he bother to pose it, for although there may be considerable discussion among those in the milieu, there is little dialectic, and arguments of extraordinary inventiveness are permitted to flourish unchallenged. The warm, permissive climate of the New Reviewing is sealed protectively against most intellectual discipline, and it has managed to foster in comfort a whole new genre of fallacy. Lionel Abel, for example, in disagreeing with Hannah Arendt about Adolf Eichmann, takes an argument of Miss Arendt's own, treats it as his, and arrives at a new form of argument altogether, a kind of preemptive bid—agreement-as-refutation: "Is there any contradiction between being morally monstrous and also comical?" he asks. "I am inclined to think that there is none, that anyone who considers the comical traits of Iago and Richard III must be of my opinion." Precisely, and of Miss Arendt's as well—but one must concede Mr. Abel the novelty of his argument; he simply restates, in less subtle terms, what Miss Arendt has said, and expects her to cry "Touché!"

"On the subject of Trotsky," Lionel Abel writes, in another article, "Mr. Kazin exhibits a harshness, intemperateness, and insensitivity which he does not show at all in responding to Herman Melville's Captain Ahab. And this is all the more striking to me since everything Mr. Kazin has to say against Trotsky could be said with equal or greater force against Melville's hero." This appears to be some sort of art/reality interchange, whereby everything that can be said against Mr. Abel can probably be said with equal or greater force against Dogberry. We might call it, perhaps, the argument-from-socio-critical-ineptitude.

Alfred Chester, on the other hand, touches all the forensic bases, and doffs his cap at every one:

> So *Tropic of Cancer*, says I, isn't a great book. So? There is a consolation prize, however; think of what pleasure it is to disagree with Karl Shapiro. And what pleasure it is to disagree with that long and laudatory list of eminent names that appears on the dust jacket like a list of vitamins and minerals: Eliot, Pound, Durrell, Anaïs Nin, Orwell, etc. And what pleasure to disagree also with the whole of the beat generation and their sycophants who have learned from Miller . . . to posture at revolutions that even Time Magazine approves of.

This passage, despite its strange, uncertain irony, calls into being the argument-from-the-stature-of-the-people-with-whom-one-disagrees.

"The sum effect is that *The Glass Bees* puzzles," writes Theodore Solotaroff, "by its technique of steadily delimiting and generalizing its particulars, to the point of turning them into abstractions that could mean this or could mean that, and producing eventually a type of moral sensationalism and sentimentalism." "Delimiting . . . particulars to the point of . . . abstractions . . . producing . . . moral sensationalism"—the sum effect is that this argument puzzles by its technique of steadily ensnarling and obfuscating its terms that could mean this and could mean that, and producing eventually a kind of logical surrealism and vertigo.

And, finally, Mr. Podhoretz himself has argued in *Show* that if two authors "had really wanted to give us a profile of the art of acting, rather than a profile of the practitioners themselves, they would have tried to induce these people to talk candidly about each other's work instead of about their own lives and careers." The argument that a book is improved when its subjects "talk candidly about each other's work" is—"for reasons," as the *Aaron's Rod* reviewer would say, "all too transparent"—a characteristically New Reviewing prescription. "Hamlet," Mr. Podhoretz says in the same piece, "would exist without John Gielgud to play him, but would the heroine of 'Sweet Bird of Youth' have existed without Geraldine Page? For me, the fact that I can't remember her name is answer enough." Answer enough, perhaps, for Mr. Podhoretz. The reader may detect the birth of the argument-from-personal-amnesia.

It is hardly necessary to go on citing instances of the inexhaustible variety of argument along the reviewing circuit. There are signs, in any case, that the cloud (catastrophe-droppers might say "the mushroom cloud") is passing. Or, in purely mechanical terms, there are beginning to be some short circuits in the New Reviewing system. Steven Marcus, in *The New York Review*, crosses three wires (anti-Everyman cliché, reviewer centrality, and catastrophe-dropping), with this result:

> It is almost as if for three hundred years the literature of Western culture had not, so to speak, conducted a campaign to

demonstrate that the middle class family is about as close as we have come to achieving hell on earth.

"The literature of Western culture," as represented by Henry James, Thomas Mann, and Jane Austen—to name authors of but three nationalities—has conducted no such "campaign." Mr. Marcus has confused "the literature of Western culture" with the expository writing of Norman Podhoretz, Leslie Fiedler, Lionel Abel, and the rest of the New Reviewing school.

One can view Mr. Podhoretz as an exponent of a group program only because, in his polemic, or *Undoings*, he insistently invites one to do so, and because (aside from an ill-informed and poorly reasoned piece on Hannah Arendt and his well-intentioned but poorly reasoned essay on the Negro problem, both of which have a kind of negative fascination) the *Undoings* have no interest except as examples of a school of critical writing. And the principles that unite the New Reviewing school are—if it is possible to call them "principles" at all—an elaborate system of cross-references that amounts to mutual coattail-hanging; a stale liberalism gone reactionary in anti-Everyman snobbery and defeatist cliché; a false intellectualism that is astonishingly shabby in its arguments; a hostile imperiousness toward fiction that results in near megalomania on the part of expository writers; and a withering condescension toward authors and readers that finds expression in a strident tendency to shout the opposition down. The New Reviewing is, more generally, a pastiche of attitudes and techniques vying to divert the attention of the reader from the book ostensibly under review to the personality of the reviewer, striving intrusively and valiantly to hold the line against the arts. And the *Undoings* in this collection are, for the most part, models of New Reviewing principle.

In the essays, however, in which Mr. Podhoretz is least interesting as a member of, or spokesman for, something—in his *Doings*, in short—Mr. Podhoretz does manage to assert himself as a genuine critic. Most of these *Doings* are included in a section called "Traditions"—non-topical, non-polemical, even noncontroversial essays—and they are the considered, sympathetic works of a young man more interested in interpreting books than in pitting himself against them.

# Early Radicalism:
# The Price of Peace Is Confusion

$A$T ALMOST EVERY MAJOR UNI-versity in the country, mimeograph machines operate by night in cluttered student apartments, coffeehouses are filled by day with animated political debate, an outdoor platform is occupied nearly every afternoon by speakers deploring some aspect of American foreign policy, and students rush home each evening to pore over copies of the *Times, Le Monde,* and the *Congressional Record* as if they contained reviews of a production in which the students themselves were playing a major part. The source of this activity is a student protest movement that offers, as the students are fond of saying, "not an ideology but a rallying cry." And the cry itself is vague and changeable enough to reflect a curious fact about America in the sixties: there are very few revolutionary positions that the Establishment does not already, at least nominally, occupy.

Students who are revolutionary in spirit, however, after protesting a bit for mere protest's sake, have come up with real social criticism in three phases: the Free Speech Movement, which
began as an attack upon the bureaucracy of the large university
and turned into a protest against the impersonality of all institutions that, like the government welfare program, have lost contact with the people and values they were designed to serve; the
Civil Rights Movement, which began as a campaign for Negro
rights and turned into a campaign for eliminating local pockets
of poverty; and the Peace Movement, which has begun as a protest against American military involvement in Vietnam and is
turning into an attempt to influence all of foreign policy. On
many campuses, all factions of the peace movement are united
in an Independent Committee to End the War in Vietnam—a
frail, tangled coalition of forces and personalities that includes
groups ranging from religious pacifists to militant supporters of
the Vietcong; sociological types ranging from children of left-
wingers of the thirties to what one student called "some of your
preppier New Englanders, who are in it for moral reasons"; a
few students who simply hope to evade the draft; a few repre-
sentatives of national, local, and ad-hoc committees; a few hard-
line members of the Young Socialist Alliance (Y.S.A.), who
are commonly referred to as Trotskyists and are known within
the movement, familiarly, as the "Trots"; and a new breed of
lonely hangers-on and demonstration enthusiasts who might be
described as Sunday Outing Radicals.

Most of the students involved regard the United States position in Vietnam as at best unjust, and most of them feel that a
post-Nuremberg ethic requires them to oppose a war that they
cannot in conscience support. How to go about it is another
matter. Since there has been, for good or for ill, no long-standing
tradition of student protest in this country (as there is in France,
and in other countries that do not regard college students as
children), American students seem to have borrowed their tactics from several contemporary sources. From Aldermaston and,
more recently, from the civil-rights movement comes the protest
march. From the Johannesburg Negroes' burning of their identity cards stems, apparently, the American students' draft-card
burning. And the extreme form of Buddhist protest against the

Diem regime seems to have inspired at least one American student to burn himself to death.

These manifestations, quite naturally, have caused alarm. The possibility that a generation of young might refuse to carry on the military business of their generally permissive society seemed, for a time, to threaten the nation in a not yet demilitarized world. There was also concern for the fact that, in their enthusiasm for the movement, many students were leaving their studies and shuttling back and forth among the campuses of the nation as vagabond dropouts in a vaguely academic orbit. And the unkempt appearance, condescending manner, and frequent acts of civil disobedience of many of the demonstrators added to an impression that this particular lot had spoiled, and that something must be done to keep the rest from being ruined. Militant counter-movements quickly sprang up on many campuses. In August, Congress passed legislation that provides a maximum penalty of five years in prison for draft-card burners. In October, Attorney General Katzenbach said that the Justice Department had found in the peace movement evidence of Communist infiltration. These developments, coupled with a certain predisposition on the part of student revolutionaries to draw a sense of risk from somewhere, confirmed in the minds of students an already widespread suspicion that the government was conspiring against them. Few demonstrators at Columbia now, to take one example, have any doubt that their telephones are being tapped; anyone who brings a camera or a notebook to a demonstration is immediately pointed out to all bystanders as an agent of the F.B.I.; and students seem to stand in hourly expectation of an academic purge of dissidents, followed by a rapid punitive draft.

But the peace movement has also matured. Most of the early leaders now concede that radical action on the peace issue was a tactical mistake. (The disruption of an R.O.T.C. ceremony at Columbia last May 7th, for instance, which was once thought of as "a milestone," or "a hairy idea," is now spoken of on campus simply as an "aberrant demonstration.") As for the charge that the peace movement inadvertently prolongs the war by misrepresenting American public opinion, it has been treated in several of the movement's countless "position papers"—most recently in "A Position Paper on Tactics," by a student named Robert E.

Bogosian, who suggests that communiqués be sent at once to Peking, Hanoi, and the Vietcong informing them that the demonstrators speak only for themselves and that theirs is a minority position, which, obviously, it is. As for the charge of Communist infiltration, the demonstrators tend to dismiss it (Students for a Democratic Society has dropped its anti-Communist clause) as "irrelevant." Post-Stalinist Communism no longer seems to these well-travelled children of prosperity a monolith, or even a particularly potent expansionist force. "If an American still wants to be a Communist, we think that's his business," says David Gilbert, a leader of the peace movement at Columbia.

The charge of Communist inspiration for the movement, however, seems particularly wide of the mark. If anything has characterized the movement, from its beginning and in all its parts, it has been a spirit of decentralization, local autonomy, personal choice, and freedom from dogma. On many campuses, even simple majority rule is regarded as coercive of the minority; policy decisions require a "consensus." As a result, very few policy decisions are made. In fact, it often appears that the movement may be, in the end, more right than left—that it may have picked up a dropped conservative stitch in the American political tradition. Individualism, privacy, personal initiative, even isolationism and a view of the federal government as oppressive —these elements of the right-wing consciousness have not been argued in such depth (least of all by the right wing itself, with its paradoxical insistence on domestic police expansion and on military intervention abroad) since 1932.

Over the Thanksgiving weekend, the student peace movement and many other groups of diverse moral and political persuasions—all apparently united by an overriding concern that the United States get out of Vietnam—converged upon Washington. By Sunday night, the student demonstrators had divided into several major factions and the student peace movement faced a crisis that had very little to do with its attitudes toward the war in Vietnam. The first split, which occurred well before the march, was down the middle, between a liberal institution and the student groups. In August, more than three hundred demonstrators calling themselves the Congress—and, later (to avoid the acronym "COUP"), the Alliance—of Unrepresented Peoples staged a sit-in on the steps of the Capitol in a protest that combined the causes of peace and civil rights. When the demonstration was over, some of the participants met to form a new group, the National Coordinating Committee to End the War in Vietnam. The Coordinating Committee was to be situated centrally, in Madison, Wisconsin. It was to have no membership and no specific policy. Its function, under its chairman, Frank Emspak (a recent graduate of the University of Wisconsin), and a secretarial staff of four, was to issue a weekly newsletter and facilitate communiction among the members of various far-flung organizations—an alphabet heap that included, among others, YAWF, W.F.P., W.I.L.P.F., P.L.P., M.2M. (for the May 2nd Movement), C.P., S.P.U., W.R.L., Y.P.Y.F., T.U.P., C.F.R., I.W.W., C.F.IV.I. (for something called the Committee for a Fourth International), Y.S.A., I.S.C., C.N.V.A., M.F.D.P., S.S.O.C., V.D.C., and S.D.S., together with numerous local "independent" and ad-hoc committees.

The Coordinating Committee successfully coordinated a number of nationwide activities, most notably the marches on October 15th and 16th (the International Days of Protest). It was decided to hold a national five-day convention of the Coordinating Committee in Madison over the Thanksgiving holidays. Then it was learned that Sanford Gottlieb, political director of SANE (the Committee for a Sane Nuclear Policy), and other sponsors were urging a national peace march on Washington on the Saturday after Thanksgiving. Since the Coordinating Committee wanted no conflict between the two events, it decided to move its convention to Washington. In time, however, it became apparent that SANE's invitation to march had been what the students refer to as an "exclusionist call." Although anyone might march, SANE reserved the right to authorize the slogans that the marchers could carry. Any poster that could, in SANE's judgment, politically compromise the movement would be excluded from the demonstration. The Coordinating Committee, which had always stressed its non-exclusionist, non-centralized, laissez-faire character, expressed outrage ("They're leaning over backwards to define not what they are but what they're not," said one student), and the march organizers, having no practical means to censor the posters anyway, capitulated. The rift between SANE and the Coordinating Committee, however, was established almost from the outset—if not in official policy, then certainly in spirit. The next jolt to the student movement came not from what it looks upon as the creeping, ineffectual liberalism of SANE but from the thirties, and from within the Coordinating Committee itself.

The first few hours of the convention in Washington ran smoothly, with the arrival on Wednesday of delegates from all over the country at convention headquarters—a basement in a predominantly Negro neighborhood of Washington. There were a few cheerful posters taped to the bleak stone walls ("God Bless This Office and All the Revolutionaries Who Work Here" and "The Price of Peace Is Confusion"), but the room was basically an office devoted to the serious business of registering fifteen hundred delegates and alternates, and assigning them—two or three to a room, if necessary—to the Harrington Hotel, where twelve workshops, or discussions, on such subjects as Peace and Freedom, National Program, Organization Structure, the Draft, and Community Organization were to be held. A few arriving delegates began to confer in the strange, conditional idiom of Anglo-American dialecticians ("I would be prepared to argue that . . ." and "Yes, well, in that case I might want to maintain that . . ."), but, perhaps because the room was overheated, most of the delegates left the basement as soon as they had registered.

Late Wednesday evening, at the Second Act Coffee Shop, around the corner from headquarters, a crowd of delegates gathered, and a kind of civil-rights alumni reunion appeared to be taking place. Ray Robinson, a tall, handsome Negro veteran of countless civil rights and peace campaigns, seemed to know almost everyone from somewhere or other. He was telling of his participation in a protest march from Canada toward Guantanamo ("Uncle Sam said, 'Man, you can't go 'cross that water. Cuba's over there'") when Stephen Frumin, an intense young delegate who had attended the University of Wisconsin, broke in. "The war and my perception of things have escalated," he said.

"We may be a minority, but at least the press is giving us equal time," said another delegate. "They think the fact that some of us have beards is interesting. It's a sign of the boredom and banality of American life."

"I hope we get some things decided at this convention," said

Vicki Cooper, a delegate from Pittsburgh. "There are so many issues that are still receiving much heated debate. If we could get some of this clarified, maybe the press would stop describing the *people* involved in the movement and pay some attention to our ideas. We might even put up political candidates, although it would have to be in a participatory, democratic way. I couldn't permit any major decisions to be made for me. If I couldn't have a major say, I wouldn't follow them."

At nine o'clock Thursday morning, at the Harrington Hotel, a meeting of the Coordinating Committee's presiding committee was held, at which, with a great deal of gravity and circumspection, very little was accomplished. Emspak conducted a low-keyed discussion of whether rigid standards should be set up for delegate credentials. It was decided that since few, if any, delegates would want to falsify their registration, standards should be loose. When the committee adjourned, a young man from Youth Against War and Fascism tried to sell a "Support the National Liberation Front" button to Mary Walker, a middle-aged delegate from the Committee on Non-Violence of Denver, Colorado. "No, thank you," she said. "I have a thousand 'Stop the War' buttons back in Denver. I think that gets the message across."

"A REVERENT SILENCE IS REQUESTED," said an old sign above the door to the nave of the Lincoln Memorial Congregational Temple, where the first plenary session of the convention was held, at twelve-thirty on Thanksgiving Day. Within moments, however, there was neither silence nor reverence anywhere in the building, for a power struggle, in a completely unexpected form and at a completely unexpected time, threatened to split the Coordinating Committee. What started it was a leaflet signed by thirty-three delegates and alternates, most of whom identified their local committees as either the Committee to End the War in Vietnam (C.E.W.V.) or the Vietnam Day Committee (V.D.C.), proposing an additional workshop "that would provide an opportunity for the independent committees to discuss their own programs, structure, and tasks." The workshop, the thirteenth, was to meet concurrently with the other twelve, which were preoccupied with essentially the same problems. This may have struck some of the delegates as strange, but only the most knowledgeable at once besieged the platform with cries of "Point of order!" "Amendment takes precedence!" "Sit down!" "Shut up!" "Let him speak!" and "Two-thirds of us don't know what's going on!" (At one point, Emspak actually had to restrain someone intent on wresting the microphone from him.)

As Jens Jensen, a delegate from Cambridge, Massachusetts, rose to say that "no one wants to be divisive in the slightest," Marilyn Milligan, Jack Weinberg, and Jerry Rubin—all members of the Berkeley V.D.C. and signers of the controversial document—gathered around Steve Weissman, a Californian, also of the V.D.C., and one of the early leaders of the Berkeley free-speech movement. "What have I signed?" asked Marilyn Milligan. "I knew we shouldn't have signed. Those so-called members of independent committees aren't independents at all. They're Y.S.A. The Trots seem to be trying to steal the movement."

"Every generation has got to learn," said Weissman. "The Trots have still got their sense of imminence. They're still listening to history and not to people."

Aside from a few converts to the Young Socialist Alliance, it was difficult to imagine what the "Trots" hoped to gain from splitting and undermining the National Coordinating Committee. Some delegates thought Y.S.A. was trying to bring the whole movement into its own sectarian line. Others thought Y.S.A. was maneuvering to form a hard-core cadre of extreme radicals within the non-exclusionist N.C.C., and others speculated that the urge to take over an organization—no matter how formless that organization might be—was simply a reflex acquired from the bitter struggles of the thirties.

The delegates on the floor, however, most of them still unaware of what was going on, voted to adjourn and to give the thirteenth workshop permission to meet after the plenary session if it chose. The meeting was held briefly in the basement of the church. There were some impassioned appeals to disband, and the workshop voted to adjourn until seven-thirty that night, when it would decide whether to adjourn for good.

The rest of the afternoon was devoted to the twelve scheduled workshops and, for those who wanted them, seething discussions about "structure." The anti-draft workshop, under the leadership of Staughton Lynd, a professor of history at Yale, began in the church balcony, with a series of reports from various regions:

"I'm from New Orleans, and the consensus out there seemed to be that a person should do anything that he feels he can do in conscience," and "I'm from Chicago, and we simply could not get even a simple majority to endorse any organized program of draft opposition. We don't feel that without an extreme consensus we ought to get into the anti-draft bag." Another workshop met in the nave of the church, in full view of the balcony. Practically every remark there was greeted with tempestuous applause, and at one point Professor Lynd leaned over the balcony to shout, "Friends, do you think you could not applaud every time somebody says something?" This was greeted by the first laughter of the afternoon.

At seven-thirty, when the meeting of the thirteenth workshop was slated to begin, the room was packed and overflowed into the hallway. Jerry Rubin rescinded his endorsement of the leaflet and pronounced it "beyond my comprehension" that he should ever have signed such a thing. Then, having moved that the meeting adjourn and having lost by a small margin, Rubin led the Berkeley delegation and many of the real independents out of the meeting and to Room 407, where the Berkeley delegation held a meeting of its own.

"That was stylishly done," said Steve Weissman in Room 407. "But now, as I see it, the Berkeley delegation, as one of the oldest, truly independent committees here, should draft the strongest statement possible denouncing the attempt to split the movement."

"Do you think we should lay it on the line that Y.S.A. is behind it?" asked Rubin. "In a way, they've packed the delegations and we're faced with a fait accompli. Y.S.A. chairs the independent committees from San Francisco, Los Angeles, and Cleveland, just for a beginning, and they've got ten years of political indoctrination behind them."

Ray Robinson bounded angrily into the room. "I've just been caucusing with the Mississippi people downstairs, and they're going to resign this goddam thing," he said. "They're cutting out. *Three times* now, they've been asked to come up to Washington for peace and they have just been *used*. The infighting has got to stop. One of the girls from down there asked me a simple question. She asked what she came up here for—you dig? She didn't come here to *meet* people, and listen to Y.S.A. interpret ideology for the ones who don't know where they're at. You college people messed up again, I tell you that, brother."

"We know, Ray," said Weissman. "And we're trying to draft a statement. But is that all—is there a bitch besides that?"

"Yeah," said Robinson. "The Mississippi people just aren't being made to feel welcome."

"I know just what they mean, and it isn't just the Mississippi people, either," said Beverly Sterner, a member of C.N.V.A. "The opening of the session was so sterile and so cold. No orientation. No word of welcome."

The Berkeley delegation didn't draft a statement that night. It didn't have to. Word came upstairs that the thirteenth workshop's meeting had been persuaded to adjourn, after all, by Rubin, who had gained admission, recanted his endorsement yet again, and confessed that he had been "taken in by Y.S.A." This last remark was pronounced "not in good taste" by members of the Y.S.A., but for the moment they gave in.

Late Thursday night, the Mississippi delegation, having decided not to leave, was holding the first of its "soul sessions" at the hotel. The soul session, which has become a tradition of the movement in the South, is a kind of marathon group therapy, with a dash of mysticism. Participants have described it as a drugless "high on talk." The Mississippi people, who were likely to have experienced more suffering at the hands of society than any of the other delegates, were trying to demonstrate that a revolution can originate in the personal sufferings of people, freely expressed, rather than in a few directives from the top. "Don't think you have to talk," Delmar Scudder, a Negro student from Swarthmore, said at the beginning of the session, "until you feel that you can get out some of the pain, and find out where it is."

In a room marked "Ideological Overflow," Al Johnson, a Negro worker for the Mississippi Freedom Democratic Party in Washington, said to Weissman, "I'm not sure what this convention has to offer the movement in the South. The argument about structure—we had it all in S.N.C.C., and look where it led. No more local autonomy. Every worker has to file a weekly report. Man, that's what I'd call a co-ercive structure."

"That's just what I think the movement is all about," said

Weissman. "To see if we can find any structures that are not coercive. Maybe it can't be done. Maybe there can't be any participatory democracy in a mass society. But you M.F.D.P. people, and the chapters of S.D.S., and the movement in New York, and we in Berkeley ought to be able to talk to each other about that."

The conversations and caucuses and soul sessions went on at the Harrington far into the night.

Breakfast on Friday in the Harrington cafeteria was a time for introspection and political realignment. ("The trouble with national structures is just what's happening here. They can be taken over." "Yes, but how can you confront a national government without a national structure?") In the lobby of the Harrington, photographers were gathering some of the more bizarre-looking people around and posing them on a sofa as a cross-section of the movement.

Very few people went to any of the workshops on Friday, and the Students for a Democratic Society held a caucus to plan its own convention in December. "I suggest that we get away from the smoke-disaster syndrome," said one delegate. "All this boring dialectic in smoke-filled rooms. I think this time we ought to go someplace where we can run in the fields." The S.D.S. discussed the meeting place for several hours and then reached a consensus: Antioch, if the delegate who had suggested it could get use of the campus.

"I think S.D.S. ought to stay away from protest for a while," said Weissman. "The other groups have taken it up, and, as they say, I'm less concerned with anything we can do about Vietnam now than I am about how we can affect foreign policy seven wars from now. It's hard for a democratic group to find the levers of foreign policy. In a way, M.F.D.P. and S.D.S. have the same problem about the convention. We don't want or need a strong central structure at present. We've got our local community-action constituencies."

That evening, at a plenary session, a delegate from Missisippi read a transcript of ten single-spaced pages of soul session, taken down the previous night. He told the delegates, "Don't applaud. We don't care if you agree. The issue is whether we can speak to one another." The delegates gave him a standing ovation. Immediately thereafter, however, the Young Socialist Alliance broke forth with a complicated new issue, concerning credentials. There was a long and bitter floor fight, which the Y.S.A. lost but which caused one Mississippi delegate to tear up his delegate card in chagrin and another to suggest the possibility of a delegate-card burning. The Y.S.A. made still another attempt to take over, through the seemingly harmless maneuver of suggesting that the movement adopt three slogans—"Let's Bring the Troops Home Now," "Self-Determination in Mississippi and Vietnam," and "Freedom Now, Withdrawal Now"—for the march the following morning. But David Gilbert, of Columbia, among others, pointed out that the "Withdrawal Now" slogan would be unacceptable to SANE and also to many constituents of the Coordinating Committee (who believe in negotiated withdrawal); that the ensuing split would simply feed the movement's enemies; and that the convention was, in any case, not empowered to adopt slogans without a mandate from the local committees. Throughout this discussion, there were jeers, cries of "Parliamentary nincompoop!" "Ideologue!" and "Let him finish!" In the end, the convention allowed each marcher to adopt the slogan of his choice.

On Saturday, the march itself went off almost without a hitch, and without much excitement, either. Veterans in the vanguard of the procession were shouting, "No more vets! No more vets!" The flags at the base of the Washington Monument made their usual applauding noise. In front of the stage below the monument, a special section was roped off by SANE monitors, to be reserved for veterans, clergymen, writers, celebrities, and, "in case there should be enough room," the old and the infirm. There were speeches of varying quality, leading up to an appearance by Sanford Gottlieb, who seemed to be showing a certain hostility toward the marchers when he asked, "How many of you can't hear me back there? Raise your hands," and then continued, "Oh, well, I see a lot of raised hands. That must mean you can hear just fine." (As it happened, owing to quirks of the wind, the marchers back there could hear perfectly at times and sometimes not at all.)

But the high point for most of the students, and for some of the older people as well, was the speech by the president of Students for a Democratic Society, Carl Oglesby, who had held himself aloof all week from the Coordinating Committee infighting and who now delivered a scathing yet considered attack not on the administration in Washington but on the institution of American liberalism itself, which, he said, had become so entrenched as to be, in an almost entirely new sense, complacent and reactionary. A bearded young man himself, he said that America had become "a nation—may I say it?—of beardless liberals." He went on, "There is simply no such thing for the United States now as a just revolution," and he deplored the government's determination to "safeguard what they take to be American interests around the world against revolution or revolutionary change, which they always call Communism—as if it were that." Later, he said, "Then why can't we see that our proper human struggle is not with Communism or revolutionaries but with the social desperation that drives good men to violence, both here and abroad?" The rhetoric of Oglesby's speech was strangely old-fashioned, but the young people present were moved, and even the older people seemed to feel reassured. The scene ended with Sanford Gottlieb advancing and raising Oglesby's arm in triumph, like a prize fighter's, to volleys of cheering.

At the Harrington, however, many students who had not bothered to march were locked in caucus about structure. (The issue of Vietnam, never very clearly in focus at the convention, seemed to have been eclipsed entirely.) Immediately after the march, the presiding committee met in a room at the hotel, while in another room the thirteenth workshop had reconvened and was making a last-ditch effort to form a movement of its own, in a meeting that was turning really ugly. Three young members of the Y.S.A. stood guard outside the door, and unlocked it only for members of independent committees who pledged themselves to vote in favor of founding a separate national committee. When one delegate, remarking that the room had been paid for by the Coordinating Committee, attempted to meet force with force and enter, he was caught for some time in the door, which the guards were pushing shut, and then was forcibly dragged some distance down the hallway.

"Goons and Storm Troopers," said one dismayed independent. "This is supposed to be a *peace* movement."

"*We've* never advocated non-violence," said one member of Y.S.A.

"And furthermore, there has *been* no violence here," said a middle-aged woman emerging from the door. "You didn't *see* any, there *wasn't* any, and if you insist on misrepresenting things that way I'll have you escorted out of here."

The final plenary session—the meeting on structure—was held on Sunday morning, in a room at the New Dunbar Hotel. Dave Dellinger, the editor of *Liberation*, presided. The Y.S.A. caucus had come up with its own proposals on structure. But Jack Weinberg received permission to make an opening statement and set what he called a "tone" to the meeting. He said that he knew some delegates had reached "the conclusion that we are going to come out of here divided," and he asked them to "destroy the split before it is carried home to every chapter and there is a vote—a majority and a minority, with two separate affiliations and no consensus—in every community and on every campus." Then a man leaped to his feet, identified himself as Albert Nelson, of the Spartacist Movement, and, in the first really open allusion in the plenary session to anything that was going on behind the scenes, claimed that "the political infighting ought to be hitting the floor," that someone was "gutting the convention of its real political issues." Condemning the Young Socialist Alliance and the Coordinating Committee for their "lack of candor" and loss of the personal touch, he announced that he would abstain from voting for the proposals made by either one. Here Dellinger interposed. "A common interest has reasserted itself," he said, "but if there are any jokers here we are trying to bring them out. If they take over the national organization, it will be only the shell, because the rest of us will continue under other auspices."

After all the votes had been cast (the Coordinating Committee's proposal on structure was adopted), Elizabeth Fusco, a worker for M.F.D.P. in S.N.C.C. overalls, asked, and received, permission to speak. She announced that the Mississippi delegation had just completed another soul session, said that "they felt they were the only people in the convention dealing with something warm—the pain they feel," and asked that everyone remain after the plenary to join in. "Will you stay?" she cried. "Will you stay?" Delmar Scudder then climbed to the stage to announce that the Mississippi people were so pleased with their sessions that they were planning to hold a "soul press conference" and to look into "travelling soul workshops and soul education and soul recreation," adding, "Maybe that's what we have to offer the American people."

When the last soul session of the convention took place, in a room at the Statler Hilton, it was packed, not only with S.D.S. and Mississippi people but with other independents. The Y.S.A. (who were caucusing again) didn't attend, nor did Emspak, who was on his way back to Madison. The session lasted for a full thirty-six hours, after which everyone claimed to feel refreshed. The Mississippi counties, and S.D.S. organizers, who were concentrating on community action, returned to their communities and campuses.

"I guess if you take the soul sessions, and the ideologues, and the kids who just can't sleep on account of Vietnam, you can get a pretty clear idea which way all this is going to lead," said one delegate as he boarded a bus to return in time for a class on Monday morning.

# Instruments

Wᴴɪʟᴇ ᴍᴀɴʏ ᴀᴜᴛʜᴏʀꜱ ᴛʀʏ ᴛᴏ register the times on a loud and epic scale, two novelists, one French and the other English, are measuring little conflicts, minor hesitations. They have no interest in writing the apocalyptic novel of a nuclear age; they are not concerned with that form of innovation which consists in beating back the censor. Each has simply used the novel as a finely calibrated instrument capable of recording varieties of experience that have not been explored in fiction before.

Nathalie Sarraute probes the minds of her characters to a depth at which they are all more or less alike. So alike, in fact, that she finds it possible to dispense with characters, as discrete individuals, almost altogether. And along with characters, she does away with plot. For reasons set forth in her collection of critical essays, *The Age of Suspicion,* Mme. Sarraute believes that the props and techniques of conventional narrative have become frozen and inert; in her latest novel, *The Golden Fruits,* translated by Maria Jolas (Braziller), she simply melts them down. What is left is a subterranean pool of social impulses and responses rippling among nameless, bodiless, characterless speakers. As the novel opens, that pool is stirred by an event—the publication of a novel called *The Golden Fruits.* Immediately there are little quivers of anxiety, tentative questionings: "Tell me . . . have you read? . . . What did you think of it?" For a time the question drifts, partly formulated, unanswered. Then it strikes something solid, an opinion:

> Listen. I'll call out, answer me. Just so that I may know that you are still there. I am shouting in your direction with all my might. The Golden Fruits . . . do you hear me? What do you think of it? And a dreary voice replies . . . "The Golden Fruits . . . it's good . . ."

It's good. The verdict washes quickly over other minds, which hasten to agree, to outdo one another in agreeing. Feminine voices obligingly pose the question; masculine voices forcefully reply:

> "And The Golden Fruits, do you like that?" . . . Yes, I like that, do you hear? . . .
>
> Tell me, rather, I wanted to ask you, I haven't really read it, I only had time to glance through it, I wish you would tell me: The Golden Fruits, what do you think of it?
>
> —It's a superb book. Furthermore, you see . . . I just happen to be writing an article . . .

An article. The matter then is borne toward the critics, where the judgment "superb" can be amplified. First it is divided into syllables: "su-perb." Further amplifications follow:

> "I don't think it is as classical as all that. In the sense that people usually take this word. It is involved, baroque, heavy and even awkward, at times. The classics, moreover, as is too frequently forgotten, were also awkward and involved when they were the moderns. This is a difficult work. . . . It reflects the spirit of our time perfectly. . . ."
>
> "This book, I believe, establishes in literature a privileged

language which succeeds in investing a correspondence that is its own structure . . ."

—We agree absolutely. Thus, an a-temporal dimension is dissolved here in the becoming of a thematic. Because of this fact, this work, down to its most structured strata, is a poem.

A poem. The current of approbation begins to carry all before it. Critical jargon, literary-cocktail-party gossip ("Intimate diaries . . . confidences . . . memoirs of dismissed servants . . . one finds . . . such baseness that it is hard, this must be admitted, not to have a very legitimate feeling of superiority"), ploys and counterploys reach such proportions that they threaten to engulf the reviewer of Mme. Sarraute's own *Golden Fruits.*

Not everyone, however, can be swept along. Some must be snubbed, cast off, abandoned, to preserve the cultural elitists' "very legitimate feeling of superiority":

—Oh you, my dear Jean-Pierre, you . . . you say that to please us, we know you. . . . People can't get in here like that. They must have given certain proofs. . . . At certain moments, certain unfortunate mistakes were made, a few too many pledges given to others when they were in power. . . . One must be very careful not to open the door to such questionable allies, to these last-minute adherents who could bring discredit on the entire community. . . .

Critical unanimity has reached its crest; no new assenters need apply. The moment is ripe, however, for a rara avis—something solid and resistant, a new opinion. Someone soon risks it: "The Golden Fruits," he says, "is flat." There follows agitation, turbulence: "Ha, ha, ha, I can't bear it . . . When I think . . . oh, you'll be the death of me . . . Now listen, is it possible you don't see that that banal, platitudinous side you speak of, is precisely what Brehier was after, he did it on purpose." The argument is an old and potent one in critical circles, but to no avail. The tide has turned, and in a short while

Those who from near or from far, openly or secretly, even in the uttermost depth of their consciences, continue to look upon The Golden Fruits with admiration or even mere liking, a bit of fellow feeling, all those who today still consort with it, uphold it, seek excuses . . . those who by word or thought give it any support whatsoever, are fools. . . .

In a sense, Mme. Sarraute's *The Golden Fruits* is satire, and she has caught in all its absurd manifestations the universal aspiration of that supernumerary in the arts, the critic: to be the first to state what everyone is or will soon be thinking anyway. She has caught the critic's self-importance ("Alone with another image that they have never ceased to contemplate, an image of themselves with gigantic proportions, more and more enormous, spreading out on every side"), his simple vanity ("Say what you talked about . . . about whom? About me, perhaps, oh joy, perhaps my book?"), his false knowledgeability, and his complete vulnerability when he is asked to document his arguments. But except for occasional lapses into broad parody (thrown in, perhaps, much as an Expressionist painter might draw a caricature or two to demonstrate that his more drastic innovations stem from choice and not from lack of talent for the ordinary), *The Golden Fruits* is not satire after all but a new kind of reporting. Critical discussions and cocktail-party conversations are as Mme. Sarraute has overheard and recorded them.

Since *The Golden Fruits* presents not a story of characters but a report of murmurs, anxieties, afterthoughts, and undertones, it is unlike the work of any other novelist. In one respect it is unlike any of the previous work of Mme. Sarraute as well. Her earlier novels, notably *The Planetarium*, were also studies of the formlessness, vapidity, and even solubility of speakers in social situations, but the technique seemed limited to the study of trivia, to small concerns. *Everything* dissolved in pettiness; it seemed that such a novel could support only a cynicism as uniform and as unpunctuated as the dialogue itself. There was nothing at stake. In *The Golden Fruits,* Mme. Sarraute has managed to cast something significant adrift on those aimless subcurrents (the publication of a book is, after all, an event of some significance) and to find at the end, surprisingly, someone firm and uncompromised: a single character, a reader—notably not a critic of the periodical or cocktail party sort—for whom the author can, without abandoning her objectivity, plead eloquently, a reader uninterested in the prevailing value judgments, a reader whom the book itself affects:

> People can say what they like. . . . No word from outside can destroy so natural, so perfect a fusion. Like love it gives us the strength to face anything. Like one in love I should like to hide it. For them not to see what there is between us, for them not to come near it, is all I ask of them. I have not the slightest desire to convince them. . . .

Such a reader, awkward and sentimental as he is, is the first bit of solid gold Mme. Sarraute has discovered in the tepid social waters she explores. His presence in the novel, however unobtrusive, means that the author's technique can now accommodate, without irony, a whole range of human attitudes and responses, not excluding the noble.

While most of the speakers in *The Golden Fruits* are subjective and interdependent, the characters in Ivy Compton-Burnett's *A God and His Gifts* (Simon and Schuster) are rigid, angular, and aloof. The novel is written almost entirely in dialogue, so formal and relentlessly logical that Miss Compton-Burnett manages to transform a convention by the very scrupulousness of her adherence to it. The novel is stylized and frozen; what upheavals occur are conveyed through a violent readjustment of surfaces, like a cracking of ice. Hereward Egerton, the hero of the novel, an author who is by his own account "a man of full nature . . . built on a large scale" and "not afraid to say it," marries a woman who is by her own account not one to "attract so many" and "a person who tends to look up." In time, Hereward seduces his sister-in-law (by whom he has a child), his first son's fiancée (by whom he has another child), and his children's nurse. He also makes advances to the fiancée of his second son and to his own daughter by his sister-in-law (with whom, by this time, his third son, unaware that the girl is his half sister as well as his first cousin, has fallen in love). As the novel ends, Hereward's son by his first son's wife is in danger of falling in love with Hereward's first son's daughter. Since the whole family is eventually gathered under one roof, and since all the characters are always in dead earnest when they speak, the situation might seem an explosive one. Yet the novel is developed with the austerity of a syllogism; no voices are raised, and nothing is said that does not go directly to the point. It is as though a situation that would do credit to the imagination of Tennessee Williams were expressed with the terse, perfect logic of the Cheshire Cat or the White Queen:

> "To think we are all descendants!" said Joanna. . . . "I have never worked for myself. It does sound egotistic."
> "Well, I have worked for myself and others in managing things," said Sir Michael. "I think it is a just claim."
> "Yes, Sir Michael. Though most work is for others," said Galleon, leaving the matter there.
> "I think all claims are just," said Joanna. "That is why they are made. I have never met an unjust claim. I suppose it is because there are not any."

That is the continuing pattern of Miss Compton-Burnett's dialogue—a gradual undercutting of ironies and frivolous remarks, a conversation that seems to come nearer the truth, a brief lapse into platitude ("Most work is for others"), and then the whole matter crumbles into mock tautology ("All claims are just. That is why they are made"). The result is that by having her characters speak with complete logic and frankness Miss Compton-Burnett achieves an effect of absolute disingenuousness: when nothing is held back, everything seems kept in reserve. It is the absurd deadpan comedy of Joseph K. and Alice. The revelation, for example, that Hereward Egerton has fathered the child of his son Merton's wife is greeted by Merton sarcastically:

> . . . " 'I will try to be a son to you, Father. Better perhaps than I have been. If I had not failed you, you yourself might not have failed. Let us learn from each other.' "
> "I am glad, Merton," said Hereward, as if accepting the literal words. "I will not say more. Again it need not be said."

And after Hereward has undercut his son's sarcasm by ignoring it, the conversation continues:

> "How wonderful everyone is!" said Joanna to her husband. "I did not know they were all like this. I know that some troubles bring out the best in people. But I should not have thought this

one of them. I suppose, when there is so much quality, anything does to bring it out. I am so proud of everyone."

"Well, I am proud of everyone but Hereward," said Sir Michael in a low tone. "I can't reconcile myself to this. I had had no thought of it. I am not a person who suspects such things. I can't understand the excuses made for him. Though of course as his father I am grateful."

"Oh, but isn't it better to be proud of him too? We should not like him to be left out. And a mother has to forgive everything. It has always been recognized."

"I suppose a father should too."

"I don't think it matters about a father. Anyhow there is no rule. Perhaps we only have rules that can be kept."

The sequence is the same—irony, missed irony, platitude, truism. And although everything is said, courteously and articulately (these are not the anxious mutterers of *The Golden Fruits*), nothing is revealed. As Mme. Sarraute deals with vague undercurrents and profits from the tension between the conversational crisis and the triviality of the speaker's feelings, Miss Compton-Burnett studies smooth surfaces and profits from the tension between the conversational urbanity and the enormity of the emotional issue. What is extraordinary about each of these writers is her complete consistency, her strict attention to only that psychological level she has chosen to study. Each is an innovator and a formalist, in the best sense of the word, and each manages to convey more truth by means of her polygraph than we are getting from many writers of cataclysmic aspiration, the seismologists among contemporary novelists.

# Selling an Enraged
# Bread Pudding

Sub-adult mystics, under-educated cynics, doctrinaire propagandists, and pop philosophers have this in common: they like to think and talk of paradox. Not the Existential, or logical, paradox that has haunted the twentieth-century mind. Not any genuine paradox at all. But a kind of muzzy half truth—with a heady whiff of portent—that conceals a simple failure to distinguish between levels of discourse. Boredom is the state of utmost fascination. The ultimate plan is to be completely random. The form of the creative work is to be entirely indeterminate. The facts are irrelevant to the real truth of the matter. The audience is the performance. Even, the medium is the message. All these are ideas that it can be useful or amusing to entertain at the level of metaphor. Taken at all literally, however, they belong beside earnest efforts to overhear one hand clapping or to find a married bachelor. They involve a serious misunderstanding of the way language works.

A sign that you have met a dealer in false paradox (usually a kind of walking absurdity himself—a proselytizing Nihilist or a publicity man from the Underground) is not merely that he trots out an entire repertory of pseudoenigmas, while you are bored. Should you take the trouble to argue, should you demolish his position—top to bottom, root and feather, in every detail—then, *then* he will draw himself up to his full intellectual height. "*That*," he will say, with a look of truly imbecile condescension, "is the whole point." This is, of course, the moment to leave him and find more interesting company—which is what most people do, and which is why the paying audience at such events as the recent "9 Evenings: Theatre and Engineering," at the Sixty-ninth Regiment Armory, is small. All nine evenings were grounded, one way or another, in false paradox; all were dull—poor in invention and shoddy in execution; and all were attended by the sort of audience for whom "That is the whole point" constitutes a crushing rejoinder to any argument.

The first evening consisted of "Physical Things," by Steve Paxton, in which the "performance" was the audience's entry into the Armory by way of an inflated plastic bag, a series of plastic tunnels, and a plastic tower. ("This piece," the author wrote in the program notes, "is not an airplane, is pretty much the opposite of an airplane, but much of the rest of it is analogous"); "Grass Field," by Alex Hay, in which the performer (Mr. Hay), whose body was wired for sound to be broadcast to the audience, distributed some peach-colored bedsheets about the floor and then, with the help of an assistant dressed in a peach-colored suit and a peach-colored shirt, gathered them up again ("The work activity is the random placement of 100 numbered six-foot squares"); and "Solo," by Deborah Hay, in which dancers took up positions on and off carts that were operated by remote control ("Solo is a white, even, clear event in space. . . . I am interested in creating a middle ground between seeing and not seeing").

The second evening consisted of "Open Score," by Robert Rauschenberg, in which a tennis game, played with rackets wired for light and for sound, caused lights to go off until, in complete darkness, a number of performers gathered and were

projected to the audience on three television screens ("The conflict of not being able to see an event that is taking place right in
front of one except through a reproduction is the sort of double
exposure of action. A screen of light and a screen of darkness"),
and "Bandoneon!" by David Tudor, in which noises played on a
bandoneon were translated electronically into blobs on a television screen (" 'Bandoneon!' uses no composing means; when ac-
tivated, it composes itself out of its own composite instrumental
nature"). On later evenings, there were five more pieces, by
Yvonne Rainer, John Cage, Lucinda Childs, Robert Whitman,
and Oyvind Fahlstrom, which were described by their authors in
program notes of a similar intellectual quality.

Normally, it would be unfair to hold artists accountable for
what they say about their work, since exposition and criticism
are not the artist's medium. But these statements actually *consti-
tuted* the works in question. For the rest, they relied upon tech-
nical gadgetry (which, despite pretentious descriptions by the
engineers and fawning tributes from the artists, was not very
sophisticated to begin with and did not, in any case, work) and
felicitous accidents (of which there were, in the course of the
nine evenings, none). It could be argued that the statements—
and the performances, too—were presented in a mood of irony.
But someone's witless ironies are hardly worth the price of admission, and irony as a blanket excuse for tedium, incompetence,
and graceless nonchalance begins to rank with the argument
from the whole point. No. It became clear as each work was
performed a first and then a second time that something quite
distinct from philosophy or theatre (or, for that matter, engineering) was being staged at the Armory—and drawing its own
special little audience.

The First Armory Show (and other *succès de scandale,* like
Marcel Duchamp's historic urinal) seems to have created a permanent cadre of viewers, critics, and collectors determined never
to be caught again outside the swim of art. They are marked by
a terrible anxiety to ferret out the New (as others, of the opposite turn of mind, seek out antiques), as though everything were
not in some sense new, while values are expressed in other terms.
But an audience whose judgment is steeped in overeager avant-
gardism and numbed by the Kahlil Gibrans of false paradox becomes submissive to performers in some very curious ways.

There was, for instance, the seating in the Armory itself: all the center tiers, front to back, comprising by far the best third of the house, were allotted to "the press." This arrangement reflected a quite common set of pop priorities (one's name in print, regardless of the circumstances: life's purest joy) and one of the more fashionable false equations (bad notices: the highest accolade). It also reflected an attitude toward the paying audience, which could hardly see.

Then, bland and flaccid though the performances may have been, it soon appeared that there was considerable lust for mayhem in them. They had a character at once soft, shapeless, and incongruously vicious—like an enraged bread pudding or a feral pulp. The audience, entering so docilely through those plastic bags, submitting to interminable pauses and interminably repeated exercises, yielded from the first to the authors' whims and predilections. Thereafter, the pulp that was performed exercised its power over the pulp that watched. Inflicting the amplified sounds of a performer's wired pulse and digestive system, flashing glaring lights (in the tennis piece) directly into the audience's eyes, turning the volume up (in the Whitman piece) to an unbearable pitch, and (in the Fahlstrom) staging a rough fight on the floor and then spraying the audience with choking incense— the inspiration, such as it was, seemed to derive from children's play gone suddenly nasty, or from scientific tests run on little human populations, or (and here a few program-note references to "Total Theatre" reinforced the impression) the gas chambers. It was a case not of the emperor's wearing no clothes but of the revolutionaries' wearing epaulets and spurs. As the evenings focused into minor orgies of pure spite, as a bust of President Johnson, for example, was used to bludgeon a pane of glass, the occasion began to seem less theatrical than political—as, say, a lynching or a burning in effigy (or a recent highly praised piece of sadistic theatrical drivel, an ugly, dead-ear parody of Shakespeare and contemporary life, *MacBird*) is political. It would not have been altogether surprising in this company if the incense had been lethal and the current in the electrodes reversed.

Mixed media were and are, in any case, better suited to propaganda than to art; they do not enlighten, they incite or numb. A rare, appropriate mixture of media—with audience participation—occurred one evening a few weeks ago at Town Hall, in a performance by the San Francisco Mime Troupe. Six actors—three of them Negro, three white—put on a minstrel show in blackface. Among its successes were a silent movie that depicted an entire country pursuing, fleeing from, making love to, and being bombed by—in short, being defined in terms of—a watermelon; an intermission during which the minstrels invited white girls in the audience to dance with them; and, in a stroke of brilliance, a rendition by the minstrels, their white interlocutor, and the audience of "Ol' Black Joe." (The expressions on the faces of members of the audience as they did or did not choose to sing along were a study in the affective possibilities of theatre.) The Mime production, however, entitled "Civil Rights in a Cracker Barrel," was not only committed satire but conscious propaganda, designed to cause an audience to go out and take social action. The Cage piece in the "9 Evenings," on the other hand (during its second performance, when the loudspeakers actually functioned), caused the audience to advance toward the performers as though mesmerized, and then, as the noise level increased, to lie about the floor in a parody of sleep or catatonia.

The degree to which theatre is "total"—that is, mixed, mindless, and engulfing—is, of course, precisely the degree to which it is no longer theatre at all but simply environment, or even ideology in motion, like a hall of mirrors, a storm at sea, a riot, or, under controlled conditions, a brainwashing. And, in the end, the audience at the "9 Evenings," small as it was, seemed less an audience than a constituency—a supine constituency in whose interests it somehow was that distinctions should be blurred, that intelligence should be numbed, that brutality of spirit should be subsidized, and that creativity should be reducible to felicitous accident. It is possible that in political terms this constituency has not been sufficiently taken into account. Aesthetically, it has no consequence except as a temptation to artists in a state of nervous exhaustion who long for acceptance by an undiscriminating public. But if one of the major struggles of the age is to rise above the disintegration of false values to new and genuine distinctions of value, and if another is to defend consciousness against induced states whose rewards rival those of consciousness, and if art, insofar as it can be said to be on any side at all, is necessarily on the side of consciousness, then "9 Evenings: Theatre and Engineering," blurring distinctions and beating its audience into a trance of boredom, was not art, bad art, or anti-art—any more than the performance of the corner dope peddler, whether or not his merchandise is cut, can be called "9 Evenings of Dance and Biochemistry."

The same constituency, or an overlapping one, seems to drift through the night life of the city in search of events that seem more or less to carry the imprimatur of art: down into the discotheques run by whip-wielding pop press agents, with inferior rock-'n'-roll bands and an inept use of film and strobe lights; up into the lofts of the financial district for improvised but uninventive happenings; even out into the fresh air of the parks for flirtations with religions of the East. Until recently, for American occultists the flight from consciousness—or, at least, from consciousness as it is commonly understood—took place in Zen, stressing the contemplation of paradox as a path to beatitude. Now it is Krishna Consciousness. On each of the past few Sunday afternoons, between two and five, a crowd has gathered in Tompkins Square Park to join a swami and a group of his disciples in chanting a single mantra: "Hare Krishna-Hare Krishna-Krishna Krishna-Hare Hare Hare Rama-Hare Rama-Rama Rama-Hare Hare." Most members of the crowd pronounce the words quite differently from the way the swami does, but they chant enthusiastically. The swami himself—dressed, by coincidence, in a peach-colored robe, and seated on a green mohair cushion on a straw mat near the center of the park—chants softly and beats a bongo drum. His disciples, playing finger cymbals and chanting, surround him. The crowd that gathers is miscellaneous: a girl in a kilt and a low-cut blouse, carrying a loaf of bread and an ostrich feather; a young man in blue jeans, a Fordham sweatshirt, and sneakers; a girl in sweater and tights, with a caste spot on her forehead (the spot has an Op design in black and white).

As the group becomes quite dense, and the chanting proceeds, several members are inspired to dance. Arms raised, they form a little circle in the center of the throng. The girl in the kilt dances a kind of hora. She is soon joined by a large girl in slacks, with pennies in her loafers, doing a sedate Frug. The swami's immediate disciples are doing a dance of their own. In the crowd, and occasionally taking a turn at the finger cymbals, are some members of the New York fashion, film, museum, and publishing worlds. They leave after a while. The chanting continues. A boy from City College, apparently misunderstanding the point of the chant, tries to speed it up. The swami goes on imperturbably at his own pace. The poets Allen Ginsberg and Peter Orlovsky arrive (having given their own recital the preceding night at Town Hall) and join the chanting, offering an almost uninterrupted pantomime of inner happiness. They go off to drive a friend to the airport, quietly promising not to miss the last appearance of a rock-'n'-roll group called the Byrds at the Village Gate. They also arrange to meet another old friend, Dr. Timothy Leary, the following day. The chanting continues without them. The idea, once again, is mindlessness. ("Turn On," says a leaflet passed among the crowd, meaning with chants, not drugs. "End All Bringdowns. . . . Stay High Forever. No More Coming Down. Practice Krishna Consciousness.")

But there is no hostility here. It is the reverse of the "9 Evenings." The audience is attuned to an equal passivity of intellect, but in this case the performance goes off in mildness and apparent fellow feeling. Here benign monotony brings on the trance. The old people who have come to the park to talk and sun themselves, and the children who have come to play, look in on the group briefly and then remain aloof. At four-forty-five, the swami looks at a clock in a plastic case beside him, puts it in a sack, and delivers a short speech. He and his disciples leave. The genuine religious experience is over. What remains is the constituency—the residue of a vaguely anesthetic cultural event.

Last Wednesday afternoon, there was, and each Wednesday afternoon for the next four weeks there will be, a showing at the Museum of Modern Art of public-relations films and television commercials that the museum and an organization called the American Television Commercials Festival consider in some way distinguished. In the initial Wednesday's showing, the humor of Cracker Jack "Card Game" (produced for Doyle Dane Bernbach by Rose-Magwood Productions), Alka-Seltzer "Stomachs" (produced for Jack Tinker and Partners by TeleVideo), and First Pennsylvania Bank "Karate" (produced for N. W. Ayer and Son by Rose-Magwood); the photography and design in Chemical Bank "New York Woman" (produced for Benton and Bowles by Cahill, Kacine and Heimann), Eastern Airlines "Birds" (produced for Young and Rubicam by EUE/Screen Gems), and Jamaica Tourist Board (produced for Doyle Dane Bernbach by EUE/Screen Gems); and the superior inventiveness, wit, and craftsmanship of Clark's Teaberry Gum "Shuffle" (produced for Leo Burnett by the N. Lee Lacy Association) and particularly, Mellon Bank of Pittsburgh (produced for Fuller and Smith and Ross by Freberg, Ltd.)—all these drew strong approval from an active and opinionated audience, which, in the course of a dull stretch near the program's end, walked out. The quality of the productions would seem to provide evidence for the suspicion that talent has, in our time, at least in part and temporarily, abandoned art for other interests. It may not be so. One thing is clear, however: the producers of television commercials create a more promising marriage of Art and Engineering than the participants in the "9 Evenings" ever could. They are honest about what a deliberate combination of art and technology must be for. It is for selling something. And that, of course, is the whole point.

# The Black Power March in Mississippi

$\mathrm{F}$OR THREE WEEKS IN JUNE, A civil-rights demonstration, under black leadership, and with local Negroes in the overwhelming majority, passed successfully from the northern border of Mississippi to the state capital, crossing several counties whose most distinguished citizens had been Negroes who died for civil rights. One of the triumphs of that demonstration—the James Meredith March Against Fear—was that none of the marchers were murdered. They were not, like the Selma marchers, protected by the federal government. They demanded protection from the state, and, with certain lapses along the way, they got it. For those weeks in June, white Mississippians and black saw state troopers surrounding Negroes not to oppress but to shield them, not to give them orders but to come to terms with their demands. With the support of federal law, and the authority of their own courage and intelligence, the

Negro leaders required the government of Mississippi to deal with them—for the first time—as men. For this reason, if for no other, the march marked a turning point in the Negro's relationship to the white community, North and South.

From its beginnings, ever since Abolition, the civil-rights movement has been the child of Northern white liberalism. The Southern segregationist has regarded the Negro as his child in a different sense. With the march, the movement proved that as long as the law prevents acts of violence against it from going unpunished, it can assume its own adult leadership—including responsibility for its own radical children. On this occasion, the children were the workers of S.N.C.C. (the Student Non-violent Coordinating Committee), and the worried parents were the workers of S.C.L.C. (the Southern Christian Leadership Conference). Other members of the family were the understanding older relative, CORE (the Congress of Racial Equality); two rich, conservative older relatives, the N.A.A.C.P. (the National Association for the Advancement of Colored People) and the National Urban League; and two industrious cousins, M.C.H.R. (the Medical Committee for Human Rights) and the Delta Ministry of the N.C.C. (the National Council of Churches). The issues, but for their repercussions outside the state of Mississippi, would not have been issues at all. All branches of the movement were united in trying to develop political assertiveness where the need is great—among the Negro masses, too poor to afford the restaurants integrated by sit-ins, too ignorant to attend the colleges now open to them, too heavily oppressed to vote. The leaders, by marching in a state where they are hated by violent men, hoped to dramatize personal courage, and to inspire local Negroes to take the physical and economic risks that still accompany a Negro's registering to vote in Mississippi. For every large minority, the vote is the key to political power, and that S.N.C.C.'s rallying cry of "Black Power!" should have proved divisive—and even dangerous—is only the latest in a series of ironies that have beset that organization from the beginning.

A campus offshoot of Dr. Martin Luther King's S.C.L.C., S.N.C.C. always comes to the national attention when it is on the brink of going out of existence. S.N.C.C. workers—young intellectuals who have tried valiantly to "speak to the needs" of a poor black community—drew the movement to the rural South, only to be outdone by better-organized and better-financed civil rights groups and by the federal government. S.N.C.C. leaders were subject to grinding pressures—personal danger, responsibility for lives, internal dissension—which seemed to wear them down. And it was S.N.C.C. leaders—whose awareness of the complexity of moral and social issues had always, characteristically, involved them in agonized conferences lasting several weeks—who came up with the simplistic "Black Power!" slogan.

To the marchers, the meaning of the chant was clear: it was a rallying cry for Negroes to vote as a bloc, to take over communities in which they constitute a majority, and to exercise some political leverage in communities in which they constitute a large minority. The local black audience—full of affection for the young radicals but all too conscious of what the power realities in Mississippi are—virtually ignored the chant as bravado. White Southerners heard the challenge to white supremacy and braced themselves. And Northern liberals, already bored or disaffected by tensions in the movement, heard only the overtones; a mob chanting anything, and particularly a spondee followed by an unaccented syllable, seemed distressingly reminiscent of prewar German rhetoric, and alienated white sympathies—which the movement will need as long as the need for a movement exists—still further. (What black extremists in the Northern ghettos heard remains to be seen.) "Black Power!" turned out to be, at best, an expression of political naiveté; at worst, it could be misconstrued as a call to violence, which would bring on retaliatory violence to oppress the Negro more heavily than ever, and cause the country to cheat itself once again of the equal participation of its black minority.

Another irony, which almost obscured the purpose of the march, was that violence should appear to be a major issue in the movement. The only marcher who seriously advocated "violent revolution" was a white college graduate, unemployed, wearing a baseball cap and a few days' growth of beard. He became known to reporters as the House Marxist, and he provoked from Negro marchers such comments as "I don't know what to say to you," "The first thing you whites want to do when you come to the movement is make policy," "Everyone has a right to his opinion until he hurts someone else," and "We gonna have a non-violent march no matter who here." The House

Marxist joined the march at Batesville and left it at Grenada—muttering that the march itself was "only a tool of the power structure in Washington."

It is true that the marchers were often kept awake for much of the night by discussions of the Negro's right to bear arms in his own defense. But the issue was always just that—self-defense—and discussions of it were largely academic. Even S.C.L.C. workers have tacitly acknowledged that the strategy of non-violence, so effective in integrating lunch counters, is simply pointless when it comes to facing armed night riders on a Southern highway. Negro communities have for years afforded their civil-rights workers what protection they could, and not even the Mississippi government has made an issue of it. The march's ideologues—mostly Northern pacifists and hipsters, who kept insisting that the argument lay "between a Selma and a Watts"—brought the question unnecessarily into the open and managed to produce what eventually became a split in the movement. (The mere fact that Medgar Evers, James Chaney, Andrew Goodman, and Michael Schwerner, among so many, are dead while Byron de La Beckwith, Sheriff Lawrence Rainey, and Deputy Sheriff Cecil Price, among so many others, are still alive should be testimony enough to the movement's commitment to non-violence. There have been no white-supremacist martyrs yet.) Marchers who, giving way under the strain, exchanged threats and insults with bystanders were quickly surrounded by other marchers and roundly scolded; but when a memorial service in Philadelphia, Mississippi, was engulfed by a white mob armed with hoes and axe handles, the marchers fought back with their fists, and no one—not even the vocal pacifists—protested.

Perhaps the reason for the disproportionate emphasis on divisive issues during the march was that civil-rights news—like news of any unified, protracted struggle against injustice—becomes boring. One march, except to the marchers, is very like another. Tents, hot days, worried nights, songs, rallies, heroes, villains, even tear gas and clubbings—the props are becoming stereotyped. Radicals and moderate observers alike long for a breakthrough into something fresh. The institution of the civil-rights march, however, is likely to occupy a long moment in

American history, and the country might as well become familiar with the cast.

THE DRONES: In every march, there seem to be a number of white participants from out of the state who come with only the fuzziest comprehension of the issues but with a strong conviction that civil rights is a good thing to walk for. The last to be informed of events and decisions—after the police, the press, the nation as a whole—the drones trudge wearily along. They become objects of hostility when Negro marchers—forgetting that the only whites within scorning distance are likely to be friendly whites—mistake who their enemies are. In the March Against Fear, the drones turned out to be the only continuous marchers. Leaders dropped out repeatedly—Martin Luther King to attend to affairs in Chicago, Floyd McKissick for a speaking engagement in New York, Stokely Carmichael for a television appearance in Washington—and most of the local Negroes could march only part of the way. But the drones stuck it out. Some were thrust into action, and reacted in various ways to dangers of which they had not been fully aware. A mustachioed anthropologist from a Northern university, for example, volunteered for a voter-registration task force in Charleston, Mississippi. When the white population proved hostile, he simply drove back to the march, leaving the rest of the task force to fend for itself. After two more incidents of this kind, he was punched in the jaw by another marcher, and wisely went home. Two drones from the North arrived in a station wagon, bringing their three-year-old son with them. The child, whom they left alone for naps in their car by the side of the road, became covered with mosquito bites, and was twice found wandering by himself, screaming in terror at the sight of a large, barking dog. On the night of the tent-pitching in Canton, Mississippi, the child was rendered unconscious by tear gas, but his parents were preoccupied with what they thought was the need to precipitate another episode. "We've got to pitch those tents again," they insisted, on the second night in Canton. "By backing down, we're only deceiving the local people." (The drones were the last to learn it was the local Negroes who decided that they had proved their point and that another act of civil disobedience would be unnecessarily dangerous.)

THE PRESS: Reporters have become, despite their neutrality

as observers, an integral part of the movement, as they cover one of the last of the just wars. Some of the time, the television networks alone had more than a hundred men accompanying the march, with planes and helicopters overhead, couriers cruising along the line of march in cars, a press truck, and walkie-talkies adding to the din of the already crowded airwaves. ( The night security guard, the Deacons for Defense and Justice, and even passing Klansmen were all equipped with citizens'-band radios. The police and the F.B.I., of course, had radios of their own.) At times when the marchers were silent, the only sounds along the route were disembodied voices on the radio.

The press was jeered by roadside segregationists, threatened by troopers during the tear-gassing in Canton, harassed by a water moccasin planted aboard the press truck in Yalobusha County, and attacked outright by the mob in Philadelphia, but all this did not make the civil-rights workers any the less unhappy with what they came to regard as their unfavorable reviews. Marchers accused the reporters of exaggerating dissension in the movement (when there was a brief argument aboard the press truck, marchers gleefully cried, "Dissension in the press! A split! A split!" Reporters responded with cries of "Press Power!"), and even of generating some dissension by distorted reporting of events.

As far as the wire services were concerned, the marchers had a point. The Associated Press, in particular, made almost daily errors in its coverage—errors that seemed to reflect a less than sympathetic view. The A.P. quoted Stokely Carmichael's cry, in the face of the tear gas, "Now is the time to separate the men from the mice!" as "Now is the time to separate the men from the whites!"—implying racism in what had been only a call for courage. It repeatedly identified Willie Ricks, a demagogue affiliated with S.N.C.C., as an aide to Dr. King, of S.C.L.C.—implying that the organization most deeply committed to nonviolence was severely compromised. The sort of story that A.P. was determined to listen for and report is suggested by a question that an A.P. correspondent asked some civil-rights workers who were arming themselves to repel a second attack on their headquarters in Philadelphia; he wondered whether the incident would "encourage Negroes in the promiscuous killing of whites."

In a sense, of course, the A.P.'s mistaken report of James Meredith's death was what brought the civil-rights leaders and the press to Memphis in the first place; but there were signs each day that subscribers to the wire service, North and South, were getting a distorted version of what was going on in Mississippi. Other members of the press were more than competent. Their mere presence contributed substantially to the safety of the marchers, and they have proved to be an important factor in the pacification of the South.

THE WHITE SUPREMACISTS: Stock characters out of the Southern bestiary, they line the route of every march. Shouting epithets, waving flags, wielding hoses, throwing objects, or just gazing in malevolent silence, they congregate most often at gas stations and grocery stores—a grotesque parody of small-town America. In conversation, they invariably protest that "our niggers are happy," express earnest worry about "niggers' raping our women," and show their only traces of real animation when they contemplate disposing of the problem. "I'd spray the whole bunch with sulfuric acid," said a Navy recruiter in Greenwood. "What I'd do," said a tourist from Arab, Alabama, sputtering over his grits, "I'd get me some dynamite, and run me a line to the side of the road . . ."

The more cultivated elements of the segregationist community have evolved their own schizophrenic logic. "Negroes have always been able to vote here," the Greenwood newspaper proudly editorialized, and added, "This country was one of the first in the country to receive federal registrars." "You better get out of here before you need an undertaker," a sheriff said to a voter-registration task force. Then he muttered to himself, "They just came in here, mouthin'."

But there are signs of progress, or at least of resignation. "We didn't want this to happen, but what the hell!" said Joseph Lee, the editor of the newspaper in Grenada—a town that had twice run out a team of COFO (Council of Federated Organizations) workers, but in which the marchers registered more than twelve hundred voters. "There are things we used to do that we don't know now why we did them. We didn't know why we did them then. There are still some people who hang back and look sore. And a man who's a little weak in the head can make as much trouble as a Rhodes Scholar. But these days I tell my own Negroes to get their fanny on over and register." The Grenada city manager, however, was reconciled in his own way. "Most of your Negroes registering are either very old or young," he said. "Your old ones—well, the vote isn't till 1967. And the young ones —a lot of them will be going to Vietnam. And some of them won't be coming back."

There are advances in law enforcement. Despite the fact that several marchers were kicked and beaten by troopers during the tear-gas episode (a medical worker suffered three broken ribs and a collapsed lung), the troopers were not—by the standards of Watts, for example—especially brutal; they exercised what might be termed self-restraint. The sheriff of Sunflower County, where the White Citizens Councils were born, is a graduate of the F.B.I. school and, like many other local officials whom the Justice Department has quietly encouraged to attend federal schools, cooperates in seeing to it that federal law is observed. Charles Snodgrass, in charge of the march for the Mississippi Highway Patrol, won the marchers' respect for his integrity; and he worked closely with John Doar—an Assistant Attorney General so respected by Negroes and whites alike that, in the words of one marcher, "He seems to be the only one left in the Justice Department who knows what's going on. Without John Doar, there'd be a lot more dead in Mississippi."

Even the most extreme elements are, almost unconsciously, changing. The mob in Philadelphia, shouting, surging forward, throwing eggs and Coke bottles, listened to every phrase spoken by Dr. King long enough to scream an ugly answer to it. (Sometimes they listened and screamed so carefully that Dr. King appeared to be leading them in a responsive reading.) And a waitress in Jackson readily conceded, "Your whites in Neshoba County, they're the meanest people in the state." (Then she added, as if overcome by her own liberalism, "They got Indian blood in them.") And there are some real liberals. "It takes about ten drinks for me to say what I really think," a lady in Jackson said. "Why, we've never done anything that's right for the Negro. All we did was starve him, and work him, and shoot him in the back. I don't see how they could run their counties any worse than the whites have been running them."

THE LOCAL NEGROES: Strong leadership is developing in the small communities, and the march left little registration teams everywhere in its wake. Canton alone already had Annie Devine, of the Mississippi Freedom Democratic Party, who, with mud still on her dress and with her eyes still red from the tear gas, rose to announce, simply, "We are not going to stay ignorant, and backward, and scared"; and young Flonzie Goodlow, of the N.A.A.C.P., who, despite white intimidation and jealous opposition from misguided workers for S.N.C.C. in the past, brought so many Negroes to vote that she could announce her own intention of running for registrar in 1967; and George Raymond, of CORE, who was a voice of gentle moderation throughout the march, and diverted the marchers at moments of crisis with singing. Then, there are the local non-leaders, like the delegation from Holmes County that came to offer the marchers lodging, and, upon learning that the march was skirting Holmes, acknowledged, "There are other places in badder shape. Whichever way they go, we're going to support it." And like Hura Montgomery, a Negro farmer in Louise, who permitted the marchers to pitch their tents on his land. "I was possibly hoping they wouldn't ask," he said, "but somebody had to let them in."

THE MARCH LEADERS: Robert Green, of S.C.L.C., a tall young professor of psychology at Michigan State, was liaison man for the march. Addressing the local police with quiet authority, planting an American flag on the statue of Jefferson Davis in Grenada ("The South you led will never stand again. Mississippi must become part of the Union"), leaping over the cowcatcher to board a locomotive moving toward the line of march in Jackson (he commanded the engineer to stop, and persuaded the angry marchers to keep marching), reassuring a troubled white worker for the Urban League ("We need the conservative groups, too. We need to engage the problem at every level"), and reasoning quietly with the few advocates of arms among the marchers ("The whites will simply seal you off and crush you, as they did in Watts. Our only course is to confront them again and again with the force of non-violence. It's the glory of the movement"), Green played a part in the march which itself changed the face of Mississippi. The police respected his fearlessness and his dignity. The towns were so shaken by his treatment of the monument in Grenada that several other monuments along the route were guarded by six Negro trusties from the state penitentiary, to prevent a recurrence of the desecration. And the marchers were sufficiently impressed by his courage and intelligence to respond consistently to his leadership.

Floyd McKissick, the national director of CORE, was always called upon to lead the marchers on days when they had to start promptly and walk fast, and to make practical announcements concerning strategy and finances. McKissick, an attorney from Durham, North Carolina, marched for the most part with patience and good humor. When a lady from Charleston, Mississippi, a Negro, came to the campsite at Enid Dam in the night to wish him well, and to tell him that "there are [liberal] whites in Charleston who are just as scared as we are," he discussed with her for an hour the question of whether it was time for the movement to make contact with white liberals in Mississippi. It was McKissick who served the marchers their lunch on days when he led them, and who, after many nights disrupted by the arguments of ideologues, the buzzing of transistor radios, and the nervous jokes of the night security guard, announced that "anyone who disturbs the marchers' sleep tonight will be hauled out and sent home." It was McKissick who mediated between S.N.C.C. and S.C.L.C. But on the night of the tear gas in Canton McKissick's patience simply broke. The contrast between police treatment of peaceful Negro trespassers on the grounds of an illegally segregated school and the reluctance of the police in Philadelphia to intervene against an armed white mob seemed to overwhelm the lawyer in him. He was almost incoherent with rage, and close to tears. "I'm tired of having to negotiate for our constitutional rights," he said. "Some people said we ought to confront President Johnson. I say the hell with it. When the tear gas came, I fell off that truck like a scrambled egg. You didn't want that school, but they made it yours. They don't call it *white* power. They just call it power. I'm committed to non-violence, but I say what we need is to get us some black power."

Stokely Carmichael, the young chairman of S.N.C.C., argued most persuasively for black political power, and when, as he saw it, he was continuously misrepresented by the press, he became obdurate and began to make himself eminently misrepresentable. What he had in mind throughout the march was a Populist movement in the South: White S.N.C.C. workers would address themselves to the white poor, black S.N.C.C. workers would address themselves to the black poor, and since the blacks would outnumber the whites, the new Populists would naturally be under Negro leadership, and would present an encouraging example of Negro effectiveness to Negroes throughout the country.

Tall, lean and intellectual, Carmichael spoke to the crowds at night, punctuating his words with a finger pointed at the ground, enunciating a phrase slowly and then repeating it rapidly, bending his knees to add emphasis to his soft, tense voice. It was Carmichael who said, "It is time to stop being ashamed of being black. It is time to stop trying to be white. When you see your daughter playing in the fields, with her nappy hair, and her wide nose, and her thick lips, tell her she is beautiful. *Tell your daughter she is beautiful.*" It was Carmichael who, wherever he went, picked up children and carried them, and who, when the marchers swarmed into a Negro lady's house for a drink of water, reprimanded them by saying, "None of you asked where that lady got the water. None of you bothered to find out that she has to carry that water in buckets a mile and a half. These are things we ought to be talking about." (Carmichael himself hauled water for the lady.)

It was also Carmichael who, having lived for six summers under the fear and strain that assail a S.N.C.C. worker in the South, became hysterical for several minutes after the tear-gas episode in Canton. "Don't make your stand here," said Carmichael, the militant, sobbing and wandering about in circles. "I just can't stand to see any more people get shot." The following evening, it was Carmichael who wanted the marchers to risk putting up the tents again in the schoolyard, and who, overruled by Dr. King and the local people, sulked. (When James Lawson, a member of S.C.L.C., and a founder of S.N.C.C., told him later that he had been wrong, he accepted the criticism and agreed.) Although on the night of the Philadelphia riot* Carmichael said,

---

* In Philadelphia, Mississippi, a voter registration crew was attacked one morning with ax handles, hoes, tear gas, and rifle butts. Dr. Martin Luther King led a return march the following morning.

"This is S.N.C.C.'s night, man. This is our suit," he never forced an issue, never exhorted the marchers to violence, never, in spite of his militancy, put people in unnecessary danger. And it was Carmichael, the militant, who, in the words of one reporter, "came all over shy" when fifteen thousand people, assembled in Tougaloo, sang "Happy Birthday" to him (twenty-five) and James Meredith (thirty-three); and the night itself seemed to break out in smiles. (As for Meredith, who had been such an enigma throughout his personal ordeal, he simply melted before this friendly, sentimental face of America. "This is the happiest birthday I've ever had," he said.) In later interviews, Carmichael (like Meredith) was as uncompromising in not urging non-violence—and in not urging violence, either—as he had ever been.

Dr. Martin Luther King, of S.C.L.C., proved on the march that he is still the leader of the movement, and perhaps the most forceful voice of conscience in the country. People came from all over Mississippi to see him, and responded to the measured, rational cadences of his voice. Time after time, he averted a crisis among the marchers, and his aides—Hosea Williams, leading gentle hymns and silent night marches, and Andy Young, making soft, persuasive speeches—called forth the same extraordinary discipline with which he is able to inspire the movement. Turning to Sheriff Rainey, in Philadelphia, and saying, "I believe in my heart that the murderers are somewhere around me at this moment," and turning back to the marchers, under attack from a far larger crowd, to say, "I am not afraid of any man," Dr. King set an example of pure courage. Exhorting the marchers in Canton to remain calm under the tear gas, or addressing a church full of Negroes in Cleveland, Mississippi, so movingly that a five-year-old girl began to sob and say over and over again, "I want to go with him," Dr. King was a superb spiritual leader. Bringing a busload of juvenile-gang leaders from Chicago to Mississippi, in the hope of diverting their energies to the non-violent cause of civil rights, Dr. King proved himself again an incomparable strategist and pedagogue. And a few phrases like "America, land of the free and home of the brave. Land of free white men, and home of brave Negroes" proved that Dr. King's rhetoric has not lost its cutting edge.

The march was led by complicated men with divergent ideologies, just as the movement is, and their differences are the same ones that divide the nation at large. The response of the white community—alarm and hurt among liberals, and, among reactionaries, alarm and threats to use the white man's undeniably superior force—conceals a failure to hear what the movement is saying. For too long, civil rights has been treated as though it were only the Negro's struggle, with some benevolent white liberal support to help it along; what the movement seeks now is not benevolence but a recognition of reality: the Negro's rights are *law*—and for the white community to resist or ignore the law implies the collapse of an entire legal and moral system. It has become intolerable to the Negro to win so slowly what is his by right, and it has become too costly, in every possible sense, to go on denying him his just place in this society.

# Conversations

THERE IS MORE TO WRITING realistic dialogue than a good ear and a sound memory, and spontaneous conversation as recorded by tape or stenography will seldom sound authentic on the stage or in the novel. (Even in newspapers, in which quoting out of context can create one kind of distortion, quoting *in* context may create another.) To convey the spoken word accurately in print, a novelist must paraphrase. For a time, the dialogue in fiction was more "literary" than the speech of fact. Stammerers or the inarticulate appeared less as real characters than as examples of something—paragons or caricatures of simple virtue; most characters in the novel expressed themselves more cogently and gracefully than speakers in the street. In recent years, however, the reverse has become true, and a twentieth-century novelist, trying to transcribe real conversation, may limit his dialogue to expletives, monosyllables, clichés, or even grunts. If the distortion factor for speech in novels of the past was eloquence, the new distortion factor is aphasia.

In both his novels, first *The Ginger Man* and now *A Singular Man* (Atlantic-Little, Brown), J. P. Donleavy resists a modern convention of flattened dialogue and coarsened sensibility as earmarks of realism. His characters are not Neanderthals in Yale or Greenwich Village clothing, and they express themselves with a certain rococo elegance. The hero of *The Ginger Man* behaved rudely enough, but in all his (often tedious) brawling, drinking, and philandering, he had, somehow, the air of the false primitive, and as a commentator on his own behavior he was flamboyant and amusing. Sebastian Dangerfield was a post-adolescent ne'er-do-well trying to take the world by physical storm; George Smith, the hero of *A Singular Man,* is completely at the mercy of the world, and he is mild, eccentric, poetic, never dull, and often funny. In all his strangeness, he bears a resemblance to many characters actually at large, and *A Singular Man* is an attempt to see how much of the eccentric part of life—the whims and lyric flights and capers, no less real for seeming literary—a modern novel can accommodate.

George Smith is a victim. His wife, from whom he is separated, exploits him financially. He is successful in an enterprise that is never defined, but he is persecuted by threatening letters ("Dear Sir: . . . What are your remaining assets . . . P.S. We will squeeze out what is left of your toothpaste") from a person who mysteriously signs himself "J.J.J." Smith is a formal, fastidious man, who even addresses two of his mistresses as "Miss" Tomson and "Miss" Martin. He talk to himself in the street: "Show people you're in command of the situation by not saying much, don't let them get in close, keep everyone at arm's length, stop smiling kindly." He has been told by his unadmiring wife that "the only time traffic will stop for you, George, is when you're dead." In consequence, he builds himself an enormous, traffic-stopping mausoleum. What Smith wants above all things is that

> . . . someone will look at me, stop, come back, see into my eyes and say I love you.
> Without later

Turning
Utterly
Treacherous.

All the characters in *A Singular Man* are, in Donleavy's words, "incorrigibly strange of spirit." Smith himself—who is described as "frond-like"—takes boxing, wrestling, and fencing lessons; he is a kind of paranoid in a time and place where delinquents, drunks, journalists, and the general atmosphere of violence made paranoia seem an evidence of sanity. By his own description "a self-employed slave," Smith owns an applause machine, which roars and cheers him when he feels depressed. His host at a party has an alligator, which snaps at guests from beneath a hydrangea plant in the conservatory. His particular girl friend has a large, vicious dog named Goliath, whom she occasionally telephones just to say "Woof, woof, sweetie."

Donleavy writes of all these characters with affection, and ascribes to them some of the incongruous mixtures of idiom that often characterize the modern American post-collegiate speaker: Edwardian ("And a most merry Christmas to you Mr. Browning. And would you divide this among the men with my compliments"), comic-strip ("Lungs gasping as Smith cleverly switched to mental power to give the muscles a rest"), legalistic ("On a Wednesday of the 19th ultimo . . . you made an unprovoked . . . attack upon our client, Mr. Harry Halitoid, which resulted in a knockment into the tracks of the said system where there was a sustainment of considerable head and body injury"), Dizzy Dean ("I do you an injustice you don't deserve"), Elizabethan, Lower East Side, and journalistic, and occasionally nonsense syllables:

> "I know you, hey aren't you George Smith . . ."
> "Beep."
> "Ha you're George Smith all right."
> "Beep."
> "What do you mean, beep for an old friend. We were prepsters together."
> "Beep."
> "Now wait a minute George ha ha. I know this is a funny situation."
> "Beep."

"Gee George is there something wrong. Are they crowding you. I can take a hint if that's it. What are you saying this beep to me for. If you don't want to recognize me say so."

"Beep. Beep."

"I'm sorry. I didn't know anything about this George. Is it permanent. . . ."

There are all kinds of slapstick-comedy scenes, some very good—as when Smith tries to buy an empty paper bag from a delicatessen, and manages to negotiate the purchase only by "buying the air rights within the said container"—and some not very good at all. There are serious scenes, too, and the author mixes the comic and the serious in strange proportions, delivering in unobtrusive little asides psychological insights that other novelists might extend, repeat, and flog to death for chapters. *A Singular Man* becomes by turns a love story, a melodrama, an unresolved detective story, a soap opera, a vaudeville routine, and a very fine light novel by a stylist who can afford to give considerable rein to his quirkish imagination.

# The Thursday Group

THERE SEEMS TO BE NO MORE persistent and serious preoccupation in the art and thought of our time than the idea of madness—perhaps because, in our century, definitions of sanity have been so carefully posed, and so drastically called, by events, into question. In purely psychoanalytic terms (sanity as freedom from crippling disorders of reason), or even in the tolerant, anthropological view (sanity as an adjustment to the consensus of one's own community), too many twentieth-century personalities—Eichmann and Gandhi, for example—may turn up on opposite sides of the border from where we should care to place them. In times when moral and social values are under stress, it is nearly impossible to tell in what an unsound mind can possibly consist. Hallucinatory states, ethically monstrous acts, radically eccentric or suicidally impractical behavior—each of these formerly clear symptoms of madness is now, for some part of the community, a social norm. The words "mad" and "insane" themselves have passed out of pathology and into the world of fashion; without a broad consensus, or word from a higher spiritual authority on what is right, it is impossible to be certain who is sane.

There is less ambiguity in cases of physical disorder, where it is relatively easy to determine who is sick and who is well, but even in physical medicine there are borderline cases: the allergic, for example, whose "disease" is, after all, only a symptom of excessive health—a heightened physical perception. In the case of those who are not sick or insane by any standard but only disaffected or troubled in their minds, the problem of whether and how they are to be treated—and, above all, whose responsibility it is to decide, and diagnose, and treat them—becomes of vital importance; for nothing defines the quality of life in a community more clearly than people who regard themselves, or whom the consensus chooses to regard, as mentally unwell.

The kind of treatment that the troubled in search of professional help have been getting has, by all indications, not been good. Although the nature of the problem makes it difficult to compile statistics (human misery in a free, affluent, and secular society is hard to quantify), two recent studies on the subject— "The Effects of Psychotherapy," by H. J. Eysenck, which appeared in the *International Journal of Psychiatry*, and a survey by Harry Weinstock, which was prepared for the American Psychoanalytic Association and never published anywhere—reveal no appreciable difference between people who have undergone psychotherapy and people who have not, and no statistical evidence that psychotherapy does patients any good at all. It is true that increasing numbers of patients feel relieved by therapy, for they continue to seek it, and there are many case histories of patients who apparently have been cured, since symptoms that existed when they began treatment had disappeared when they terminated it. The same claims, however, are probably made with more validity for other, non-scientific, approaches to emotional disorder—notably friendship, prayer, ritual, the laying on of hands, and the passage of time. The religious comparison, in particular, has been reinforced by the intolerance or indifference with which members of the various schools of psychotherapy often regard one another's work; professionals who deal constantly with the troubled seem to find it difficult to communicate on an equal basis with observers from other disciplines or colleagues within their own. Psychiatrists quite commonly treat (and charge) observers as though they were patients, and intradisciplinary conferences in psychotherapy more closely resemble ecumenical councils than free exchanges of scientific information among peers.

In addition, there is the peculiar problem of appraising a "cure," or successful outcome, for mental disorder in the first place. With what are generally termed psychotics—schizophrenics, paranoids, depressives—the most valid approach seems to lie not in psychotherapy at all but in somatic medicine. Drugs, tranquillizers, and amphetamines are providing the only results —the control of radically undesirable symptoms—that can be appraised in scientific terms, and some psychiatrists now favor discarding the old psychoanalytic definitions of mental illness altogether and defining each psychosis solely in terms of the drug to which it responds. (There are also psychiatrists who have declared themselves ready to testify for the surviving family in malpractice suits that involve the treatment of potential suicides by psychotherapy alone.) With neurotics, however—patients who are simply troubled and who have difficulty in adapting their behavior to their own standards or to those of society—the problem of appraising outcomes is practically insoluble. A "cure" can consist only in adjusting the patient's world view and behavior to some arbitrary system of values (not the patient's own, for he is presumably sick, and not society's, for its values are vague and variable, and occasionally sick as well)—usually those of the therapist and the particular tradition in which he has been schooled. In other words, a cure may be no more than a sectarian conversion.

Among people in search of treatment, there are signs of disillusionment with the old orthodoxies. Most prospective patients have, in any case, assimilated the principles of psychoanalysis so thoroughly that the tenets themselves are no longer insights but may represent an entirely new order of symptoms; it is possible that the Oedipus complex, for example, is now less a common mental disorder than a debilitating obsession with the doctrines of Freud. The doctrines themselves have been cast into doubt, not only by somatic medicine but also by anthropology, which by comparing different societies reveals that the principles of traditional psychoanalysis do not hold universally but only in a particular cultural context; by sociology, which by observing emergent generations suggests that the principles of sexual repression and sublimation in work may have held only at a particular time; by zoology, which suggests that—in monkeys, at least—complexes are induced less readily by traumas associated with parents, or the lack of them, than by the absence of a peer group in childhood; by sociometry, which reveals that in all but the rarest individuals perception, and even reason, can be distorted or corrected by group pressure or group support; and even by historical criticism, which tends to place Freudian analysis within the limited context of a literary movement: Symbolism.

In addition, post-Freudian orthodoxies have tended toward the increasingly simplistic and banal, culminating in what appears to be a policy of flat attempts to reverse behaviors; that is, the practical analyst assumes that whatever behavior his patient exhibits is the one he must be seeking to reverse. The results, observable in many analysands: the aggressive attempt to make themselves amenable; the timid become inconsiderate. The mental hypochondriac attends what is, in effect, a private psychiatric charm school. For whatever reason, the troubled are turning in increasing numbers to an unorthodox form of treatment—group psychotherapy.

In 1905, Dr. Joseph H. Pratt, of Boston, found that the best way to persuade his tuberculosis patients to follow the regime of absolute rest over a period of months or years prescribed for them was to treat them in groups, which he called "classes," at which star patients were frequently called upon to testify. The classes proved well worth the exertion that the patients made each week to attend them. Members cheered up, followed their regimes, and got better. On the basis of this early, modest experiment, and as a compromise among psychotherapists with conflicting claims to having been the pioneers, Dr. Pratt is widely considered to be the founder of group psychotherapy in the United States. In the years since Dr. Pratt, the practice of group psychotherapy has proliferated enormously. There are group programs affiliated with all the major analytic schools—Freudian, Adlerian, Jungian, Sullivanian, Horney. There are groups in hospitals and prisons, in urban centers and small communities, in universities, schools, offices, barracks, and factories.

There are special groups for veterans, teachers, adolescents, married couples, families, homosexuals, stutterers, and alcoholics, and heterogeneous groups that combine the troubled of all sorts. Some of the best results in group psychotherapy have been achieved with aged patients thought to be senile on physiological grounds; babbling, memory lapse, incontinence, psychosis—many supposedly arteriosclerotic symptoms—have been reduced among senile patients in groups all over the country. At the Long Island College Hospital in Brooklyn, there are groups for children afflicted with cerebral palsy, and groups for their parents. The private practice of a psychiatrist in Beverly Hills includes in one group a convicted dope pusher and in another the detective who arrested him. In Utah, there are therapy groups for Mormon foster parents of Indian orphans, and for Mormon youths doing their two-year term of religious service. At the Postgraduate Center for Mental Health on East Twenty-eighth Street, there are several special kinds of groups for members of the New York Police Department, and in Bethel, Maine, each summer the National Training Laboratories (a division of the National Education Association) run what they call Sensitivity Training Laboratories—two-week-long group-therapy sessions for, among others, practicing group therapists.

One of the reasons it is almost impossible to find any meaningful data on the extent to which group therapy (or, for that matter, individual psychotherapy) is practiced in this country is that, as far as the law is concerned, almost anyone may practice. The federal government has set no standards for the accreditation of psychotherapists. A continuing feud between the American Psychiatric Association (which considers psychotherapy a branch of medicine, and would require a medical degree for all practitioners) and the American Psychological Association (which considers psychotherapy a branch of psychology, and would require only a degree in psychology) has effectively blocked legislation in most states; the result is that untrained, unaccredited, unregistered, and unsupervised "therapists" may set up practice, for individuals or groups, almost anywhere. An organization called the American Group Psychotherapy Association has existed since 1942, but although its educational requirements for membership are minimal (a Master's degree in social work), and although it now claims more than seventeen hundred members (who alone can account for at least six thousand therapy groups), it seems to include only a small fraction of the group therapists, trained or self-styled, now at work. In this situation of professional anarchy, or in this professional morass, the techniques, the vocabularies, and even the sources of American group psychotherapy, far from being traceable to the experiments of Dr. Pratt, have become as disparate and eclectic as the situations in which groups naturally occur. The open confessionals of the early Church, the Quaker meetings, the secret society, the progressive-school classroom, the popularity contest, the family, the theatre, the symposium, the television panel, and, not least, the tradition of evangelism have all made their contributions to the therapy group.

Freud himself never treated patients in groups, although in "Group Psychology and the Analysis of the Ego" he set forth some of the principles upon which psychoanalytic group therapy is based. The theory is, briefly, that the group re-creates the family unit—that the therapist becomes a parental figure, and that members form transference relationships with the group parent and group siblings which will reactivate old neurotic patterns, subject them to analysis, and ultimately eradicate them. Some more immediate and pragmatic reasons given for the spread of group therapy (or Group, as it has come to be called) are the scarcity of therapists qualified by any professional standard (there are only eighteen thousand clinical psychologists in this country, while the number of troubled people in search of professional help is impossible to estimate); the possibility that patients find the private session—a one-sided confession to a person who reveals nothing in return—demeaning, and prefer the reciprocal emotional responses of a group of acknowledged fellow-patients; and the fact that as psychotherapy ceases to be the prerogative of the rich, the group has the happy characteristic of costing the patient less (from five to twenty-five dollars a session instead of from twenty-five to a hundred dollars for a private session), while earning more for the therapist (there being, normally, about eight to ten patients in a therapy group).

The major respect in which a therapy group differs from any

other social gathering is in its high regard for frankness and spontaneity. If the participants were not, in some sense, more honest than they would be at a cocktail party, the group would lose its point and fall apart. A therapy group, however, is normally among the most enduring of social units. One therapist tells of a group of seven that met twice each week for seven years. Eight years ago, all members having been pronounced "cured," the group disbanded as far as therapy was concerned. Yet one patient has called every other patient in the group every day since the group was first convened. Through cohesion and a demand for honesty, group therapy has evolved a special order of freedom: a group member is free to say or do anything, short of committing acts of physical violence, that he likes, without consequences for his life outside the group. He cannot lose his wife or his job or his friends or his social position as a result of anything that occurs within a session. In many groups, discretion is assured by the fact that members know one another only by first names, but, in any case, the basic condition of trust—or perhaps the fact that all members, having been equally candid, are equally compromised—guards against breaches of confidence.

The group thus presents the paradox of being both less and more real than everyday life: It is artificial, an irrelevance, perfect theatre in the sense of being divorced from the practical consequences of normal social behavior, and it is genuine in the sense that freedom from practical consequences permits an honesty that everyday life does not encourage. A therapy group is self-absorbed, a meta-group occupied primarily with its own immediate feelings, and its most remarkable characteristic appears to be the willingness with which adults from every walk of life and level of sophistication are drawn into its peculiar conventions. The fact that normally reserved adults do confide in one another and respect the confidences of what are, in real life, strangers may indicate that the therapy group satisfies, at the very least, a recreational need. It may serve as a substitute for the old units of tribe and family—a cross-section of strangers having more in common in these times than the old groups of cousins, aunts, and grandparents who used to share their lives and hold their secrets from the world. Or it may provide a kind of emotional park or playground for the troubled, whom modern society (with its emphasis on lack of candor as a means to personal and social ends) may have confined too rigidly, and whom private psychotherapy (with its theory and professional detachment) has been almost powerless to liberate.

A therapy group may have all sorts of routines and embellishments. It can be combined with individual therapy for some or all of its members, and with alternate sessions at the homes of members without the therapist. Some fairly unorthodox practitioners encourage what is called "acting out": impulsive behavior like running about the room or lying on the floor, exchanges of clothes between male and female patients, exhibitionism, affairs between patients, or mass collapsings on the floor in a heap. More traditional therapists, taking the family metaphor literally, consider affairs between patients regressive and incestuous, and encourage talking about physical impulses rather than acting upon them. In most groups, there is a custom called "going around," in which, at various times, every patient gives his reaction to every other, and the reaction itself is appraised and modified by the group. Some groups do occasional improvisational drama or solo singing, or engage in unlikely forms of social activity, like making anatomical drawings—all with a view to relaxing the members' inhibitions in each other's presence.

There is a special kind of Group called Psychodrama, begun by Jacob L. Moreno (who, in 1913, became one of the first practicing group therapists when he organized a circle of prostitutes in Vienna), in which members act out roles of people in each other's personal lives. In some groups, conversational material is predominantly sexual; in other groups patients may talk about art, politics, sports, careers—whatever happens to be on their minds. Most therapists try to include the widest possible variety of patients in a given group—excluding, for obvious reasons, very severe stammerers, the mentally retarded, and patients with hallucinations or homicidal tendencies. Ambulatory schizophrenics are now considered exceptionally valuable in a mixed group; the schizophrenic's essentially private world seems to give him direct access to the meaning of symbolic material—notably dreams—which may have eluded both the dreamer and the therapist. One psychiatrist tells of having been puzzled by a patient who refused to sit down, either in a group or at any other time. A schizophrenic provided the explanation: the patient, having in childhood observed his parents in the lavatory, concluded that sitting down was a sign of femininity; he remained standing as an expression of his maleness. The insight accelerated therapy, and the patient soon sat down. A recent text, *Group Psychotherapy and Group Function,* edited by a psychiatrist and a doctor of psychology, now states unequivocally, and apparently without humorous intent, that "every group might profitably include one or two well-chosen schizoid personalities."

Some groups, again interpreting the family metaphor quite literally, are conducted by co-therapists, male and female. (At an A.G.P.A. meeting in 1966, a therapist complained that one of his groups had dwindled to four patients and that he and his female co-therapist, of whom he claimed to be extremely fond, were somehow unable to find new patients suitable for the group. The diagnosis on all sides was quick: unconscious family planning.) Aside from peripheral innovations, however, the basic methodological categories for group therapy appear to be five: The Slavsonian, originated by Samuel R. Slavson, in which the therapist himself deals with each person in turn, and which is, essentially, individual therapy in the presence of commenting bystanders; the exhortative-inspirational, in which the therapist, with the backing of the group, attempts what amounts to the reeducation of every member; the Whitaker-Lieberman, in which the therapist regards the whole group as an independent organism, encourages acting out, and treats the feelings and actions of individual members merely as symptoms of ambivalence within a single group personality (a characteristic remark on the part of the therapist would be "I feel the group is hurt and angry today"); the Bionite, in which all group behavior is analyzed in terms of the three phylogenetic motives that the English psychiatrist Wilfred Ruprecht Bion postulated for man's gathering in groups in the first place—pairing, flight or escape, and work— and in which the therapy group serves as a model for the social world outside; and the self-determining, self-analyzing group, with mixed technique, in which the therapist is simply a trained (and, preferably, himself a previously analyzed) occasional participant as well as guide.

There exist groups in special situations, which cut across methodological categories, and for whom therapy has become a way of life—with no therapist at all. One such group has been in operation since September, 1963, at Daytop Village, a converted mansion on the south coast of Staten Island. Daytop is a haven for about a hundred drug addicts, of both sexes and mixed races, who have been free of drugs for periods ranging from a single day to six years. Group therapy begins the moment the addict arrives at the Lodge to seek admission. In the front hall, he may recognize inhabitants who were formerly his companions on the street. They ignore him. The bond with the non-therapeutic world, the camaraderie that exists among addicts in their addiction, is broken at once. After a long and lonely wait, the candidate is admitted to an interview in a small office, and an initiation group, seated in wooden chairs around a desk, asks him why he has come to Daytop. The candidate invariably replies that he has come to kick his habit for good. Immediately, the group, composed entirely of ex-addicts, breaks into derisive comment. Remembering their own reasons for coming to Daytop, the members tell the candidate that they are aware he is lying, and that the precondition for existence at Daytop is truthfulness. They tell him that he has come, as all of them came, under pressure from the law, with the intention of getting some rest and breaking the habit only temporarily, so that he can return to taking smaller doses on the street. The remainder of the interview is frank and brutal. When it is over, the candidate is taken to another room and searched for any drugs he may have smuggled in to tide him over. Thereafter, he is warmly welcomed to Daytop and brought to the living room, where he spends the remainder of the day and night in conversation with "older" members. (He is discouraged from talking very long with other recent arrivals, for fear they will dwell on the subject that is likely to be uppermost in their minds.) Interestingly enough, although he is likely to be uncomfortable and to long for drugs, the new member exhibits none of the withdrawal symptoms—cramps, chills, and other forms of physical agony— that have been so widely publicized as invariable reactions to kicking the habit cold. Since the group consists of former addicts, who would consider such behavior theatrical and make no concessions to it, it simply does not occur. The new member is treated without pity, but with interest and concern.

The following day (or, if his addiction has been particularly heavy, the day after that), the new member is put to work in a group to perform some menial chore. He is assigned a room with three other members, whose Daytop tenures have been of various lengths, and he is expected to act "on the floor" (that is, in the normal course of the day) "as if"—as if all were going well, as if he felt no hostility, as if he were a member of an unusually polite society in the outside world. If he fails badly in his work or in his manner, he is either "dumped on" (that is, scolded by another member) or given a "haircut," verbal or literal, by a whole group of older members. He is not expected to reply. If he commits a mere oversight, he is given a mild reprimand, to which he responds, quite cheerfully, "I accept the pull-up." When the morning chores are over, group members attend a seminar, in which quotations from Dostoevski, Nietzsche, Proust, or some other writer are discussed. If a member claims he is not educated enough to participate, the substance of the discussion is explained to him, and he is required, after a time, to make a comment or express an opinion. The result of the seminars—and of various courses, plays, and concerts that are continually being given at Daytop—is that addicts who have always felt excluded from the "square" world of arts and letters develop a rare confidence and poise. In later phases of treatment, many inhabitants go off to attend universities, to work with troubled children in schools, or to become most persuasive and sought-after speakers on behalf of welfare groups and at prisons.

MICKY DON'T WANT TO HEAR FREUD. HE ASKED YOU A QUESTION: There are other activities at Daytop that correspond closely to non-therapeutic group activity in the outside world, but at least three evenings a week life "on the floor," the "acting as if," comes to a temporary halt and a special, acute form of group therapy takes place. Any member who in the course of the day has felt a grievance against any other member, old or new, simply writes his own name and that of the offender on a slip of paper and drops the paper into a designated box. On the evenings of "encounters," all the inhabitants of Daytop are divided into therapy groups of eight or ten, and any two members whose names appear on a slip of paper together are assigned to the same group. The encounter is likely to release all the hostility that has been suppressed during the "as if" day; it consists largely of shouting, at a pitch and volume seldom heard in the outside world. Insults, threats, accusations, and screams of apparently directionless rage are uttered in the peculiarly obscene vocabulary that has always been characteristic of the underworld and the world of the oppressed. The atmosphere of pure, unanalyzed fury may be sustained for hours. Fists are clenched under chins, chairs are jerked violently back and forth, and the shouts of the encounter in the basement are clearly audible among the shouts of the encounters elsewhere in the mansion. Then, when the shouting has subsided a bit, one of the older members is likely to take over—although each member has in effect already chosen his personal therapist for the evening.

"Scumbag," one of the participants said to another, in a milder moment of a recent encounter in Daytop's dining room. "How come you gave me a order at lunch today? What makes you think you got the right to order me? You think I'm your trick or something?"

The boy replied, between clenched teeth, that he hoped he would soon find an opportunity to slit the questioner's throat.

"Luis," an older member named Micky said quietly to the first speaker, "how long would you say you've had your trick complex?"

Luis just stared. Then he frowned and leaned back in his chair. "I don't know," he said.

"Well, you better think about it. And you, Paul," Micky said to the second boy, "how come you always wearing your shades on visitors' day? Think you're a *movie* star?"

"Naw, man. They're prescription," Paul said.

Micky said nothing.

"Look, Micky," Paul said, "my old man *and* my mother both wore—"

"Spare us your mother, will you, man?" another older member said. "Micky don't want to hear Freud. He asked you a question."

"O.K.," Paul said, cracking his knuckles and staring down at a tattoo on his arm. "I guess I'm ashamed on visiting day. Being a junkie. Being here."

"Got it all figured out," Micky said coldly. "Thought about it. Think you're cool in those shades. Where'd you get your stuff out there? Ever been in jail? Ever get beaten up?"

Paul replied that since his father was a doctor, he never ran the risks of making a connection.

"A doctor," Micky repeated very quietly. "No cops. No connection. Who you putting on? You taking us on a trip, or what? I bet you been beaten a hundred *times*."

"Yeah," said Paul, grinning. "I guess I did get beaten a couple of times."

"How come you're smiling? You think it's funny?"

"No," Paul said. He stopped smiling.

"Cool, ashamed, shades. How about blowin' that image," Micky said. "Might as well do it while you're here."

"I'm trying, Mother."

"Well, don't just try."

Micky then spoke to the other members in turn, drawing them out, replying to them, letting them talk to one another. ("I'm hung up, Micky," one of the older members said. "I feel as though sometimes my 'as if' was burning out.") The encounter lasted four hours, and by the time it broke up, at around midnight, the members were either engrossed in their private thoughts or united in a bond of released energy and concern. From encounter to encounter, the newer members apparently find that their bouts of rage diminish and their introspection and their intuitive response to one another increase. The no-holds-barred encounter after the pent-up "as if" day is, after all, the principle upon which all group therapy in the outside world is based.

Since Daytop has been in existence for little more than three years, it is impossible to predict its long-term results, but at least the immediate outcome of this form of therapy is fairly easy to appraise. Charles Dederich, the founder of Synanon (which originated some of the Daytop methods, though in a simultaneously more mystical and more paramilitary setting, in California), has suggested that the cure rate among drug addicts can be measured only in "clean man-days." By that standard, absolute cures —that is, up to the present time—have been achieved with seventy-five per cent of the addicts who have come to Daytop's doors. (Measured in similar terms, the Public Health Service Hospital for drug addicts, in Lexington, Kentucky, has, according to a recent statement, a cure rate of under ten per cent.) A peripheral outcome has been that the Staten Island community in which Daytop is situated, after reacting to its founding with petitions, epithets, and even rocks, has now accepted it to the extent that neighboring stores contribute merchandise, neighboring residents attend the open houses that are held each Saturday (and even, when they are troubled, participate in occasional encounters), and neighboring schools seek out Daytop inhabitants for their extraordinary facility in dealing with troubled children. It is true that some hard-line conservatives, still unreconciled to Daytop's presence, complained some time ago that addicts in search of the Lodge had stumbled, looking unkempt and criminal, onto the doorsteps of several houses in the neighborhood. Daytop's management, having always seen to it that candidates had explicit directions for reaching the Lodge, became suspicious, and eventually traced the rumor to the fact that a visiting congressman had lost his way in the night.

Other special needs or special problems have generated other groups that, like Daytop, have no particular therapist and have become more or less a way of life. There are, of course, Alcoholics Anonymous, Gamblers Anonymous, and a new, rather frivolous group called Neurotics Anonymous. There is also a highly serious and successful group called Recovery, Inc., of which the only member who might reasonably be considered the therapist has been dead for several years. Recovery, Inc., is a group of former mental patients, who meet with the aim of preventing one another from relapsing into psychotic states, and of easing the transition from the psychiatric ward into what passes for normal life. The therapist is present only in the form of a book, *Mental Health Through Will Training*, by the late Abraham Low, from which members draw a vocabulary and a philosophy ("When you have done something good, endorse yourself") to help them with the problems they present and discuss at evening meetings. (The vocabularies of groups without therapists, idiosyncratic though they may be, are likely to be more tolerable than the jargon therapists use, which ranges from polysyllabic hyphenated constructions of vaguely Latinate origin, through jarring usage like "to obsess upon" and "conflicted," to a kind of professional baby talk. "I always advise young parents to stay together until their children have grown up," a marriage counsellor said in a recent lecture at the Postgraduate Center for

Mental Health, "because every child needs two legs to stand on —the mama leg and the papa leg.")

One type of group therapy that is diametrically opposed in principle to Daytop, Alcoholics Anonymous, and Recovery, Inc., is a crash program consisting of a single session under the complete domination of a therapist. The session, which is known as a group-therapy marathon, lasts thirty uninterrupted hours, after which it permanently disbands. The theory behind marathons is, briefly, that sleep deprivation induces a feeling of portentousness—not unlike a mild reaction to a psychedelic drug —and that inhibitions and resistances are lowered much more rapidly than in regular groups. Marathons conducted by a therapist called in from outside (who may never see the members of the group again when the session is over) have become quite fashionable as an approach to solving problems of industrial management, and they are also popular with patients who are familiar with more conventional therapy groups. For what one practitioner has termed "therapy virgins," however—members with no previous experience of group therapy—the marathon is not without its dangers. Ordinary neurotics well within the borders of any definition of sanity often undergo in their daily lives states that verge on the psychotic; a marathon may push these persons over the line into an actual psychosis.

SHARING: A marathon was recently conducted in New York by a well-known psychologist from the West who had run more than twenty marathons in cities from coast to coast. The session had been convened (the cost was a hundred and twenty-five dollars per person) by a hospital administrator from New Jersey, who brought along three members of his staff. The other participants were two young New York psychiatrists, one of whom had brought a troublesome patient, a middle-aged landscape painter, along; a television actress from California, who had been a patient of the therapist, and who brought her distraught dachshund; a receptionist from a brokerage firm, the group's only therapy novice, who arrived alone; a silent observer invited by the therapist; and the administrator of a home for unwed mothers, who also arrived alone.

The session began at ten o'clock on a Saturday morning, in a single room of a suite on Central Park West. The members were introduced by first names to one another, and a list of rules was passed around and read. No one was to leave the room except to go to the bathroom; conversation was to be continued throughout meals, which would be served in the room; no one was to go out of his way to protect any other member from verbal assault; no physical violence would be allowed; and the identities of the participants were to be held in strictest confidence. (The names of the members, like all names in this article, have been changed to disguise their identities.) The rule about leaving the room was waived for the actress, so that she might walk her dog from time to time.

The first three hours of the session were spent in denunciations of the hospital administrator by his staff members. He was accused of megalomania, of eavesdropping on his assistants electronically in the name of "scientific research," of overworking his staff for the sake of expanding his clinic to become the largest of its kind in the country. After a long recital of grievances by one of the assistants (a man in his early thirties dressed in white T-shirt, khaki pants, and sneakers), the administrator (also in his thirties, but wearing a dark cashmere suit) sighed and loosened his tie. He said, "What I'm hearing is this—proletarian envy and an infantile feeling of rejection." The assistant leaned back, groaned, and bit his fingernails.

Throughout this exchange, the therapist from the West, a chubby man in his early fifties, wearing a maroon sweater, a brown wool scarf, baggy pants, and loafers, had been sitting curled up on the floor, stroking the leg of one of the shy members of the staff under the trouser cuff. "When are you going to *say* something, Harry?" he asked, in a heavy Middle European accent. "When are you going to *share* something with us?"

"Oh, he'll talk," the administrator said. "Harry never says anything until the twenty-third hour."

The therapist resumed stroking Harry's leg.

There was more talk. Lunch arrived, and the therapist homed in on the receptionist. "We know nothing about you, Elizabeth," he said. "Come. Share something with us."

The receptionist, wearing black net stockings, loafers, and a skirt belted at the hips and looking rather ill at ease, gave a brief outline of her early life and education, and, after a moment's hesitation, a description of a young man with whom she was going out at present.

"You bore me," said one of the New York psychiatrists.

The receptionist looked nervously about the room. "I don't know what you want me to say," she said. "I'm so afraid something awful is going to happen."

"Well, Lizzie," the therapist said, "you must share *more* with us than that. I warn you, if you allow nothing to *happen*, after the session you are going to feel depressed. Very depressed."

"Gosh," the receptionist said, smiling awkwardly and casting an alarmed glance about the room. No one smiled back.

"What are you smiling for, Lizzie?" the therapist asked. "Are you really very happy at this moment?"

"And you might cut out that 'Gosh' number, too," said the actress suddenly springing to life. "You're a big girl now. What did you come here for? Aren't you interested in becoming a real person?" The receptionist choked and said nothing.

One of the New York psychiatrists lunged across the room and took off one of her loafers. "Maybe that will loosen you up," he said, looking at the therapist.

The girl sat frozen, with one loafer on, and abruptly re-crossed her legs.

"Perhaps you ought to take your skirt off, too," the therapist said, rolling his eyes. "Perhaps then you could share with us."

"I don't know what you want me to say," she said, now close to tears.

"Why don't you leave her alone?" said the landscape painter. "She looks like a sensitive person, and she's never been through this before. Why do we all have to jump on her at once? Why is it always breaking people down?"

"Remember the ten commandments of the marathon," the therapist said, with obvious annoyance. "No protection . . ."

"O.K.," said one of the psychiatrists, turning to the landscape painter. "Let's talk about you. What's your hangup?"

The painter said he had been in therapy with the other psychiatrist in the room for seven years, and that they both felt they had come to a point where they were making no further progress. This was discussed for a while, and several members implied that although it took considerable courage to come to a marathon together, there must be a homosexual undercurrent between them.

It had grown dark, and supper was brought in. "Why are you

sitting there like that?" the actress suddenly said bitterly to the landscape painter. "With your head drawn in and your arms hanging down like some kind of ape or something? And what would you call those boots you're wearing? Why don't you sit there like a human being?"

"I guess I don't have a very high opinion of myself," the painter said, glancing over toward his psychiatrist. "These are special therapeutic shoes. I have trouble with my feet."

"Diana is a very special patient," the therapist said, turning to the actress. "And I want to share this with you. I once made advances to her, and she turned me away. When she left our group in the West, she was given a trophy for being the most giving and sharing member of the group. Tell them about yourself, Diana. Diana is a very serious artist."

Diana began to weep, and remained in tears for the rest of the session. It turned out that she was a kind of therapy nomad, travelling from group to group, and that she had not yet lit in a group in New York. (One of the New York psychiatrists immediately handed her his card.) Diana's current problem, as she saw it, was that after two unsuccessful marriages she was having an affair with a textile merchant from her former group who had gangster affiliations and was pressing her to marry him.

"Tell them the truth," said the therapist. "Tell them that Sol is impotent. Tell them that he is *imprinted* on his former wife."

Diana allowed that this was true. "But he loves me," she said, pushing her dachshund aside and crying into a fresh handkerchief.

The group discussed for an hour or two what this might mean. Then other members began to talk about their own extramarital affairs. One of the New York psychiatrists, a bachelor, said, when the conversation turned suddenly to him, "I don't have any real hangups at the moment. I just came to watch what you all were doing and feeling. My life is satisfactory. I go out with Swedish air hostesses. I learned the secret in Paris. You just talk to their navel and they come around."

"Have you ever been in analysis?" said the actress, narrowing her eyes.

"No," the psychiatrist said. "But I'm a pretty smart guy. I can fix my patients up all right. I just don't have any real hangups at the moment."

"Would you like to sleep with any of the girls here?" the therapist asked.

"I would," said the shy member of the hospital staff.

"Well, you can do it when we make subgroups after the marathon. Tell us, Lizzie, do you think you are a good lay?"

"I don't know," the receptionist said. "I guess so." Then, apparently startled by the turn the conversation had taken, she looked suddenly agonized.

The remainder of the night was spent in discussion of sexual adventures. The therapist, prefacing each remark with "I want to share this with you," shared several of his own and gave the young men advice in the conduct of theirs.

After breakfast Sunday morning, the hours were spent in "going around."

The bachelor psychiatrist with no hangups suggested that unless the receptionist went into therapy immediately she might soon slash her wrists.

The painter suggested to the actress that she stop attending groups for a while. "Do you know what I mean when I say that?" he asked kindly.

"I know what *you* mean," she said, glancing slowly from his head to his feet, "but I'm afraid I won't take your advice."

The hospital administrator said to the therapist (in a perfect imitation of the therapist's voice and accent), "You know, Emil, I'm puzzled about you. I *respond* to phonies, and if somebody outside asked me about you, I'd say you were phony clear through. You hear what I'm *shar*ing?"

"Do you think you're a*mus*ing?" asked the therapist, with real rage. "Are you en*joy*ing yourself? If you ever say anything like that outside, I'll ram it down your throat. I'll make your name a dirty word in every hospital in the country."

The administrator backed down and apologized.

At four o'clock Sunday afternoon, tea with rum was served. The therapist insisted that members join hands and sing, to the tune of "O Tannenbaum," "Oh, marathon, my marathon, without you I could not go on." Then several members exchanged addresses, and the therapist and the actress embraced. She was still in tears, and the dachshund scrabbled and whined at their feet.

"I wanted to ask you something," the landscape painter said

earnestly to the therapist. "So many Americans go to foreign analysts, when you might think understanding the language was so important. Do you think a foreigner means the Dark Father to them—something daemonic?"

The therapist giggled.

"And what's the control?" the painter continued. "I mean, you ask everybody to form 'subgroups' after the marathon and everything. How do you know it's not going to get out of hand?"

"I am the control," the therapist said. "I have a very therapeutic personality."

The receptionist asked the therapist for a cigarette.

"How many are left?" he asked.

The receptionist examined the pack on the table. "Two," she said.

"Then you may not have one," the therapist said. "I like to have a b.m. in the evening and one in the morning, and I need a cigarette for each of them."

The receptionist waited until the therapist looked away, and then, with her first cheerful smile of the occasion, calmly smoked both of his cigarettes and left for home.

The therapist, giving one last, detailed account of an adventure he anticipated for that night, picked up the empty package of cigarettes and returned to his hotel room for a short rest before beginning another marathon, for a group of executives from an electronics company, the following morning.

Far more common and far less concerned with the mystique of "therapeutic personalities" are the weekly or semi-weekly therapy groups conducted by relatively orthodox analysts for urban neurotics, or just the urban lonely. One such group convenes each Tuesday night in the office of a therapist in the upper Seventies, near Park Avenue. This therapist is highly qualified, possessing a degree in psychiatry, a Ph.D. in psychology, and a degree from a psychoanalytic institute, where he was himself psychoanalyzed and of whose faculty he is now a member. He is of the non-directive school, saying very little, interpreting only now and then, but he is also receptive to innovations in the field. He speaks with particular interest, for example, of a widely respected colleague who created a television program, which ran for six months on a major network and which consisted solely of reenactments of one of the colleague's therapy groups from week to week. The program, although it ultimately failed for lack of a sponsor, attracted a devoted following, and the therapist noted that the members of the group profited enormously from seeing themselves portrayed each week on the screen. Some initial worry on the part of the patients that they might be identified by their families or friends was laid to rest when one member, a woman who complained constantly of lack of communication with her husband and their adolescent son, watched the program with both of them one evening when the session was devoted almost exclusively to her problems. At the end of the program, her son turned to her husband and said that he did not understand why such a nice and obviously normal lady should be in therapy at all. The group was disbanded, and all but two of its members were pronounced "cured," a few months after the television series came to an end. The two remaining members became the core of a new group, and were cured themselves a few months after that.

The therapist's present Tuesday-evening group consists of seven members, all of whom have reason to consider themselves failures in some widely accepted meaning of the term. A physicist in his early thirties cannot bring himself to move out of his parents' home, because, he claims, his mother needs him around the house and his father needs the use of his car. A former burlesque comedian in his fifties, who is now a night clerk in a hotel, cannot bring himself to move out of his mother's apartment, because, he says, it would be too much trouble to pack his books. A middle-aged scholar who also lives with his parents had a nervous breakdown in the middle of teaching a class in history at a girls' college, which gave him leave of absence to undergo treatment. A psychiatric social worker in her thirties is having trouble at the office, because she is distracted by a feeling that she ought to move back to Tennessee, where she fears her aging parents are going to die in her absence. A forty-nine-year-old secretary with an exceptionally loud, shrill voice (because she says, her older brother never listened to her and her father always silenced her when she hummed) weeps frequently because, on the half-dozen dates she has had in her life, she has found that "all men are after the same thing." Another woman, who is twenty, and who both overeats and gets migraines whenever her mother comes to visit, is heavily dependent, despite being married and a mother, on a girl friend. A fifty-year-old liquor salesman, who complains that his wife talks too much, occasionally goes on binges with prostitutes, whom he longs, but does not dare, to beat up. ("Maybe when you get better," one of the women once said to him, smiling, "you'll have the courage to beat one up, and get it over with.")

The therapist also has a seven-member Wednesday group, which includes the night clerk from the Tuesday group; the twenty-one-year-old husband of the twenty-year-old woman in the Tuesday group; a wealthy young musician who has not been able to work in two years; a receptionist in a law firm who, at twenty-two, has an illegitimate baby and is living in her mother's apartment (she cannot afford an apartment of her own at the moment, because she uses the money for therapy); a woman in her early sixties who cannot decide between two lovers, and who is thinking of changing her job from secretarial work to kindergarten teaching; and two lonely graduate students who dread their Ph.D. exams.

Both the Tuesday and the Wednesday groups are likely to spend their hour and a half in the doctor's office recounting the nagging problems of their daily lives—people who have spoken sharply to them, people to whom they have spoken sharply, setbacks at the office, guilt, loneliness, frustrated ambition, problems in breaking away from their parents. The doctor, who normally looks rather sleepy, offers words of encouragement now and then, but for the most part the members seem to draw their consolation from each other's presence. After the session, both groups adjourn to Phebe's Whamburger, where the conversation becomes indistinguishable from any ordinary social exchange. The doctor does not encourage his patients to meet outside the office. "I find that sooner or later, if they see each other outside the group," he has said, "a couple of patients will have an affair. And sooner or later one of them—usually the male—will tell the group about it. Then the girl drops out. I don't call that therapy; that's acting out. The important thing is that the group should provide a new experience within the session—the experience of being listened to, and criticized, and understood. When the results of that experience are carried into life, the old neurotic patterns break and improvement starts."

Not all groups, or even the majority, are composed of what could be called, in worldly terms, misfits or failures. Some are composed of people who would strike the casual observer in their social or professional set as having fewer problems than are to be found among random guests at a cocktail party. One group, which for some months recently met each Thursday, at four, in the same building as the Tuesday and Wednesday groups—but with another therapist—had ten members, of whom five were "old," having attended meetings for more than a year, and five were "new," having joined the group within the past six months. The group also held an open-end session each Monday night at a member's apartment, without the therapist, who said he was unworried by the possibility of acting out. Patients who wanted to sleep together, he said, would do so with or without alternate sessions—and if marriage should result, they would at least know more about each other than couples who had never been in therapy together ever could.

The old, or core, members were Leigh, a successful stockbroker in his middle forties, who had been twice married, twice divorced, and was about to be married again, this time to an Italian movie star; Dinah, a beautiful woman of forty, who had been married at fifteen and then, after a brief career as a model, had got a divorce and married an accountant with three children by a former marriage (they had three children together); Jonathan, an advertising executive in his early thirties, married, and a part-time alcoholic, homosexual, and drug addict; Alvin, a record-company executive, who had been four times married, four times divorced; and Don, a bachelor lawyer, who was on vacation in South America during the time the new members came in. The new members were Benny, a sportswriter for a newspaper; Clara, Benny's wife, who was a dietitian in a girls reformatory, and who had transferred from another group to be with her husband; Max, a diamond cutter from Czechoslovakia, who lived with his mother (with whom, as the youngest of six children, he had slept in the same bed until he was five); Emily, a twenty-three-year-old substitute kindergarten teacher, who painted in her free time; and Fern, twenty-nine, the wife of a psychoanalyst and mother of two. All members of the group were rebounds from unsuccessful earlier analyses, and they addressed the therapist by his first name, Reuben.

Reuben's office was painted a bilious green, with several ambiguous paintings (including an androgynous-looking portrait, a picture of a couple of uncertain sex) hung between bookcases filled with works on psychotherapy. The chairs were arranged around a coffee table, on which there were five ashtrays with bases made of beanbags. ("If table ashtrays are used," says a textbook called *A Practicum of Group Psychotherapy*, "they might be preferably of the bean bag variety, because if they are thrown, the relatively soft bean bags are likely to hit the target first.") Reuben sat in a stuffed chair in one corner, drinking cherry Cokes and smoking a pipe, while the patients sat wherever they liked. Seating arrangements are regarded as very important in any therapy group; sitting on the right of the therapist is likely to be interpreted as evidence of a need for reassurance, while sitting in the same chair every session is regarded as a sign of rigidity.

IF YOUR PARENTS HAVE BROKEN BOTH YOUR LEGS: One Thursday in midwinter was Emily's and Fern's first in the group. The other members introduced themselves, and both new members looked tensely about the room. Emily, a shock of hair dangling over one eye, was dressed in a suit, smoked constantly, and smiled tentatively at members of the group in turn. Fern, in a tight silk dress pulled her legs up underneath her and blinked continuously over contact lenses.

Leigh, the stockbroker, began the session by telling about an argument he had had with Dinah, the former model, at the alternate session on Monday evening. He had been speaking bitterly of his parents, and Dinah had suggested that he try to understand and forgive them. "My feeling is that if your parents have broken both your legs, you don't forgive them," Leigh said with considerable heat. "First you try to learn to walk. My father's a psychiatrist, but when I was little we were so poor they had to put me in an orphanage. I had the most horrible dream last night. I dreamed I had a cataract in my left eye, and—"

"Left eye?" said Jonathan, the advertising executive. "Left I. Left me. Your dream was about rejection. I went to a psychiatrist when I was eighteen, and in love with a girl, and he told me I was really gay. So I became gay. Later, I found out why he said it. I met the boy he was living with."

"Left me. That's good, Jon," Leigh said. "I know in my mind the reality was not rejection. But that's the way it felt, and I can't forget it now."

"I'm sharp with my children sometimes, Leigh," Dinah said. "That's part of the reason I'm here. But I like to think someday they're going to remember the good things, and forgive."

"That's your problem, Dinah," Leigh said. "And you're going to have to face the fact that behind that beautiful façade you're seething with hostility toward your mother."

"I'd like to tell you a dream I had," said Max, the diamond cutter, a short, stolid-looking man with crew-cut, graying hair and a constant expression of bewilderment. "I don't know if it means anything. There was a crippled man walking an enormous dog, and I felt this great—I don't know. Anxiety."

"That crippled man was you, Max," Leigh said without hesitation. "And the dog was your hostile impulses. Can you tell us any more about the dream?"

"No, I can't," said Max. "But, frankly, I think I prefer to be in private therapy."

"That's just why I think you ought to be in Group," Reuben said. "I think you need to learn to relate to other people, unleash the dog."

Fern tugged at the hem of her dress and cleared her throat. "I feel, as a new member, I ought to say something," she said. "My reaction is fear." She turned to the sportswriter, a tall, slightly overweight man with a pink and friendly face. "I think I'm afraid of you, Benny," she said. "I think you're really hostile to me."

Benny smiled, and lighted his pipe.

"Everyone feels frightened the first time in Group, Fern," said Clara, a large, handsome woman, who had a flower pinned to the jacket of her suit. "You don't have to be afraid. In fact, my complaint is that no one in this group is very open. Nobody interacts."

Several group members protested, and accused Clara of trying to run things. Clara suddenly began to cry. "I miss my old group," she said. "I was with them for four years, and I think about them all the time. Last night, I wanted to call them. I feel I'm only in this group for Benny, and it's making me terribly isolated and angry."

Fern uncurled her legs. "I like you, Clara," she said.

"Women," said Alvin, the record-company executive, a tall, dark man with a thin neat mustache, wearing a gold wristwatch studded with diamonds. "This morning, I had the most awful scene at the office. My secretary didn't show up on time, and it made me think of Gloria."

Reuben sighed, and asked Alvin to tell the new members about Gloria.

Alvin said that Gloria had been his girl for three years, that she used to be a patient of Reuben's, and that before going into treatment she had often tried to commit suicide. Just the night before, Alvin had felt alarmed when Gloria got out of bed to go and read in the living room.

"Like your mother," said Reuben. "She was always having fainting spells. When she fainted, you used to think she was abandoning you—is that right, Al?"

"Oh, Christ. I guess so," Alvin said.

"Somehow," Benny said, "I'm always depressed after these sessions in your office, Reuben. I wonder why that is."

Reuben smiled. "I always want you to feel free to challenge the Father," he said.

With that, the group adjourned for a hamburger, not at Phebe's but at Mayhew's, a few blocks farther down Madison Avenue.

ALVIN: The alternate session—Fern's and Emily's first—was held in Alvin's apartment, a penthouse on the upper East Side. In the foyer was a round red velvet sofa, of the sort used in beauty parlor waiting rooms, on which the members dropped their coats. The living room was filled with antique furniture, many shiny creeping plants, potted palms, and statuary (an angel reaching down to touch the breast of a nymph, and so on). Benny and Clara arrived early. Jonathan arrived soon afterward, with his bicycle, which he brought up in the gilded elevator and left outside the apartment door. The rest of the group all arrived at once—Fern wearing slacks and glasses (instead of contact lenses), Emily wearing the same suit she had worn Thursday afternoon. Alvin received them in a red turtleneck and red socks, a gray cashmere sweater, black slacks, and red-trimmed slippers. On a coffee table he had set out fruit and cheese, and there was instant coffee in the kitchen.

"I want to talk about Gloria," Alvin said after everybody sat down. "I've been so depressed all week. I didn't think I was going to talk about it, but I found myself looking forward to the group like it was my family. I wouldn't even let the maid pick out the fruit. I picked it out myself. I'm in bad shape. Gloria and me, you know, we were going on a cruise. And she said she felt she ought to have some dresses—maybe a couple. So I said, 'Go ahead.' So she comes back from Bergdorf Goodman with eleven dresses. *Eleven* dresses. I said, 'Gloria honey, when you said you were going to buy a couple of dresses, did you have to buy *eleven?*' She said, 'Honey, these dresses weren't five hundred dollars. I'm used to five-hundred-dollar dresses.' So you know what I said to her? I said, '*Then, for Christ's sake, why don't you find yourself a five-hundred-dollar John?*' So the cruise is off. She walked out on me."

"Alvin, sweetie," said Dinah. "Don't you understand? She was only buying her trousseau."

"I don't know why, Dinah," said Clara, "but you always seem to me like the group mother."

"Not to me," Fern said bitterly. "She seems to me more like a whore."

"Trousseau," Alvin said thoughtfully. "You know how it was when I first met Gloria? I was dying for her to marry me. After four marriages. I was pleading. She was seeing Reuben at the time, and she used to bite her fingernails, and she said, 'Al, I'll marry you when my nails grow long.' So one day she wasn't biting her nails anymore, and I said, 'Gloria honey, your nails are long. Let's get married now.' So you know what she told me to do? She told me I should see Reuben myself. Now I'm not sure I want to marry her. I been seeing other broads since we broke up. I told Reuben about them, and he just sort of snickers. I think he likes to hear about it."

"Alvin, you're how old—fifty—now?" said Jonathan. "You

don't want to die alone, do you? I have to make the same decision every day in my marriage—whether I'm going to stick with
Sandy or start going gay again."

"Please, Jon, for Christ's sake, don't start that gay stuff," Alvin said.

"I don't know why I'm so hostile sometimes," Fern said, pulling her legs underneath her on the seat again. "My husband is a
successful analyst. Everything he does he does just right, and I
want to slap him. In a way, I'd like to see him fail at something.
It seems like everything I feel I also feel the opposite. I want you
to like me, but I can't seem to find the real me. And I think if I
stop being hostile, if I try to repress it and make you all like me,
*I'll lose the last little bit of the real me that I've got.*"

Emily had seemed for some time on the verge of saying
something, and Leigh asked her what her problem was.

"There's not much to tell," Emily said. "I teach, and sometimes
I paint, although I never seem to do very much. Lately, I don't
even want to see my friends. I go out with a homosexual artist,
but I'm just so tired of dates, and parties, and people. I'm becoming a secret bitch. I double-book dates for no reason, and
then I call up, or dial the telegraph office in some faraway place
direct and send a telegram, to say I can't show up. It's sort of a
joke."

"Freud tells us there are no jokes," Leigh said.

"There's nothing wrong with you, Emily, except you ought to
wear shorter skirts," Alvin said. "You got good legs. And you
ought to get that hair out of your eyes."

Benny mumbled something, and Clara asked him to repeat
it. "There are years of my marriage I just can't remember at all,"
he said.

Fern interrupted. "That's strange," she said. "You know, in all
the years since my mother died, I've never gone to visit her
grave."

Dinah was crying softly, and Clara asked her why.

"I'm crying for Leigh," Dinah said. "He's getting well." Then
she smiled. "Sooner or later, every girl in this group falls in love
with Leigh," she said.

WAIT A MINUTE. I HAVE TO THINK: The next Thursday, in
Reuben's office, Dinah said that the night before, when she

couldn't sleep, "instead of counting sheep" she had rated the group members in her mind, and found that she would like to spend time with Emily and Max, in spite of the fact that they were relatively new in the group. "I think they look as though they had a sense of humor about themselves," she said. "Although I suppose it's only a guard against the trauma of treatment."

"I don't think of you as having such a great sense of humor, Dinah," Jonathan said. "Irony, maybe, but not humor. Most of the talk you produce is pain talk. Beautiful pain talk, but pain talk all the same."

Fern said she felt hurt by being left out of Dinah's rating.

"Sweetie," said Dinah, "you were pretty hostile to me the other night. You called me a whore. In the adult world, that gets a reaction."

"You've got to realize that Dinah is Miss Tailored Woman of 1966," Jonathan said, "and if you offend her she's going to hit you with her handbag."

"Anyway, Dinah's ratings are like a tennis ladder," Leigh said. "Next week, you may be on top. You never know."

"I had a funny dream," Fern said. "I was feeling hostile and I went with this man to a chichi hotel—"

"Chichi," Jonathan said. "She. She's your mother, obviously. The hotel was your mother's house, and the man you were going with was your father."

"Wait a minute. I have to think," Fern said.

"I might as well say that I'm feeling good," Jonathan said. "I'm a success at the agency, my marriage is going well, and I even bragged about the group. You're not losers. You're winners —a record tycoon, a sportswriter, a model, the wife of a successful analyst."

"Jon," Reuben said, "maybe if you could mute your high moods you could mute the lows a little."

"For Christ's sake," Jonathan said, picking up an ashtray, "you're down on me when I'm on dope or picking up boys in the street. Now you're even down on me for being burgherish."

"Jon," Dinah said, "maybe your highs are so high because your lows are so convulsive."

"It may just be a bid for his father's attention," Reuben said. "You know what your father said—he said you were either a criminal or a twinkle-toes. Your father was always judging you."

"One night, my brother and I came home late from being out with a couple of girls, and my father kept asking us where we'd been," Jonathan said, putting down the ashtray. "Finally, he beat us up and sent us to bed. Next day, I found out why. A family of five had been murdered, and he thought we must have done it."

"That's funny," Emily said. "Once, I was out on a date in high school with my boy friend and I came home late. My mother said, 'Oh, God, I thought he must have strangled you and thrown you in the lake.'"

"Jon," Clara said, "did you ever think that just because you have impulses you don't need to act them out?"

"You don't give a damn about me, Clara," Jonathan said, really angry. "And neither does Reuben. I believe in hypocrisy and repression all right. 'Hypocrisy is as natural to man as slime to a fish'—that's Kierkegaard. But we're all hung up on our impulses, baby. That's why you're here."

"We're here because we're caricatures of the people we ought to be," Leigh said. "Sometimes I feel there's this invisible hand reaching out of our childhood and making us do the neurotic, stereotyped things that keep us from being really alive."

Dinah informed the group that she would miss the following session, because she was going to Los Angeles to visit her mother. "I'm just telling you in advance," she said, "so there won't be any anxiety."

If Anything Genuine Is Said, I'll React To It: The Monday meeting was held in Jonathan's apartment, on the fringe of Harlem. (His wife was off at a meeting of another group, to which she belonged.) The living room was painted dark blue, the walls were covered with paintings of nudes, and there were life-size papier-mâché statues of royal personages standing about the apartment. What served as a coffee table was a broad, rough piece of timber supported at each end by bricks, and Jonathan, who began to talk as soon as the first members came into the apartment, continually stabbed the timber with a cheese knife for emphasis. "I don't know what's wrong with me," he said. "Last week, after Group, I picked up five men in the public bath, and then afterward I felt so bad I shot some junk. And last night, in bed with Sandy, I had a pain under my arm and I thought I was dying of cancer."

"I want to talk about something," Clara said. "I've been having trouble at work with my director."

"Does she remind you of anyone?" Leigh asked.

"Yes, she reminds me of my mother," Clara said. "She never really related to me or my sisters. My sisters used to fight a lot, and I always stayed out of it. All I had was a sense of danger. I can remember living on a farm, and there was this window looking down from the staircase into the kitchen. I just used to sit on the stairs and look in, and feel isolated. Sometimes I went to the meadow, and then I felt—I know this sounds silly, I'm so fat now—like a daffodil. You know, I had this terrible dream. There was a two-headed, four-legged baby with no body in between. In the dream I kept thinking, It can be fixed, but the operation will leave scars. It will hurt, but they can fix him."

"That baby is you, Clara," Jonathan said.

"And the operation is therapy," said Alvin.

"Maybe that's why I eat so much," said Clara. "To get a body in between." Then she burst into tears. "I'm crying because you listened to me," she said. "I feel so helpless. No one at my job knows it. I'm not helpless in the world."

"I feel so frustrated and hostile," Fern said. "No one understands me. When Reuben called a few nights ago to ask how I felt about being in the group, I made a joke. I said I was in a state of shock. He took me seriously. He never gets a joke. Analysts don't. I've got to tell the group something. The other night, I slept on my husband's side of the bed. I wanted to be nearer to the children, in case they needed something. You know what he accused me of? He said I was trying to take his rightful place as a man."

"Maybe he was right," Alvin said. "When you arrived at my apartment, and here tonight, in slacks and glasses, you looked such a mess I thought at first you were Emily."

"I want to get back to Jon," Emily said. "I feel we haven't given him anything. His trouble is *serious*. He thought he was dying."

"I'm not trying to make a thing about its being serious," Jonathan said, glancing anxiously over at Leigh.

"When a child has a tantrum, you don't pick him up," Leigh

said severely. "Jon wants us to pick him up. We've been through this a hundred times before. He wants attention."

Jonathan began to complain about Reuben—that he could never be reached in a crisis, and that he left the group three times a year for vacations.

Benny chimed in with a complaint that Reuben was growing hard of hearing and refused to wear his hearing aid.

Max told about having spoiled a diamond he was cutting in his hurry to get to an appointment with Reuben the week before. "Finally, I decided to take a taxi," he said. "At a dollar a minute for individual sessions, it's cheaper to take a taxi."

"The last session I had with Reuben, I spent the whole fifty minutes talking about Gloria," Alvin said. "Fifty minutes. Fifty dollars. I thought, It's cheaper to talk to the group, and from now on I'm only going to talk about Gloria to the group. I can tell Reuben's dying to know about her, but he's not getting another word from me. If he wants to know so much, let him get her back in therapy."

"I can't stand the idiotic grin on his face," Clara said. "Once, I told Reuben to get that idiotic grin off his face and stop drinking that goddam cherry Coke, or I would scream."

"What did he say?" Fern asked.

"He started to cry," Clara said. "He's really O.K."

"You know what that grin reminds me of?" Emily said. "When you're a child, and you're singing or dancing, and suddenly you notice that somebody in the corner is just sitting there, with a sort of secret smile. An I've-got-your-number-you're-just-showing-off sort of smile. It makes you self-conscious forever, and it can blight every spontaneous, joyful thing you ever do."

"Maybe we're all complaining about Reuben because it's easier than talking about our own problems," Leigh said.

"You're a fine one to talk," Benny said. "Ever since I've been in this group, you've been sitting there like a sphinx, dropping your little pearls of wisdom, never telling us anything about yourself. The function of this group is to interact, and you never respond to anyone."

"Look, Benny," Leigh said. "I've been in this group longer than any of you, and I can tell the new members are not really working. If I feel I can't be genuine, I prefer not to say anything. If anything genuine is said, I'll react to it."

"You don't know how much better Leigh has got," Jonathan said. "You're new, and you think you know what it's about, Ben baby. But when I first joined this group, Leigh was always cleaning his nails or playing with something. Why don't you wait around before you start judging other people?"

Alvin got up abruptly and put on his coat. "I'm going out and meet a broad," he said. "This is the most depressing session we ever had."

"And as for what you said, Benny," Leigh said as everyone got up to leave, "I guess I've got a certain amount of hostility toward the new brothers and sisters. I guess I'll just have to realize that everyone in this group is a slice of life, and adjust myself to it."

Don's Dream: At the following session, in Reuben's office, Don, the lawyer who had been in South America, returned to the group, looking tanned and rather shy. Reuben introduced him to the new members and asked whether he had had any interesting experiences on his trip.

"Well, I had this dream," Don said, and he drew out two sheets of paper, typed, single-spaced, and began to read in a slow and stammering voice. The dream was a complicated one, about having tried to follow some girls into a hotel and having been diverted by a prior social commitment to a group of bachelors.

When Don had finished, Max drew himself up in his chair and announced that he thought the dream was boring. "So much detail," he said. "Frankly, I had the feeling no one was listening. No one interrupted, or said anything."

"Nobody interrupts a man who's telling a dream," Alvin said.

"You've known the guy for maybe five minutes," Leigh said. "Can't you give him a chance? What's the matter, Max? Do you identify so strongly with—"

"I just happen to love Don," Jonathan said. "And maybe his *copy* isn't as *bright* as some of ours, but, Max, *yours* isn't exactly the most—"

"We've been pretty patient with the boring copy of the new members," Leigh said.

Benny, Clara, Max, and Fern turned on him at once, and the

group suddenly divided between old and new members, with Emily taking no side at all.

"Leigh thinks he's the doctor," Benny said. "I frankly think this group is going to break up. The old members have no room for us."

"The hell it is," Jonathan said. "It was going a long time before you—"

Reuben interrupted briefly, to return the conversation to Don, and the remainder of the session was spent in interpreting Don's dream. Reuben said it had to do with trying to make contact with the opposite sex. He put the new girls on notice that they must be prepared to interact with Don. Don blushed and stared at the floor. When the group adjourned to Mayhew's, Leigh, Jonathan, and Alvin said they had other plans and left. Don went with the rest, but he did not attend any of the following sessions of the group.

MAXIE FELDENSTEIN, YOU'RE A SHELL: The next alternate session was held at Benny's and Clara's rather bare apartment, in a housing project in the East Village. Dinah had returned from her trip to Los Angeles. Max came very late. Leigh did not come at all.

"I called him, and he said he had a brokers' meeting," Benny said ruefully. "I don't believe him. I'm afraid I really hurt his feelings."

Dinah spoke of having visited her mother and her married sister. The sister had just completed her own analysis, and Dinah wondered whether she herself should now leave the group. "Reuben says the group needs me as a mother figure," she said. "But I don't want to be a *figure* for anyone. I feel I could leave the group now and function perfectly adequately, but I think I'm still getting something out of it for myself. I felt I was functioning just fine before I began analysis, and then suddenly one day I had this dreadful fear of planes, and I knew it was time to start doing something about myself."

Benny told of a recurrent dream, based on a real incident in his life. On a vacation in Florida, he had heard a sound in his baby daughter's bedroom and gone to investigate. A Negro was climbing through the window. Benny had immediately moved his family to another hotel, but the dream was with him still.

"That's not so unnatural, Benny," Jonathan said. "Most fathers have a sexual attraction to their daughters. I wonder if that's what's bothering you."

Fern started to say something, and Alvin interrupted. "Don't interrupt me, Al!" she screamed. "I feel I'm not being listened to. I'm feeling so hostile and guilty about my children. I feel my parents were crazy and I'm crazy and I'm passing the craziness on to them."

"How do you visualize craziness, Fern?" Jonathan asked. "My idea of it is that I'm simply going to fall into a coma and die."

"No," Fern said. "I feel I'm going to have a nervous convulsion and be carried away. Like the way I feel when I see a bug. This weekend, Irv and I went to the country, and I saw bugs, and I felt everything was covered with bugs—me, Irv, the kids, everything."

"What kind of bugs?" Jonathan inquired.

"Here. I brought one," Fern said. And she took from her purse a neatly folded piece of Saran wrap containing a dead bug. It was passed from hand to hand and studied.

"I think it's a flea or a louse," Emily said.

Fern sighed.

"Bugs," Leigh said. "I think the association is insanity. Your fear of bugs is a fear you're going to go insane."

"I think Fern was just making a statement about the group," Clara said. "She wanted to tell us what she thinks of us. She brings us a dead bug."

Fern acknowledged that she was feeling hostile.

Dinah brought out a breadstick and laid it on a table beside her. "I brought this to eat in case of anxiety," she said. "This session is turning into a kind of show-and-tell."

Max walked in.

"Where you been, Maxie?" Alvin asked.

"With my mother," Max said.

"Look, Max," Alvin said. "You ought to get out more, and meet girls. I was married—one of my marriages—six years to a call girl I met. They were the happiest years of my life."

Max said nothing.

"What's your last name, Maxie?" Alvin said.

"Feldenstein," Max said.

"Well, then, why don't you ever say anything, Max Feldenstein? Why don't you ever do anything? You know what I'm going to say to you, Max?" Alvin said. "I'm going to say to you, Maxie Feldenstein, you're a shell."

"And you, Fern, with the bugs," Dinah said, picking up the breadstick. "You know what you'll have to do with your fear? You'll have to rise above it. Therapy or no, it's one of those things you have to rise above."

THE GROUP ALWAYS SEEMED TO BE TELLING DON TO GO, GO, Go: In Reuben's office the following Thursday, Leigh came under fire again for his reticence.

"Look, you won't believe this, but I cried for hours after the last session," Leigh said. "Maybe some of you don't know it, but I'm in private analysis with another psychiatrist, and I tried to work it through with him."

"But then all you are in this group is another non-directive therapist," Max said, scratching his head.

"You're scratching your head, Max," Leigh said absently. "Look, maybe it's just that in my private analysis I like to work things through without other people's counter-transferences getting in the way. I know in my head that's what it is. You're just projecting your own problems, and seeing me as your mother or father or brother, or something. But it hurts all the same, and it's going to take me some time to get used to it."

"But in the meantime you owe us something," Clara said. "If you can't ask anything from us, what are we getting from you?"

"All right," Leigh said. "Right now I have two problems. I'm scared to death the stock market will go down to 725, and I can't have orgasms. You want to talk about that?"

"Yes, I do," Clara said. "That's a kind of withholding I can identify with."

"All right, sweetie, identify," said Leigh.

Dinah pulled a slip of paper from her purse and read it aloud: " 'On my trip to Los Angeles, I noticed, not for the first time, that my mother thinks she always has to be right. I'm beginning to wonder if I'm the same way. I listed all these qualities in myself—beauty, intelligence, understanding, forbearance. I wonder if I need to think of myself as perfect.' " Dinah began to cry.

"I feel terribly lonely these days," said Max. "I feel somehow no one is interested in what I have to say, except maybe Dinah."

There was a long silence.

"I feel Max is asking the group for some kind of reassurance," Reuben said. "Don't you all feel that you should give him something, even if it's only your hostility?"

Everyone expressed a liking for Max.

"You were late to the alternate session, though," Dinah said gently. "When you come late, you can't expect not to feel left out a little."

"I asked Maxie to have a drink with me after the last Group, and he turned me off," Alvin said. "I think he's afraid to relate."

"And I think he feels guilty for having pushed Don out of the group," Jonathan said. "I think he identified with Don, because Don is just as retiring and just as boring as Max. *That's* his problem."

"Don's dropping out had nothing to do with Max," Reuben said. "He had an insight that he wanted to work through in private sessions. Then he'll be coming back to the group."

"I think what pushed him out was Reuben's asking him to interact with the girls," Emily said. "I thought that really put the pressure on."

"Yeah," Alvin said. "Don's a virgin, you know, and before you new members came we were always asking him, after he had a date, 'Did you make it? Did you sleep with her? Did you at least make a pass at her?' "

Dinah said, "The group always seemed to be telling Don to go, go, go."

"Maybe I just identify with Don, but I have the feeling he's really gay and he won't admit it," Jonathan said.

"I don't care if you finally turn straight or gay, Jon," Dinah said. "I like you anyway."

"I've just asked Jon to stop acting out his gay impulses," Reuben said. "I wondered what would happen if he analyzed them instead of acting them out. Maybe he'd find out he wasn't gay after all."

"Is that why you counselled me not to sleep with Leigh?" Dinah asked. "So we wouldn't be acting out and could analyze?"

"Yes," Reuben said.

"I just want to say I'm terribly depressed," said Benny. "I've been trying to distract myself by painting, and I find my paintings the most depressing I've ever done."

"Are you taking any pills?" Reuben asked.

"Just a Miltown at bedtime," Benny said.

"Well, stop taking them," Reuben said.

When the group went off to Mayhew's, Max and Alvin broke away. "I have to relate to Alvin," Max said, and they walked off together.

"Cop out!" Dinah suddenly screamed at Leigh as he got into a cab to go back to his office.

STRUCTURING TIME. INTIMACY. THE ULTIMATE REJECTION: That week, some members of the group got into the habit of calling one another. Telephone conversations, instead of beginning with "How are you?" would begin with "Are you all right?" Benny and Fern began calling each other daily, as did Jonathan and Emily. All the rest except Max (whose last name nobody could remember) called all the other members from time to time. At the Monday meeting, held again in Alvin's apartment, Benny and Clara were early, as usual, and even Max was not late.

Leigh, who was in an expansive mood, said he and his analyst had reached the insight that Benny and Clara were not interacting with the group and were projecting their lack of communication onto him.

Benny replied that he felt no one had ever done anything for him or could really understand him. He recounted a long anecdote from his childhood, involving his mother and some girdles at Loehmann's. "I go out on my job every night now and I see all those people at the track and they don't seem left out," he said. "They know what they're doing, and why. They even look happy to me, and I just feel lonely."

"Those people at the track are lonely, too, but they're not doing anything about it. It's all a matter of intimacy and structuring time," Leigh said. "They're not in Group, they're not working on their lack of intimacy. We're here because we won't settle for less than being really intimate."

"You know what makes me feel I really belong?" Fern said. "When I parade for a cause. I almost don't care which cause anymore. Last week, I went on an anti-Vietnam parade, and I felt—I don't know how to describe it—so much warmth for everyone."

"I want to go back to what Benny said about nobody understanding him," said Clara, who had been chain-smoking ever since the conversation began. "I left a group that I loved in order to come into this group—"

"There you go again," Benny said, flaring up. "You'll never let me forget this big sacrifice you made by coming here. Whichever side I'm on, Clara takes the opposite. Our older daughter wants to drop out of the church choir this week to take a part in her high school play. I told her she had a prior commitment to the choir. Clara told her to take the theatre part."

"Are you always so moralistic?" Dinah asked.

Clara fought back tears. "I don't want to cry," she said. "If I cry, Benny will think I'm trying to gain sympathy and he'll only get angry again."

"So what if he does get angry?" Max said. "So you'll get angry back. Is that so terrible?"

"You're a fine one to say that, Max," Alvin said. "You're afraid to get angry at anyone—even your mother. That's why you can never make it with women. You're afraid of your anger."

"I can make it with women all right," Max said, bridling. "It just isn't that much fun. Maybe the women I've had are not as attractive as I'd like them to be. Once, I had an attractive girl named Sarah. I thought when I went to my analyst, To hell with all this Freud. I don't want Freud. I want Sarah. And the analyst said I wasn't being realistic. Sarah didn't want me."

"It must have been terrible," Fern said.

"Well, frankly, I guess I was too dependent on Sarah," said Max.

"You mean you loved her," Emily said. " 'Dependent' makes it sound like a pathological condition."

Max told a long, stammering anecdote about a woman he suspected of having made advances to him at a wedding reception, in the course of a conversation about diamond cutting. He was furious at himself for not having responded at once. "I'm always having delayed reactions," he said. "When Dinah said she liked me, a few sessions back, I didn't feel gratitude just then. I waited until I got home. Now I wonder why I didn't just say to that woman, 'Come off it about the diamonds.' "

"You couldn't have been that blunt, Max," Dinah said, smiling. "You'd only have made it impossible for her to do it."

"You say everyone was drunk at that reception," Leigh said. "Maybe you were right not to do anything. Maybe you just reminded her of somebody out of her past."

"For God's sake, Leigh," Fern said. "Isn't it possible that she wanted Maxie for himself?"

"I wondered about my feeling for Max," Dinah said. "I used to have the same kind of feeling for Don. It's a kind of attraction for the losers. I feel I have a duty to sleep with them. Maybe I'm even beginning to understand my feeling for Leigh."

"Well, I'm getting well," Leigh said. "And I think I understand your feeling. I'm an attractive male, that's what it is."

"But you don't fit into my life plan," Dinah said. "I've got a perfectly happy marriage of my own."

"Dinah, it wasn't very nice of you to say that about my being a loser," Max said. "That doesn't make me feel very good, frankly."

"I didn't mean it, Max," said Dinah. "Of course I like you for yourself. You have lovely qualities, and I bet when you're drunk you're the life of the party. If I called you a loser, that was only my own transference."

Max did not look consoled.

"I'm beginning to understand some transference behavior of my own," Leigh said, and he traced a complicated connection between his father's dark complexion and his own attraction to Negro women.

"Oh, Leigh," Dinah said with irritation. "Can't we drop parents for a change? I know your last analyst was a Freudian and mine wasn't, so we have a conflict about this. But just for once I wish you'd leave parents out of it."

"You're overreacting, Dinah," Leigh said.

"What about Leigh?" Fern asked. "Have you been having orgasm?"

Leigh did not reply, and there was a long silence. Jonathan was fiddling with a torn flap of his wallet, and he asked Alvin for some Scotch Tape. At the word "Scotch," everyone asked for a drink.

"That's acting out," Alvin said as he cheerfully fixed the drinks. "Alcohol in groups is always acting out."

"I'm very depressed by what Leigh said about intimacy," Emily said. "Sometimes I feel unsporting for not being willing to settle for less. After all, that's life, and you might as well face it with dignity. Life always draws away from need."

"That sounds sick," Dinah said.

"No, that's right," Leigh said.

"No, Dinah's right, too," Emily said. "But what bothers me is that nobody can ever be totally there for somebody else. It's all little betrayals—the first one who leaves a party, the first one who hangs up the phone. Getting out of bed to go the bathroom, even. I feel to be really there for somebody else you'd just have to fall into each other's arms and subside, or go up in smoke. I feel that's why the group can never really work. Every time we break up, it's a little betrayal of intimacy."

"Well, Gloria and I got together last weekend, and that was intimacy," Alvin said. "We were really working, really communicating."

"Let me tell you something about breakup and betrayal," Leigh said. "Years ago, I had an analyst I really loved. Every summer, when he went on vacation, I just about cracked up. Then one summer it didn't happen. In September, I mentioned it to him. I said, 'For the first time, I didn't go to pieces when you left.' 'I know why,' he said to me. 'It's because you used to have an infantile fear that when I went away I was betraying you. You were afraid I would never come back. But now you're an adult, you know better. You know I'll always come back to you.' And you know what happened after that?" Leigh burst into tears. "He died. He was old, and he died. Isn't it ironic? When you're a child, rejection is confused with the metaphor of death. And then when you're an adult you find out you were right all the time. Death is the ultimate rejection."

ANYTHING NICE YOU'D LIKE TO SAY TO ME, DOCTOR?: The following Thursday, Reuben announced that he would be going away for a three-week vacation. Jonathan said he would miss the next session, because he had to travel upstate for an account.

"Anything you'd like to tell us about Gloria?" Reuben asked, turning to Alvin.

Alvin said nothing, and all members of the group simply smiled.

"I want to say something," said Clara, who was again wearing a flower. "Last Saturday was Benny's and my anniversary. We went to see the film of Marat/Sade, and he kept criticizing everybody. I felt he was trying to cut us off from everyone, make me feel it's us two against the world."

"What sort of thing did he say?" Emily asked. "Maybe wanting to cut you off from the world on your anniversary was a kind of tribute."

"It wasn't," Clara said. "He was even trying to destroy the group for me. He said the audience looked gay enough for Jon."

There was a silence, and Clara struggled to hold back tears for the rest of the session.

"I've got to say it," Fern said. "All week, I've felt cut off and hostile and lonely. The only time I felt good was when Benny called. My husband is such a perfectionist. If his socks aren't folded just right, he has a fit. And if I do fold the socks, he goes wild when he comes home after work because I left the baby food in front of the seltzer bottles in the icebox. He thinks that's love—folding socks and rearranging seltzer bottles. And if I try to talk more, to communicate, he just becomes a washrag, or he shuts his eyes and calls me clutching, whining, clinging, domineering, and turns away from me."

"You're not getting into my old thing about sex being the only thing that counts in life, are you, Fern?" Dinah said.

"No, I want people to like me. That counts, too," Fern said.

"She just wants more sex, that's all that's wrong with Fern," Alvin said bitterly.

"You say that because you don't like women!" Fern shouted.

"Come off it, Alvin," Dinah said. "Maybe she's just getting it so beautifully she wants more."

"Maybe if you gave up folding his socks so carefully your husband would find the *real* you," Reuben said. "Perhaps you ought to start by trying to relate to all of us here. Go around. Give your real opinion of every one of us. No one will stop liking you."

"I can't," Fern said weakly. "I feel Alvin doesn't like me already. And even Leigh. When I asked him last week about his sex life, he wouldn't talk to me."

"You were perfectly right to ask me that question, Fern," Leigh said. "I didn't answer it for my own reasons. It had nothing to do with not liking you. You've got to realize that some-times other people, for their own reasons, can be wrong. Like your husband. Just because he's an analyst doesn't mean he's not an obsessive-compulsive about his socks."

"I'd like to mention something about being wrong," Dinah said. "Last week, after Group here, Reuben, I found myself screaming 'Cop out!' at Leigh when he got into a cab. Later, I realized why I was so angry. I wanted him to kiss me. That was all. But I had no right to shout at him like that. Everyone, after having made himself vulnerable in the group, has the right, when he leaves this room, to have that vulnerability respected."

"Fern, what did you mean by that remark, I don't like women?" Alvin asked quietly.

"You don't, Alvin," Fern said, smiling rather triumphantly. "I can tell."

"Shut up!" Max suddenly shouted. "I want everybody to shut up for a minute." There was a moment's silence, and Max leaned back and shook his head incredulously.

"Good for you, Maxie," Alvin mumbled. "It's nice to see you reacting to something. I'm glad you could express yourself."

Clara was still struggling not to cry, avoiding the gaze of everyone in the room.

"Clara, before I go on vacation, there's one thing I want to say to you," Reuben said. "You are not in this group to help Benny. You are here for yourself, and you'll both be better for it."

"Don't say anything," Clara said, bursting into sobs. "I don't want to *stay* in this group, and I'm leaving right now." She rushed out of the room. Benny followed.

"Anything nice you'd like to say to me, Doctor?" Dinah asked.

"I feel *I* was saying something, and I got cut off," Fern said, also crying. "I always feel cut off."

Alvin took Fern, and Clara and Benny, whom he found out-side in the lobby, not to Mayhew's but to a bar around the cor-ner, where, since Benny and Fern had been calling each other daily, Alvin's attention to Clara made a kind of symmetry.

WELL, WHAT DO YOU WANT US TO DO, LEIGH, JUST PUT OUR HANDS ON THE TABLE AND LEVITATE?: The next Monday's meet-ing was held at Emily's apartment, on Bleecker Street. The apartment was filled with books, hi-fi equipment, armatures, and easels, but there were no paintings on the walls. Emily had arranged nine chairs in a tight little circle, as though for a meeting of suspects in an Agatha Christie novel. One chair remained empty all evening; Max, it turned out, had dropped out of the group until Reuben's return from his vacation.

When Alvin arrived, he asked at once for an aspirin. He had been having terrible stomach cramps. "I don't know what it is—mental or physical," he told the group. "The other night, I was lying in bed with this broad, and Gloria called. I told her I had somebody with me, but after that I just couldn't make it. She was a nice broad, too, and I just had to tell her to go home. Nothing like that has ever happened to me before."

Everyone began to complain about Reuben, his absence, and his deafness.

Emily said that she had gone to see him before he left and he told her she felt abandoned as a little girl and that she needed someone to trust. "He said I could lean on him and depend on him at any time," Emily said. "Then I started to say something else, and he looked at his watch and said he was sorry, he had another patient coming in. I know he couldn't help it, but it was funny all the same."

Dinah said she was worried about Jonathan—that he might have got into trouble on account of Reuben's absence. Fern said that she felt hostile, and that her husband had offered to plead his cause before the group but that his own group had urged him to postpone it until Reuben returned. Clara accused Dinah of reticence about her childhood. Dinah obligingly recalled breaking a tooth, stealing pennies and getting caught, being sent out to buy a box of middle-size noodles and being rebuked because the noodles were a size less than middle-size, and bossing the other children on the block and, when the gang broke up, going with the boys.

"You were right that time a few weeks ago, Fern," Dinah said. "I was sort of class whore at eleven. Then I married at fifteen, and since then I've been in the adult, respectable world."

Alvin and Leigh looked extremely bored, and Fern remarked upon it. "We've heard all this before—Dinah's little-girl thing. She's not really working at all," Leigh said.

"Well, what do you want us to *do*, Leigh, just put our hands on the table and *levitate?*" Dinah said.

"If your parents have broken both your arms—" Leigh began.

"We know, Leigh," Benny said. "You don't try to forgive them, you try to learn to walk. But you know what? You used to say broken *legs*. Now you're saying arms. I think that must mean an improvement."

"I don't know whether I did this just to have something to tell the group," Emily said, and then she told a complicated story of having nearly slept with a friend of her father's.

"Did you want to sleep with him at all?" Dinah asked.

"Well, yes and no," Emily said.

"Then, why didn't you?" Dinah said. "Everyone sleeps with everyone these days."

Emily said she thought that if she managed to do nothing out of line for a while she would fall in love and live happily ever after. "If you see what I mean," she said.

"I see what you mean," Fern said. "I see that meanwhile your life is going by and you haven't got anything."

"And I'm afraid you're going to smother in your own loneliness," Dinah said. "You sure set it up for rejection."

"Look, Emily," Alvin said. "Before, when I asked you for an aspirin, you brought it, with a nice smile, and a minute ago, when I left my cigarette over there in an ashtray, you brought it over to me. Now, how come there isn't any *sofa* in this apartment? How come you got only these chairs?"

Clara suggested that Emily "go around."

Instead, Emily recounted a dream in which she was trapped in a brick house with her family while her mother unaccountably told a school principal that Emily had had an abortion. Emily had felt that her privacy was lost and had cried through the rest of the dream. "I woke up with a sentence in my mind," Emily said. "It was: I once had a million dollars, and there's not a bit of hope left in me now."

Leigh asked whether Emily had ever had an abortion.

Emily said no.

Fern said she thought her husband, the analyst, had become jealous of the group.

"Of course, he feels hurt," Dinah said. "I used to feel like a

fool going out every Monday night and finding my husband
sullen when I got home. Now I just feel self-sufficient."

Alvin said he was worried about Jonathan. "Last time I spoke
to him, he told me that he was staying away from the boys and
the junk, and that he was taking Antabuse for good measure,"
Alvin said. "I hope he hasn't screwed up again."

THE HOT LINE TO THE DEEP END: By the following Monday,
when the group met at Benny's and Clara's, Jonathan had still
not appeared, although there had been many telephone calls,
including calls to Jonathan, in the meantime.

"The group has really got to help me," Fern began. "I'm really getting manic. My husband and I have taken a house for the
summer, with another couple. Last weekend, we went out there,
and it was sheer hell. The other girl, Doreen, she's everything
I'm not—good figure, competent, everything just so. I know I'm
pretty sexy, but my husband's such a perfectionist, I can't tell
you. Doreen's what he really wants."

"How do you know?" Benny asked.

"He's already said he's tempted," Fern said. "But he says he's
not going to act upon it."

"My advice is let Doreen have him," Emily said. "He doesn't
sound very good to me."

"I had a dream," Dinah said. "In fact, two dreams. No, three.
In one, I was being held by Leigh, and it felt so good. My husband isn't the sort of man who cuddles, except when he's drunk,
and it felt so good and warm to be held by Leigh. And then
suddenly he evaporated. In the second dream, I was in bed with
a girl I've never met. All of a sudden, spotlights flashed across
the ceiling and the police arrived. We were very sorry to see
them come."

"When you dream you're in bed with a girl, that usually
means something else," Leigh said. "It doesn't represent a girl at
all."

"I know," Dinah said. "But we were certainly pretty excited.
Anyway, the third dream was that I was in a car driving down
the highway, very fast, when suddenly the car vanished and I
was steering the bare machine. I had to turn into a side street,
and when a policeman came and stopped me and gave me a
ticket I was very glad to see him."

"I think all the dreams are about Leigh," Benny said. "They're all illicit somehow, and that's adultery. The policeman is probably Reuben, or your father. Or just some symbol of conventional morality."

"Yes," Dinah said. "I think of myself as a pretty conventional person."

"I don't think of you that way at all," Fern said. Dinah thanked her.

Then Jonathan arrived, red in the face and extremely agitated. He delivered a two-hour monologue, in great detail, about boys he had picked up, amphetamines he had taken, sheer fear, and a sense of abandonment by Reuben. "What I really want right now is to sleep with Leigh," he said.

"Poor Leigh," Benny said. "You're really getting it from all sides tonight."

Leigh pulled out a steel nail file and set to work on his nails.

Emily asked whether Jonathan couldn't find his kicks in everyday life. "Maybe there are some normal highs you haven't tried yet," she said.

"I'm scared to death of Jon when he's like this," Dinah said. "I feel he has a great capacity for violence."

"Well, *I'm* not scared of him. I feel *furious* at him," Clara said. "For two solid *hours* he's been talking, and he hasn't related in any way to the group. Why don't you relate to us, Jon? How do you feel about me, for instance, right here and now?"

"You asked me, baby. And I'll let you know," Jonathan said. "But first I want to say something about this group. Whenever somebody has a problem, I can just predict the reaction every member is going to have. Somebody will point out that the person is full of *hostility* and *anxiety*, and then somebody really intuitive will ask whether it might—just might—have something to do with the person's feelings toward his parents. Well, I say the hell with that. It sounds like Reuben. If I had cancer, he'd think the most important thing was how I *felt* about it. We're all so deep in therapy we think every problem is brought on by a neurosis. That's a kind of psychoanalytic power fantasy. There are some reality problems that couldn't care less about hostility or anxiety. As for you, baby"—he turned to Clara—"I'd a hundred times rather be me than you. Drugs, gay world, and all. Because you're fat and ugly, and I at least have a lovely body. I realize you look that way because of your neurosis, but that's the way I feel. What I'm asking the group to do—and I realize I'm not asking it in the most endearing way—is just to keep me from drugging myself to death."

After half an hour more of this, everyone but Jonathan got up to leave. Jonathan, suddenly contrite, asked whether the group would forgive him and meet at his place the following Monday. "I won't do this again," he said. "Leigh? I promise."

Benny was clearly moved. "Maybe we ought to have an extra meeting on Thursday," he said. "Maybe a week between meetings when Reuben is away is just too long, for Jon and all of us."

The rest of the group, however, thought Monday would be soon enough.

The next day, there were many phone calls, and all the members sooner or later called Jonathan, who was practically incoherent. Finally, Jonathan's wife told Benny that Jonathan was in no condition to leave the apartment and that she was thinking of having him hospitalized. She dreaded the thought of committing him to Bellevue, she said, because he had been there before and he hated it. Benny suggested the group might help, and convened an extra meeting. ("Who hurts?" Dinah asked when he mentioned the extra meeting to her.) In the end, the meeting was held on Thursday afternoon at Jonathan's place, but only Leigh, Benny, Clara, and Emily were able to attend.

Jonathan was lolling on the sofa, alternately sound asleep and in a spastic half-waking state. His coloring was bluish green, and he had a dark-red welt under one eye. Jonathan's wife said that she did not know how much dope, or what kind, he had been taking, since he had lied to everyone about it, but that a bottle of Seconal had been emptied within the last two days. Clara, suddenly brisk and competent, reached into Jonathan's shirt pocket and pulled out a bottle of Doriden, which she recognized as a sleeping pill. She flushed the contents down the toilet. Then, accusing Jonathan of "putting on a good show" for the group, she tried to pour some hot coffee down his throat. It dribbled down his shirt. He mumbled, said, "Ow, ow," and rolled over onto the floor.

"Well, if he's really unconscious, we might as well have our own group meeting as though he weren't here," said Leigh, who was shaking. "I was feeling so anxious about getting married I was going to pick up a girl I know, around the corner from here. But now that I've seen this, I'm just going to play it as straight as I damn well can."

"Why do you look so upset?" Clara asked Emily. "I know it's not pretty to watch, and you have a special thing with Jonathan. But why don't you talk about it?"

"I don't know," Emily said, looking nearly as green as Jonathan. "Jon seems to define the deep end for me. I feel he's acting out for all of us. The rest of us have our little problems, but he seems to keep the hot line to the deep end open. I'm afraid he's going to die. I think we ought to call a doctor."

The group, after vainly calling several doctors (including Reuben's stand-in, who never returned the call), finally got Jonathan awake enough so that he checked himself into St. Vincent's Hospital. There his stomach was pumped, and it turned out that he had taken a near-fatal dose of a number of drugs. Jonathan stayed at the hospital only for a weekend's rest, however. He managed to return to work on Monday, and he participated eagerly in a flurry of phone calls that occupied the major portion of the day. It was decided that the meeting that evening should be held at Alvin's apartment, since Alvin was now having acute stomach pains and appeared to be the member most immediately in need of help. ("Where else in the city can you get eight people to come when you're in trouble?" Fern asked Benny on the telephone. In another call, Dinah said, "We could meet at my apartment, but the group sometimes uses language I don't think I could justify to my children.")

You're Not Unprecedented: The meeting at Alvin's, the last one before Reuben's return and Leigh's marriage, began with a virulent attack on Jonathan by Clara and Fern.

"I feel you were doing just what Reuben does to me," Clara said. "Making me take responsibility. I'm a responsible person in the world, but in the group I just can't cope. I'm not in therapy to cope. I'm here to get help, just like you are, Jon, and I don't think it's fair for you to become the group baby just because Reuben's away."

"If you're going to carry *on* like this, Jon, monopolizing and *wasting* everybody's *time*," Fern said, "you can just leave the group."

"Who are *you* telling to leave the group?" Alvin said. "Just say what your own feelings are, Fernie, and don't presume to speak for the rest of us. But, Jon, if it's still just to get attention, it's not going to work."

"I don't think it was to get attention," Emily said. "I think Jonathan really tried to kill himself." And then she said that a few nights before, when the only ex-junkie she knew invited her out for a cup of coffee, she wound up sleeping with him.

Dinah asked whether she had enjoyed it.

"Yes. Well, no, no, no. I was furious," Emily said. "When he went to sleep, I got so angry I took a shower, and then I went into the next room and made an awful lot of noise. At five, I went out and got the next day's edition of the *Times* and did the crossword puzzle. I wished I could put him away in a closet. He kept talking about love and the struggle, and I thought maybe he was right. In that kind of world, you might as well sleep with everyone who breathes down your neck on the subway."

"Jonathan, you looked close to tears when Emily was telling that story," Alvin said, stroking his mustache. "I think you knew she was really sleeping with you."

"I know," Jonathan said. "And I'm really touched, baby."

Dinah said she would like to have a drink, and everyone except Jonathan had a drink.

"I'm really mad at Max," Fern said, looking around the room. "It seems like the most hostile thing you can do is not come to the group."

Benny said that he had called Clara officious for being brisk with Jonathan at his apartment and she had become so depressed that he feared she would commit suicide. She had gone so far as to take the screen out of a window. Then she had suddenly turned to Benny and asked for help.

"What happened then?" Fern asked.

"Don't ask stupid questions," Alvin said. "They went to bed, that's what happened. Everyone seems to have gone to bed with somebody this week."

Leigh stretched his arms above his head and said that his

marriage would take place the following Sunday. Everyone congratulated him. He said that his lovemaking problem was solved. He had diagnosed his problem as "premarital anxiety," and was taking Thorazine.

Dinah said that one of her reasons for being in the group was that she feared her husband was going to die. He smoked and drank too much, and he coughed in his sleep. One night, he had drunk so much that in the dark he had mistaken his study for the bathroom and had tried to flush the toilet by pulling a lamp cord. When she had told this to Reuben, he had only laughed. "I don't know if my fear is justified or not," Dinah said. "It may not be a reality problem. But that's what I'm afraid of. And it's awful to realize that what I'm getting from the group is exactly what I came for. The feeling that if he does die I'll be perfectly able to carry on."

Emily suddenly confessed that she had left out something about her brick-house abortion dream. She had once thought herself pregnant and had started to arrange an abortion before realizing she wasn't pregnant after all.

"Why didn't you tell us at the time?" Benny asked.

"It seemed irrelevant," Emily said. "And I thought I'd already talked more than my share of the time."

"It's not irrelevant," Benny said. "How can you say it's irrelevant?"

"I had an abortion once, at eighteen," Dinah said.

"I might as well tell the truth of it," Emily said. "I had one, too."

"All right," Jonathan said. "Just for a change, I'd like to alter the script and talk about an ordinary neurotic problem I've got. The other night, I was lying in bed with my wife and I couldn't sleep. I got so damn angry that *she* could sleep I thought I'd go out of my mind. Then, I thought, O.K., buddy, there are probably three million other people in this city who can't sleep tonight, either. I thought, Jon old boy, you'll have to face it, *you're not unprecedented.* I can't tell you what it meant to me to say that to myself."

"That's wonderful, Jon," Emily said.

"I guess I'm the only one who's really hung up this week," Alvin said. "My nerves are shot, and my stomach is out to here.

And this time you know what I want to tell the group? It's me. It's not Gloria at all, although I'm always talking about Gloria. It's me—Alvin."

"And you know what's wrong with your stomach?" Jonathan said. "It's the new Alvin you're pregnant with."

"Aw, come off it, Jon," Alvin said. "Why don't you have a drink, like the rest of us. I've got an ulcer. No, the thing of it is, the whole business with Gloria is coming to an end. Last week, I was tired from the office, and Gloria and I passed a cake shop and she wanted to stop. I said, 'Gloria, I'm tired and hungry, and I don't like cake.' So she said, 'Al, you're selfish.' I said, 'Gloria, let's not work now. I'm *tired*.' So she kept calling me selfish. I'm still paying her *bills*, and she's calling me selfish."

"Paying her bills is selfish in a way," Benny said. "That way you keep her to yourself. You won't let her go."

"He doesn't want to let her go," Dinah said. "Can't you see he loves her?"

Everyone had another drink.

"Sometimes I feel there's so little emotion in the things we do," Dinah said. "Being in Group is separate—like a shipboard romance. I don't know why, of all the things we could say to each other here, we say the things we do. But the rest of the time it's as though we were living under glass."

"I'm leaving," said Alvin, suddenly distraught. "I can't take any more."

"But this is your apartment," Emily said.

"Then I'm going to bed," Alvin said. "I just can't *stand* it. Jon was working. You were working. Me, Dinah, everybody. Everybody's getting well. I just can't take any more."

Everyone left, a little drunkenly.

Dinah gave Leigh a ride home in her car. "Aren't we well enough now so you could start saying *nice* things to me again for a change?" she asked, smiling. "Before you get married, couldn't you say just one nice thing?"

Leigh kissed Dinah on the cheek and went off to get married.

There is no way of telling how the members of the Thursday Group—or, for that matter, the members of all the Monday, Tuesday, Wednesday, Thursday, Friday, and Saturday groups that now meet in the city—will fare in the future. However, it seems likely that if the theoretical underpinnings of traditional psychoanalysis continue to erode, if the results of such treatment continue to prove inconclusive, and if the question whether a science of mental equilibrium is possible or desirable in the first place is cast more and more into doubt, people will, in increasing numbers, seek out other people to talk with. That these others should at the outset be strangers and that the resulting conversations should be in some degree unstructured and absurdist is not surprising. An overinsistence on structure in a field in which so little is known is likely to be more absurdist still. At a recent meeting of the American Group Psychotherapy Association, for example, when one of the earliest proponents of group therapy was reading to his colleagues a learned paper on countertransference, an enormously loud, deep, and sustained moan arose from somewhere in the auditorium. Since, at an earlier meeting of another psychological association, several Pop artists had been invited to stage a Happening, everyone in the audience looked immediately upward to the chandeliers, expecting to see Robert Rauschenberg or perhaps Andy Warhol there. As it turned out, the moan had been of the sort that announces the onset of an epileptic seizure. A psychiatrist was having such a seizure in the front row. Another psychiatrist, who had been sitting beside him, kept repeating that he would have done something but that when his stricken colleague had first risen from his chair he had only appeared to be about to sneeze. The distinguished speaker on the podium had, throughout this commotion, continued imperturbably to read. Finally, he paused to ask whether anyone was listening. Several people shouted, "No!" The speaker then instructed four colleagues in the front row to carry the stricken psychiatrist from the room and to assist him. While this was being done, the speaker offered to reread the portion of the manuscript that, being something of a traditionalist, he was certain had brought on the seizure in the first place. The second reading passed without incident, and the whole matter was subsequently discussed in therapy groups composed of A.G.P.A. professionals.

In any case, the therapy group, in one form or another, has become a widespread phenomenon in American life. The soul session, in which civil-rights workers discussed their problems for hours or even days on end, has occupied a special place in the civil-rights movement. Turning on together is the form of group therapy that has the greatest appeal to members of the marijuana generation. Business brain-storming sessions are a group form of creative free association. And industrial conferences at which professional and personal grievances are aired may become as common as the self-criticism groups. A group in pursuit of its own happiness, seems, in any case, almost by definition, one of the more promising areas for the exercise of participatory democracy. From all sorts of quarters, there is evidence that, in the words of one believer in this form of therapy, group conversation itself can be a "special high." The National Institute of Mental Health has plans to start group-therapy programs all over the country, so that dropping into one's neighborhood group may become as common as going to the park or gymnasium for some physical exercise. When the special vocabularies of all the kinds of groups already in existence meet, when the phrases of hipsterism, brainstorming, political cadreism, pocket Freud, and Movement slang are brought together in a local consultation room, it may even be that some useful conclusions about the human condition—at least at a particular historical moment—will emerge.

# Letter from the Six-Day War

In the years since 1948, when Israel fought its war of independence against Egypt, Jordan, Syria, Lebanon, and Iraq, the Israeli government had to prepare for, among other undesirable contingencies, what the defense establishment referred to as Mikre Hakol (the Eventuality of Everybody)—a concerted attack upon Israel by all the Arab countries along its uneven, militarily and geographically unsound frontier. Until two weeks ago, the possibility of Mikre Hakol seemed quite remote. Then, by an incredible series of overlapping miscalculations by almost everyone involved in the Middle East, Israel was brought to the brink of annihilation, the United Nations—which, in a sense, had been born as a peacekeeping force in Palestine in 1949—was about to dissolve as even a useful forum over the same question in 1967, and the Soviet Union and United States narrowly missed a nuclear confrontation. The rapidity with which Israel won the war (for such a small country there could be, in fact, no such thing as winning slowly) seems to have bailed out the great powers and the U.N. (although a statement by French Foreign Minister Couve de Murville, on June 7th, to the effect that France had foreseen the satisfactory outcome of events was greeted with hoots in the French Assembly, and British Foreign Minister George Brown found it necessary to remark, on the same day, in Parliament, "I deplore this tendency to giggle whenever the United Nations' authority is mentioned").

The war for Israel was a costly one, brought on in part by the refusal of the Western nations, in a kind of displaced intellectual racism, to take any statements—including racist threats—made by the Arab nations seriously. Israel won, at great risk and with great sacrifice, alone. This time, it would not, for the sake of the good will of its friends (whose good faith had been tested and found wanting in events at the Gulf of Aqaba), subject itself to the same risks and sacrifices again. The victory would, with tact and statesmanship, lead to that cooperative revival of the Middle East which had always been one of the dreams of Zionism. Israel has much to offer the Arab states; and for Israel itself peace would mean an end to the strain of maintaining a constant posture of defense, of being forced to trade at a distance of thousands of miles instead of with its immediate and natural neighbors, and of being economically dependent on help from Jews in the Diaspora. But it is impossible to negotiate with someone who does not know where his own self-interest lies, and the radical regimes of Cairo and Damascus would have to negotiate reasonably, recognizing at last the existence of the Israeli state, or go.

It is also impossible to inhabit a geographical absurdity. The Gaza Strip, which leads like a boarding ramp into Israel along the southwest coast; the wedge of Jordan that protrudes into Israel from Jenin to the Dead Sea (and that made possible the shelling of Tel Aviv on Israel's west coast from a point well beyond its eastern border); the division of Jerusalem, which leaves its civilian population virtually indefensible; and the Syrian positions above Galilee, which made impossible any accommodation over water rights (and which made the shelling of Israeli settlements, farmers, and fishermen such a common occurrence that for nineteen years northern Israelis have referred to mortar fire as "Syrian rainfall")—in all these cases the boundaries would have to be redrawn. The Israelis would have to contribute to, and the Arab nations cooperate in, a resettlement of Arab refugees. But a simple (and, as recent events have proved, meaningless) guarantee by the United Nations would not do this time. All parties would have to work out the conditions under which they could live together and return from a twenty-year siege to their domestic concerns.

To this end, Israel did not settle for a simple military victory, as it had in the campaigns of 1948 and 1956. It persisted to the point of virtual annihilation of the Arab professional armies. The victory could bring—by force or by reason—stability in the Middle East. It could even, by preempting the news and capturing the popular imagination for a while, take some of the pressure off conflicts in other areas, notably Vietnam. The West, without risking a soldier—without even, in fact, honoring one of its firmest commitments—had shared in a resounding victory over a Russian-supported totalitarian regime. The balance of power, or even the idea of the balance of power, and the relationship of the great powers to the small had been altered in ways that have yet to be fully explored; the United States might have some new room, and Russia some new incentives, to negotiate. (The fact that the Russians should have been supporting the Arab countries at all was one of the historical ironies of the situation. The Arabs had originally opposed the establishment of a Jewish state in Palestine not out of anti-Jewish fanaticism but out of the Arab chieftains' reasoned fear of what effect the sight of prospering Socialist cooperatives might have on their feudal sheikhdoms and caliphates. Russia, expecting an ally, had been one of the first nations to recognize the State of Israel. Now the prospering immigrants found themselves viewed as colonialists, and the Arab regimes were using the arms of Moscow and some of the rhetoric of revolution.)

All this, of course, has been altered by the outcome of the Eventuality of Everybody. The speed and thoroughness with which this outcome was achieved make it seem in retrospect like a foregone conclusion. It was not. Even the fact that war should come, with anyone, in any form at all, at least so soon, did not seem, in the days preceding June 5th, anything like a certainty.

Thursday, June 1st: An American Jew of German descent who now makes his home in New York arrived at Lod Airport, in Tel Aviv, and got into a battered old taxi, which was already carrying a few passengers, for the ride to Jerusalem. His daughter was spending her junior year abroad at the Hebrew University, and he was going to try to persuade her to come home. He thought he recognized a pattern to events, and he was afraid. He had been merely depressed by previous violations of international guarantees to Israel—free passage through the Suez Canal, for example, or free access to the Old City of Jerusalem—but the blockade of the Strait of Tiran had made it impossible for him to sleep. While the great powers temporized and rationalized, he felt that a little country's territory and morale were being worn away. It reminded him exactly, he said, of the dismemberment of Czechoslovakia. Foreseeing, as he thought, its inevitable consequences, he wanted his daughter home. The taxi picked up several passengers along the road (which was nearly deserted but still lined with the carapaces of armored cars destroyed in 1948), and on the outskirts of Jerusalem the worried gentleman got out.

The city itself resembled, on that Thursday before the war, a sunny sparsely populated colony for the infirm. Even the taxi driver wore a leather glove concealing an artificial hand, and most of the pedestrians (there were few cars) were either old or lame or very young and scruffy and truant-looking. The King David Hotel was nearly empty, except for some journalists and a few indomitable tourists. Zvi Avrame, the large, middle-aged manager of the King David, engaged his guests in merry conversation, and new arrivals at the reception desk were offered rooms overlooking the Old City ("There you have the view") or overlooking the Y.M.C.A. on the Israeli side ("There it is more safe"). The entrance to the Y.M.C.A.—the scene of bitter fighting in 1948—was concealed by sandbags, but aside from these, and from the strange emptiness of the streets, Jerusalem had made no obvious preparations for a state of war. From some windows, the sound of radios tuned to Kol Yisroel, the Voice of

Israel, drifted over the city. Since the early stages of mobilization, Kol Yisroel had been broadcasting only Israeli songs, Hebrew news, and (recognizing that few Israelis over twenty-five speak the national language perfectly) two news programs each day in French, Rumanian, Yiddish, English, Hungarian, Russian, and Ladino. On Thursday, June 1st, Kol Yisroel announced in eight languages that the Mapai Party of Premier Levi Eshkol had at last formed an emergency Cabinet with the Gahal Party and with Ben Gurion's Rafi Party (although BiGi himself, as the Israelis call him, had remained aloof), and that the Rafi Party's General Moshe Dayan had been appointed Minister of Defense.

Friday, June 2nd, in Tel Aviv was listless and stiflingly dull. The city was uncrowded, but it seemed as though everyone might merely be taking a siesta. In fact, quite a number of people were off at the beaches and swimming pools. Several international journalists, having exhausted their color stories about a proud, encircled people unafraid in the face of overwhelming odds, or the economic impossibility of maintaining a civilian army on perpetual alert, were preparing to go home. It began to seem that even the appointment of Dayan had been only a bit of stage business in the little off-Hot Line theatrical productions to which the small nations seemed now to be reduced. It appeared that Nasser's production had all the angels, and that even *lack* of initiative had passed out of the hands of Israel to London, Paris, and Washington. The oppressive sense that nothing at all was going to happen created the feeling that access to the world's attention was being closed along with passage through the Gulf of Aqaba. Israel seemed about to drop out of the news.

At the Chaim Weizmann Institute, in Rehovoth, on Friday night, however, people seemed both more active and less sanguine than in Tel Aviv. The Orthodox rabbis in Jerusalem had announced that for the Army the obligations of the Sabbath were temporarily suspended, and some of the inhabitants of Rehovoth felt that war might begin the following morning. (The rabbis had earlier suspended their campaign against autopsies, and this sort of concession had led some people to expect war on every Sabbath since the beginning of the crisis.) The Weizmann Institute—whose cornerstone was laid to the sound of distant gunfire in 1946—has become over the years a kind of dream haven for pure science, an intellectual aerie amid green lawns, orange groves, and bougainvillaea between Jerusalem and Tel Aviv. Agricultural research at the Institute had contributed vitally to Israel's unprecedented programs for reclamation of the soil. Theoretical research in nuclear physics and chemistry had succeeded so well that scientists were turning their attention to newer fields, like high-energy physics and research with RNA. One of the country's crowning and yet most characteristic achievements, the Institute had for weeks been on an emergency footing. (For one thing, a prevailing myth among the Arab nations that an atomic bomb was housed there made it a prime target for enemy bombing.) Of forty-three men at work on constructing a new building for the Institute, forty had been called up into the Army. Those members of the scientific staff who had not been called up as soldiers or military advisers, or put to work on special scientific projects related to mobilization, were busy taping windows or wrapping up sensitive or explosive instruments against the threat of attack. The children of the community were taking first-aid courses. Research biologists who had taken medical degrees but never actually treated patients were setting up emergency clinics. Sandbags and supports for basement ceilings were being put up in all the buildings of the Institute. In addition to their other work, scientists with walkie-talkies strapped to their waists took part in patrolling the Institute's grounds at night.

War, of course, did not break out on Saturday morning. Instead, wives and children took advantage of the Sabbath to join their men for picnics at the front. In effect, the front in a country of Israel's size was everywhere. But border kibbutzim like Nir Yitzhak and Shalom Karem, at the edge of the Negev and the Gaza Strip, were particularly full of families reclining with picnic baskets under the trees near the webby, shapeless tents in which the soldiers had been living for two weeks. The station wagons parked by the side of the road, and the tanned, rangy aspect of the men, made it look as though there had been an unlikely suburban commute from Scarsdale to the land of Owen Wister. The men—masons from Beersheba, bank tellers from Haifa, curtain manufacturers from Tel Aviv—were all dressed in highly personal variations on the Army uniform. In an army where no officer may order his men to charge, but only to follow him, there is a great deal of informality. "Tell my mother I am beautiful in my uniform," a soldier helping the civilians of Nir Yitzhak to harvest peaches said to a visitor from home. But, without any actual battle eagerness, the general attitude seemed to be "What are they waiting for?" and "Let's get it over with."

On Saturday afternoon, in Tel Aviv, Moshe Dayan held a press conference in which he apologized for having nothing to announce. He answered every question urbanely, with a crooked smile, looking confident and slightly sinister. He remarked that he would be "glad and surprised" if a diplomatic solution to the blockade could be found, and, in answer to a question about disposing of Egypt once and for all, he said, "I don't think in war there is any such thing as 'once and for all.' I don't think 'once and for all' can be applied to war." Although Dayan had been able to infuse with all the drama of his person an interview that contained no news at all, the fact remained that there was no news and no clear way out, and that patience was wearing thin.

That evening at Rehovoth, some friends gathered for coffee in the living room of David Samuel, grandson of the first British High Commissioner for Palestine, and himself a professor of nuclear chemistry at the Institute. Three friends—Amos de Shalit, Michael Feldman, and Gideon Yekutieli—were professors there as well. One, Peter Hansen, was a young English research chemist, doing post-doctoral work at the Institute, who had chosen, for the duration of the crisis, against his embassy's advice, to stay. Hansen said he had read in a column by an English correspondent that if Dayan had not been appointed he would have been brought to power by a military coup. Everyone laughed. "How can they say a military coup?" said Mrs. Yekutieli. "When an entire country has been called into the Army, a military coup would be an election." There was a discussion of the restlessness of several men who had not been called up: a frogman, a paratrooper, and a middle-aged pilot. (The pilot subsequently offered his services as a crop duster.) Mrs. Samuel said that she thought an insufficiently hearty welcome was being accorded the volunteers who were coming into Israel from other countries to fight, to give blood, or to work. She felt there should at least be a poster to greet them at the airport. "It could be a tourist poster also," someone suggested. " 'See Israel While It Still Exists.' "

On Sunday, June 4th, a number of soldiers—a tenth of the

Army, according to some estimates—were given a day's leave, and several of the North African soldiers (sometimes referred to euphemistically as the Southern French) took advantage of their leave to return for a day to their families in the port of Elath. Elath seemed confident that war would not break out there. In the first place, people said, the port was now too strongly fortified, and, in the second, at the first sign of trouble the soldiers would blow up the neighboring port of Aqaba, Jordan's only outlet to the sea. In tents all along the beach, near the empty resort hotels, was the remnant of an international collection of waifs and strays with long hair and guitars whom one now finds in so many unlikely places, and who had long been making Elath a beatnik nomad's rendezvous. When they needed money, they presented themselves in the morning at a café called Leon's, where they were recruited to dig trenches or to work for a day in King Solomon's Mines. At night, they gathered in a discotheque called the Half Past Midnight (where there were also several African students who had been stranded in Elath when their passage home through the Gulf had been postponed by the blockade). Asked why the nomads had not taken the advice of their various embassies and left the port, a long-haired guitar player from Stuttgart looked up cheerfully and said, "*Was? Wenn es grad lustig wird?*" (Soldiers emplaning on a civilian flight from Elath to Tel Aviv were asked to check their guns in the cargo section.)

On Sunday night, at Rehovoth, the professors' wives were just completing their course in how to render assistance at the Kaplan Hospital if war should break out. The cement walls of the still uncompleted building in which they met were lined with stretchers and sawhorses to put the stretchers on. The women were issued forms, in duplicate, on which they could check off a doctor's diagnosis, and thereby save him the time of writing things down himself. The lecturer, normally a gynecologist, warned the women that even to a seasoned medical man a casualty of war looks different from any other sort of patient. After the first four hours, he assured them, they would get used to it. He reviewed the forms with them, the ways of ascertaining the wounded man's identity (the pockets of civilian casualties, who did not, of course, have dog tags, would have to be searched), and he went down the checklist for gravity of wounds—mild, medium, serious, mortal. There were several questions about the word "mortal." The doctor had used the wrong word in Hebrew —one meaning "mortal" in the sense of "human being." The matter was soon cleared up. One of the women crouched on the floor with her hands locked behind her head to show the position her daughter in kindergarten had been taught to adopt in case of bombing. " 'This is how the bunny sits,' she told me," the woman said. " 'See the bunny ears?' "

Late Sunday night, the Army informed the civilian guard at Rehovoth that they might let up on the security watch.

On Monday, June 5th: at 8 A.M. the air-raid sirens went off all over Israel, and everyone knew that the country was at war. In one of the bomb shelters at the Institute, five languages were being spoken, with absolute calm, by scientists, children, visitors, and maids. A few minutes later, the all clear sounded, and everyone went to work, as though it were an ordinary day. General Dayan's voice came over the radio, speaking to the troops and announcing that tank battles were taking place at that moment in the Negev. *"Attaque à l'aube,"* one of the scientists said as he walked to his laboratory. "That's good for us. It means that we've got the rising sun in the east behind us. In the Negev, the sun is pretty blinding."

At 10 A.M. Monday, in his office, Meyer Weisgal, the president of the Weizmann Institute, an important Zionist, a good friend of the late Chaim Weizmann, and one of the greatest fund-raisers of all time, was dictating—to his wife, Shirley— some telegrams to Americans, appealing for funds for war relief. Guns could be heard in the distance, planes were screaming overhead, and sirens, which the Weisgals ignored, went off from time to time. "Send them full-rate, Mrs. Weisgal," said Yaki, their chauffeur and handyman. "We're going to win this war." When Mr. Weisgal had finished dictating, the telegrams were taken into the next room for his secretary to type. As guns, planes, and sirens continued to sound (by this time, it was becoming nearly impossible to distinguish the alert from the all clear, so that half of Israel was undoubtedly going down into the shelters while the other half was coming out of them), Mr. Weisgal told a joke. A Jew, he said was walking down the street, crying bitterly. A friend approached and asked him what was the matter.

"You see," said the Jew, "I am an optimist."

"An optimist?" said the friend. "Then why are you crying?"

"So," said the Jew. "You think in these times it's so easy to be an optimist?"

Someone turned on the radio, where the code names of units designated for full mobilization were being read out: Alternating Current, Pleasant Shaving, Peace and Greetings, Electric Broiler, Bitter Rice, Silver Lining, Wedding March, Gates of Salvation. There were twenty-three in all, and buses were lining the main street of Rehovoth to pick up the men called to duty.

There were more thundering sounds, and Mrs. Weisgal said, "When I think of the casualties. When I think of the mothers." The siren went off again.

"Don't listen," Mr. Weisgal said, and instructed her to read him a letter that had arrived that morning. The letter, written five days before, was about the situation in Israel. " '. . . I was afflicted by a sense of absolute despair,' " Mrs. Weisgal read aloud, " 'which has since left me.' " Everyone laughed.

Toward eleven o'clock, a man with a helmet, a briefcase, and a civil-defense armband came in. "The news is good," he said.

"What do you mean?" Mrs. Weisgal asked.

"I can't say," he said, and left.

Toward afternoon, the sirens became fewer. In a taxi gathering hitchhikers on the route to Tel Aviv, someone, apparently American, said, "There is always the Sixth Fleet, in case something happens."

"My impression is that something has happened," an Israeli replied mildly.

A passenger suddenly announced in Yiddish that he had four sons at the front—he was not at liberty to reveal which front—and that since he himself had been a member of the Palmach, the commando unit of the pre-independence Army of Israel, he had written them that he hoped they would not give him cause to be ashamed of them. Three of them had been born after the war of 1948. *"Aber zie machen gut,"* he said firmly. *"Unzere kinder machen gut."*

Tel Aviv, on the first afternoon of the war, was not much changed, except that all windows had been taped in accordance with instructions delivered over Kol Yisroel. Word had come that several kibbutzim along the Gaza Strip were being shelled, that Ein Gev, near the Syrian frontier, was under fire, that Haifa and Jerusalem were being attacked, and that for some reason the resort of Nethanya and the Arab village of Safad were being bombed. People seemed most worried about the civilian population of Jerusalem. An English translation of Dayan's speech to the troops was broadcast, announcing that the Arabs were being supported from Kuwait to Algeria. "I need not tell you," he added, in brief remarks to the civilian population, "that we are a small people but a courageous one. . . ."

On Tuesday morning at five, in Tel Aviv, there was an air-raid alarm (it turned out to have been a mistake); there had been none during the night. Bus service to Jerusalem was almost normal, except that, on account of Israeli Army emplacements, buses had to make a detour of several kilometres through En Karem. On one bus, Kol Yisroel was audible, and, looking over into Jordan from the highway, one could see smoke rising from a town on Jordan's wedge into Israel and verify the report that Israeli troops were taking Latrun. Because Jerusalem had been shelled throughout the night (the Egyptian general, who, under the terms of the Hussein-Nasser pact, had been put in charge of Jordan's Army, had often in the past expressed his belief in the shelling of civilians, since it diverted troops to their defense), and was still being shelled by day, most of the population of the city was in shelters. Israeli troops were attacking gun emplacements in the Old City, taking care to observe the order to preserve the monuments of all faiths, if possible. The King David Hotel had incurred minor damage—a tree down, a few broken windows, some slight injuries to members of the staff, but Zvi Avrame, who had been called up, was now wearing a uniform and seemed enormously gratified.

In the streets outside, a few helmeted civilians and some restless little boys kept telling one another to walk close to the walls and to run across streets leading toward Jordan. From several directions, there was the sound of machine-gun and mortar fire. In the early afternoon, three journalists walked into the government press office and were received with cheers. Accredited to Jordan, they had been stationed in the Old City, unable to file copy, for several days. When the Israeli troops came, they had simply walked across into the New City to file their copy there. Then they walked back again. It was announced that General Dayan had had tea on Mount Scopus that morning.

Sometime in the course of Tuesday, an Army official called a meeting of intellectuals in an office in Tel Aviv. He had invited delegates from Rehovoth, from Technion, from the Academy, and from the Hebrew University in Jerusalem. (Because of the peculiar configuration of the shelling at that hour, the professors from Jerusalem were unable to attend.) He wanted to ask their advice on a number of questions, and to brief them on the progress of the war. The war was succeeding so far beyond the most optimistic expectations that there were problems that must be faced at once. The entire Egyptian Army had been mobilized at the front when the war began, but Israel had spent the tense waiting period retraining reserves and repairing machinery, and the Egyptian Air Force had been destroyed in the first hours of Monday morning. Apparently misled by the true reports over Kol Yisroel that many Israeli border settlements had been attacked, and by the false reports from the Voice of Thunder in Cairo that Beersheba had been taken and that Tel Aviv was in flames, King Hussein of Jordan—to the surprise and special regret of Israel—had entered the war by noon, and in the afternoon the Jordanian Air Force was destroyed as well. The Syrians, originally the country most rabidly committed to the immediate extermination of Israel, were apparently enraged by the reconciliation between Nasser and Hussein, whom Damascus was still determined to overthrow. Syria had entered the war by degrees throughout the day, and by nightfall the Syrian Air Force was destroyed.

Fighting was going well on the ground on all fronts, and the problem was where to stop. Hussein, it seemed, was powerless to forbid the shelling of Jerusalem by Jordanian troops under Egyptian command, so it would be necessary for the Israelis to take the Old City. (The Rockefeller Institute, containing the Dead Sea Scrolls, the Army spokesman announced, smiling ironically at the particular stir of interest that this aroused in his scholarly audience, had already been captured.) It was clear that Jerusalem could not be divided again. Would it be a good idea to announce plans to internationalize the Old City before it was completely in Israeli hands? There was another problem, he

went on: captured Egyptian documents, which had been translated only the night before, revealed that Nasser was far more
seriously committed to the destruction of Israelis as Jews, and
far more taken with the old Nazi programs, than had been supposed; plans, on the Nazi model, had been drawn up for the
time after Israel's defeat. The question was whether to release
these documents. What Israel wanted from this war, after all,
was a lasting peace with its Arab neighbors. The two primary
obstacles to this peace were the problems of Jerusalem and the
Arab refugees. These problems could be solved. What purpose
would be served in humiliating an already defeated Arab people
by revealing the plans its leader may have had for destroying
civilians? The question was discussed, inconclusively, for some
time.

Finally, the spokesman raised a question that had been puzzling the administration: What had happened to Egypt's mis-
siles? Were the ones shown so often on parade merely dummies?
He mentioned the other possibilities: mechanical failure, fear of
a mythical superweapon at Rehovoth, or pressure from Moscow
to avoid what would have been purely futile destruction of cities.
This led him to another matter: the Russians were not famous
for their loyalty to losers, and the Arabs had lost. Was there any
point in approaching the Russians now—or, at least, the Ruma-
nians, who had declared themselves in such moderate terms?
Several professors of Russian descent expressed themselves emo-
tionally on the prospect of a rapprochement with their native
land, but the others seemed skeptical. Certain questions, the
spokesman said, in concluding the discussion (several professors
present had to return to their laboratories or their military
units), would simply be resolved by events, but, he said, "We
will settle for nothing but peace this time."

In the blacked-out living room of Professor David Samuel, on
Tuesday, the second night of the war (which had ceased, after
its first few hours of uncertainty, to seem, except at the front,
anything like war in the movies), the members of the household
were gathered: Professor Samuel; his wife, Rinna; Tally, a girl of
eighteen, who had been studying for her baccalaureate examina-
tions; Yoram, a boy of fifteen, who had been compulsively vol-
unteering for every kind of service since the war broke out; and
Naomi, a girl of three, who had slept on Monday night in the

shelter, and who now went to bed making siren noises. Tally said that her English exam for the following morning had been cancelled—"obviously." And Yoram announced that not only had he been put in charge of any fractures that might occur if his school were bombed but he was being called out that night for courier duty. "Well, if you think I relish the idea . . ." his mother began, and then simply advised him to change his undershirt. At nine, Professor Samuel left on some errand about which no one asked, and which was to occupy him until morning.

Kol Yisroel reported, with the understatement that it was to display throughout the war, that fighting had now penetrated to the Egyptian side of the Sinai border. (In fact, Gaza had fallen, and soldiers were already beginning to find pairs and clusters of boots in the desert, which, they knew from the 1956 Sinai campaign, meant that the Egyptians were in barefoot rout.) The *Jerusalem Post* for the day, in mentioning the fact that casualties were beginning to come into Israeli hospitals, and that all of them were patient and brave, did not neglect to mention a soldier who, with one eye shot away and the other damaged, was as brave as the rest. He was a Jordanian legionnaire, the *Post* reported and he kept repeating the only Hebrew words he knew: "We are brothers. We are brothers."

Someone mentioned that a Hebrew idiom for Arabs is "cousins," or "sons of our uncle," and that although the connotation was slightly pejorative, it need not always be that way. Someone praised the bravery, in particular, of the Jordanian legionnaires.

"I really think the reason we fight better is because we have no hinterland," Yoram said. "We can't swim to America. We simply have nowhere else to go." He left through the blacked-out doorway and went into the moonlight, to begin his courier duty. "A perfect night for bombing," he said, looking into the clear sky. But there were no alarms at all that night.

On Wednesday morning, the casualties began pouring out of buses into the Kaplan Hospital, where the Rehovoth wives were waiting to work. Tally's class at school was called to help out, and Professor Samuel remarked as he drove her to the hospital, "I don't know what these girls are going to see there." The wounded were silent, and as each stretcher was brought in it was immediately surrounded by many volunteers of both sexes, solicitous of the comfort of the wounded man. It turned out that among those critically wounded on the previous day was the son of the gynecologist who had had difficulty with the word "mortal" three nights before. "For us, you know, the Army, it isn't an anonymous thing," someone remarked. "To us, everyone killed at the front is a tragedy."

By nightfall, Kol Yisroel reported that the Israelis had taken Sharm-el-Sheik, the shofar had long been blown at the Wailing Wall by the chief rabbi of the military, and Meyer Weisgal, sitting in his own darkened house with his wife and a group of friends, was contemplating the offers of help for the Institute he had received from patrons and scientists all over the world. Later still, Professor Samuel (doubtless like many other professors at the Institute, and like citizens all over Israel) put away a pistol, which had served him in former wars (he had been in four of them: in 1939, 1948, 1956, and 1967), and with which he had been prepared to defend his family—in that oasis of technology, in a nation of two and a half million—if the war had gone otherwise.

# Radicalism in Debacle:
# The Palmer House

THE NATIONAL NEW POLITICS
CONVENTION, which was held at the Palmer House in Chicago
over the Labor Day weekend, began as a call from the National
Conference for New Politics—an organization that has given
financial support to radical candidates in various elections since
early in 1966—for delegates from all radical and liberal groups
opposed to the American involvement in Vietnam to unite on a
course of political action for 1968. The convention presented,
from the first, a travesty of radical politics at work. In the quality
of its radical dissent, the no longer New Left—which had
seemed in its youth somewhere midway between the plain fri-
volity of a college prank and the struggle of a generation out of
apathy into social consciousness—now seemed a vulgar joke,
contributing as much to serious national concern with the problems of war, racism, and poverty as a mean drunk to the work-

ings of a fire brigade. Throughout the convention, delegates seemed constantly to emerge, wet-lipped and trembling, from some crowded elevator, some torrent of abuse, some marathon misrepresentation of fact, some pointless totalitarian maneuver, or some terminal sophistry to pronounce themselves "radicalized." Being "radicalized" had, among alumni of earlier New Left conventions, two possible meanings: voting against one's principles with an expression of Machiavellian deviousness, or discussing one's politics as a most interesting turn in one's personal psychology. Among novices, being "radicalized" meant having been persuaded of something by radicals.

One of the reasons for the complete disintegration of the New Politics was the convention's persistent debasement of language. The word "revolution," for example, was used for every nuance of dissent. There were the electoral revolutionaries, who meant to change American foreign policy simply by voting the present Administration out. And there were the moral revolutionaries, like Dr. Martin Luther King, who sought to bring about certain kinds of social change by the pressure of non-violent civil disobedience. Closer to violence were the therapeutic-activity revolutionaries, former members of S.D.S. (Students for a Democratic Society), F.S.M. (the Free Speech Movement), and Vietnam Summer, who seemed to find in ceaseless local organizing—around any issue or tactic demonstrably certain of failure—a kind of personal release, which effective social action might deny them; and the aesthetic-analogy revolutionaries, who discussed riots as though they were folk songs or pieces of local theatre, subject to appraisal in literary terms ("authentic," "beautiful"). There were the historical, after-them-us syllogist revolutionaries, who applauded all riots as pre-revolutionary, an incitement to right-wing repression, which would, in turn, inevitably—presumably as it did in prewar Germany—bring on popular revolution and lasting peace; and the amphetamine revolutionaries, who seem to regard uncontrollable, permanent upheaval, on the model of the Red Guard, as both a prescription for restoring personal vitality and the most vigorous expression of participatory democracy at work. Finally, there were some local criminals, who, despite the determination of the "radicalized" to view them as revolutionaries, pursued their isolated acts of mugging in the elevators and vandalism in the halls, and who, as a closing touch, stole three hundred dollars from the only people present who had defied a genuinely oppressive power structure at great risk and in the name of genuine new politics—the delegation of the Mississippi Freedom Democratic Party.

It was obvious that the only way all these "revolutionaries" could find common ground—the only way Steve Newman, of the (Maoist) Progressive Labor Party, could agree in any detail with, say, Dr. Benjamin Spock, of the baby book—was by jettisoning meaning from vocabulary. Within a short time, such a phrase as "bringing down the system" was used equally for the program of a citizen who sought to speed along by legal means the natural evolution of his country—which, he would readily concede, was already the noblest social experiment, on the largest scale, in history—and for the program of an arsonist committed to the country's literal destruction. When words are used so cheaply, experience becomes surreal; acts are unhinged from consequences and all sense of personal responsibility is lost. At the Palmer House, the word "genocide" began to be tossed about as though it could apply to acts of simple rudeness, and eventually speaker after speaker—from Arthur Waskow, of Washington's Institute for Policy Studies, in plenary session, to the Reverend William Sloane Coffin, Jr., Chaplain of Yale University, at table—could argue that a list of thirteen proposals submitted, along with an ultimatum, to the convention by what was called the Black Caucus should be endorsed without modification of any kind, regardless of the substance of the individual proposals, in a spirit of interracial unity. That this implied a paternalistic white racism that would startle a South African plantation owner seemed not to enter the minds of these speakers—or of the convention at large, which endorsed the list and delegated to the Black Caucus all authority for amending the proposals in the future.

The list ranged from an accusation that blacks had been systematically excluded from "the decision-making process" of the convention (one of the convention's two chairmen, Julian Bond, the Georgia assemblyman, was a Negro, as were its keynote speaker, Dr. Martin Luther King, nine of the twenty-five members of its Steering Committee, and six of the twenty-four members of its executive board; moreover, no actual "decision-making" had taken place before the adoption of the thirteen Black Caucus proposals), through a condemnation of "the imperialistic Zionist war" (the Black Caucus itself subsequently reversed this condemnation, so the convention found itself in the position of having both endorsed a proposal and pre-endorsed, carte blanche, so to speak, its reversal), to demands for the formation of "white civilizing committees" to deal with "the beast-like character" of "all white communities . . . as exemplified by George Lincoln Rockwells and Lyndon Baines Johnsons," for "immediate reparation for the historic physical, sexual, mental, and economic exploitation of black people," and for support of all resolutions passed by the Black Power Conference in Newark. No white person could in good faith endorse the substance of all the proposals. Certainly many of the white people at the convention knew the statement about decision-making to be false, and many did not know what the resolutions of the Newark Black Power Conference were, since no official list was ever issued and it is not certain that any was ever drawn up.

From the moment the ultimatum was accepted, the convention became a charade. To disregard substance in favor of a spirit of unity was to justify McCarthy's empty lists of names on account of the spirit of patriotism in which he waved them about. But the real white-racist presumption lay in thinking that a specious endorsement of inane proposals was an act of support for Negroes—or, for that matter, in thinking that most Negroes could endorse the resolutions either. From the beginning of the convention, the "radicalized" whites had resolutely refused to deal with any competent or intelligent Negroes—any rational Negroes, as it turned out—as authentic blacks. Non-failed non-whites were simply regarded as sell-outs to the system, and ignored. The effect of this was to produce what can only be described as a new, young, guerrilla-talking Uncle Tom, to transact nitty-gritty politics with his radical white counterpart. The assembled revolutionaries (whose voting strength was determined on the basis of the number of "activists" they cared to claim at home) selected such Negroes, on the model of H. Rap Brown, to speak for the romantic, rioting, "authentic" children of the ghetto (for "the ten thousand activists in Newark," as John F. Maher, Jr., of the Cambridge Vietnam Summer, put it, in a meeting, "who were willing to die to change their way of life"), for the Black Caucus, for all the other Negroes at the convention, and for the nameless, faceless, personalityless black monolith that the American Negro has now—in the white-radical racist imagination—become.

The tragedy is, of course, that no one speaks for the young rioters, since no leader has emerged from them yet; and Rap Brown seems merely to tag along rhetorically after them. The Black Caucus, which never consisted of more than fifty delegates, sometimes spoke for the majority of the Negro delegates to the convention and sometimes did not. Its composition changed often. It occasionally broke into groups or disbanded, and entry to it was often denied to some Negroes by goons at the door. By choosing to empower the Black Caucus to speak for the entire convention, the convention simultaneously abdicated in its favor and denied it respect. A radicalism whose one worthy aim had been "to give people more of a voice in the decisions that affect their lives" relinquished its own voice at once, and celebrated the birth of the New Politics by voting itself totalitarian.

Two days of pre-convention sessions—called, in the prospectus, "the pre-convention"—had started off quite differently, as a gentle convocation of kooks. The main factions of plotters and counter-plotters, traditional at New Left reunions, had not yet arrived to present their strategies. (The Socialist Workers Party, together with other Trotskyists, favored the establishment of a third party; in default of a permanent party, they were willing to settle for a temporary national ticket, with their own candidates for President and Vice-President. The "non-electoral local organizers"—like the S.D.S. and Vietnam Summer people who believe in organizing rent strikes, cooperatives, and demonstrations, rather than in the vote—came mainly for the purpose of blocking any national ticket and getting some money. The W. E. B. DuBois Clubs and the Communist Party would have liked a national ticket, but in order to preserve unity and avoid alienating the non-electoral bloc they were willing to settle for local organizing and the option for a national ticket later on. Their position corresponded closely with the one taken by Mrs. Donna Allen, of the Women Strike for Peace. The California delegation—which was also known as the New Politics group, because its position corresponded most closely with the original position of the National Conference—favored leaving each state free to have a national ticket if it wanted one, and possibly maintaining the Conference as a nationwide hookup for the various national tickets of the states. The likely candidates for President and Vice-President in California were, respectively, Simon Casady—co-chairman of the convention, and a former head of the California Democratic Council, deposed for his opposition to the war in Vietnam—and Robert Scheer, managing editor of *Ramparts* and a former candidate for Representative from California. In default of local options for locally chosen candidates, the California group was willing to settle for a national ticket chosen by the convention. Democratic Councilman Theodore Weiss, of Manhattan, together with other Democrats, favored working through the regular parties for candidates opposed to the war in Vietnam. In default of that, they were willing to settle for a national King-Spock ticket. A Chicagoan named Arthur Rubin was running for President himself; his platform consisted of an explanation of "the generally misunderstood film *Blow-Up*" and a map of the universe "available in a variety of versions." A group called the Student Mobilization Committee came to recruit demonstrators to immobilize the Pentagon on October 21st. And some young people came only to look for jobs with established radical organizations.)

Within hours after registration, on the Tuesday evening before Labor Day, other delegates, less firmly committed politically, were roaming the corridors of the Palmer House—a huge, ornate, labyrinthine hotel, with a basement arcade, a sub-basement arcade, gusty, arctic air-conditioning, and small, transient-looking rooms. The obvious intention of these delegates in coming early was to have truly sweeping reforms to offer for consideration when the convention began. Non-political guests at the hotel that Tuesday seemed to view the delegates with tolerant smiles, pointing them out in the lobby as "the student convention." (On Wednesday, the hotel closed the swimming pool "for repairs." By Thursday, the convention was being described bitterly as "those draft-card burners." Saturday morning, the lady clerks at the newsstand were worriedly insisting that the *New York Times* had not yet arrived: "I told you we shouldn't have opened early, Bea. Here's one of them just won't go away." But by Sunday—the day before the convention ended—things were fairly normal: players in a local bridge tournament regained their concentration, and Sandra Max and David Wasserman, two apparently apolitical Chicagoans, were married without incident in the Red Lacquer Ballroom, where a White Radical Caucus had met the night before.)

Wednesday morning, after a welcoming speech by Co-Chairman Simon Casady, a kindly, bewildered-looking gray-haired man, the preconvention delegates split into committees: one for Resolutions, one for Perspectives, and one for Structures. The Black Caucus, which has been a tradition of radical conventions since the early days of S.N.C.C. (the Student Nonviolent Coordinating Committee), was already in separate session. S.N.C.C. itself (sometimes referred to as the Non-Student Violent Disintegrating Committee) is now—except as a source of publicity measured in column inches detrimental to the cause of civil rights—to all intents and purposes, defunct. Somehow, it never quite recovered from the federal government's passage of the Civil Rights Act of 1964 and the white radicals' defection to the more fashionable causes of campus free speech and Vietnam protest. The Black Caucus, however, remains, as though to preserve in memory the idealistic, soul-searching band that S.N.C.C. once was.

The Structures Committee met on the third floor, in Private Dining Room 8—a tiny, dimly lit imitation-Romanesque chapel, featuring cloudy chandeliers, a false hearth, false timbers decorating the ceiling, old branching wall lamps, folding chairs, and a medieval bestiary, with false heraldic devices, painted on its walls. The committee spent the two days before the convention discussing whether it ought to present to the conference a proposal that the New Politics disband altogether and leave its delegates to their local organizing. (Many delegates, it turned out, had come to the convention committed to its dissolution.) The Perspectives Committee, which met in the Red Lacquer Ballroom, on the fourth floor, spent the pre-convention days deciding whether to propose to the convention that it endorse a permanent third party, that it choose a third-party ticket only for 1968, that it endorse no ticket or party or nationwide hookup of tickets, that it disband for non-electoral local organizing, or that it endorse a platform set up by a Subcommittee on Perspectives, which concerned Mexican-American relations, the Dominican intervention, the Greek regime, strip-mining in Appalachia, the inequities of the income tax, and a number of other issues over which there was considerable indignation.

The Committee on Resolutions, which met in the Wabash Parlor, on the third floor, was by far the most thorough and animated. Under the dual chairmanship of Steven Jonas, a bearded young man from New York's Medical Committee to End the War in Vietnam, and Bertram Garskof, a bearded psychology professor from Michigan State University (and a member of the convention's Steering Committee), the Committee on Resolutions immediately split into four subcommittees to revise the American political and social system from top to bottom. The four subcommittees all met in the same room, but each sent a courier to each of the others every fifteen minutes, to make sure there was no duplication of effort. By Wednesday noon, Resolutions had abolished the capitalist system. By evening, it had revised policy in detail, solved the problems of the cities, deplored alimony, and endorsed sexual freedom for citizens under twenty-one. ("We'll pick up votes on that when the youth reaches voting age," someone said approvingly. Jonas, normally the kindest of chairmen, looked reproachful. "I was hoping we were above winning votes," he said. "I hoped we were working on principles.") By Thursday morning, it had legalized marijuana, pronounced heroin medically harmless, established more humane old-age homes, and resolved that "if police agencies would do their jobs, organized crime can be smashed." (Garskof proposed that all white police be removed at once from black communities. "But there are understanding white cops," someone protested. "Then let them work in Scarsdale," Garskof replied.)

By Thursday afternoon, so many resolutions had been passed that the committee established a subcommittee to improve the literary style of all its previous resolutions. Then, perhaps dissatisfied because there was so little left to do, Garskof deplored the lack of black representation on the Steering Committee. Since he was on the Steering Committee himself and should have known better, it was odd that he should make such a complaint, but his beard—even in the context of new radicalism—was an eccentric one, running straight, dense, and furry back along the underside of his chin, never touching his jaws at all, and it is not unlikely that he was just trying to liven things up a little. Two resolutions were immediately passed: one expressing grief over the separatism of the Black Caucus, and the other deploring the lack of black representation on the Steering Committee. Martin Peretz, an instructor in government at Harvard and a member of the convention's executive board, objected. "You are trying to railroad chaos through this convention," he said, and he deplored the committee's "militant ignorance." (Later, Peretz said to Todd Gitlin, of Chicago's JOIN Community Union, that he resented the implication that the Steering Committee had been "coopted." "Don't let's get up tight about cooptation," Gitlin replied.)

In any case, more than half the Committee on Resolutions ultimately walked out, to form a Whites in Support of the Black Caucus Caucus, and what turned out to be the major preoccupation of the convention—attitudes toward the Black Caucus—was established. From then on, there was so much talk of caucuses of one sort or another—the White Radical Caucus, the White Revolutionary Caucus, the Radical Alternatives Caucus, the Poor People's Caucus, the Women Strike for Peace Caucus, the Mobilization Caucus, the Labor Caucus, the California Caucus, the Anti-King-Spock Caucus—that delegates seemed to be not so much discussing a New Politics as croaking mating calls to one another from adjoining lily pads. On Thursday evening, the Black Caucus itself consisted mainly of local Chicago teen-agers and Black Nationalists, who ordered (and charged to the convention) a lavish meal, and who advocated withdrawing from the New Politics Convention altogether, to join a Black People's Convention to be held on the other side of town. The Reverend Ralph Abernathy, of Dr. King's Southern Christian Leadership Conference, however, briefly entered the group with what he called "some of our folk," and persuaded the others to remain— for a while, at least—with the still nominally integrated New Politics Convention.

Thursday night, in Chicago's Coliseum, a large, ugly stone fortification on the South Side, the full convention met for the first time. Julian Bond, the convention's co-chairman, was introduced by the moderator, Ossie Davis, as "a black terror in tennis shoes." He spoke briefly and then left the Coliseum, and he took no further part in the convention. Dick Gregory delivered one of his less effective monologues, in an apparent attempt to unite the convention by offering an apologia for its more extreme elements

("Every Jew in America over thirty years old knows another Jew that hates niggers. Well, it's even, baby"). He remained with the convention another day and then left to march for open housing in Milwaukee. And Dr. King delivered his keynote speech, a long and, for him, rather flat peroration, in a tired voice. As he spoke, some local Negro teen-agers shouted threats and insults at him from the back of the room. Negro members of the audience tried to quiet them down, but within moments a few self-styled members of S.N.C.C. were charging through the crowd whispering "Make way for Rap Brown." (This never failed to produce an awed "Where? Where?" from whatever white radicals were nearby.)

The Reverend Andrew Young, of the Southern Christian Leadership Conference (a member of the convention's executive board), turned to a white liberal lawyer with whom he had worked on many campaigns in the South. "These cats don't know the country has taken a swing to the right," he said. "I wish the violence and riots had political significance, but they don't."

"They just have political consequences," the lawyer said.

"Yeah. All bad," the Reverend Mr. Young said. He left the convention that evening.

Some teen-agers marked a cardboard box "Contributions for Our Black Brothers in Prison," and laughed loudly whenever whites dropped money in it. Two photographers who attempted to take pictures of these transactions were threatened ("You gonna lose that camera"), and it was only the quiet appearance of Dick Gregory, who caught two boys in a rather firm, friendly grip around the neck from behind, that dispersed the teen-agers. "Why, here's Brother Dick Gregory," they said, and they walked away, laughing and slapping each other's palms.

Dr. King left the convention the following morning.

At the convention's first official plenary session, on Friday morning, at the Palmer House, Gary Weissman, the chairman of the plenary (he had been an officer of the National Student Association but had abandoned it for the S.D.S.), announced to the delegates, whom he addressed as "Brothers and Sisters," that "the purpose of this convention is to enable the delegates to do what they wish to do."

Arthur Waskow, of the Steering Committee, immediately introduced a motion for the democratization of the Steering Committee with "members of all regions and all caucuses, if they feel they are not represented."

Sidney Lens, of the Labor Caucus, said, "Brother Chairman, I would move that the proposal be amended to include on the Steering Committee fifty per cent of the black people, to represent the thousands and millions who for four hundred years . . ."

In one of the long speeches that ensued (there were references to "this convention, with all its beauty and power" and to "this Chicago palace, with the country looking on"), someone referred to Appalachia as being in "the South," and a delegate rose to denounce this symptom of insensitivity to the problems of Appalachia. Someone proposed an amendment to Lens' proposal, and he accepted it. The chairman pronounced this acceptance out of order. Lens disagreed. "Brother Chairman," he said, "I've been thirty years a labor bureaucrat, and if I don't know that I don't know anything."

Many delegates questioned whether the plenary should continue to meet unless the Black Caucus joined it.

Paul Booth, a former national secretary of S.D.S., rose and threatened, if the discussion went on much longer without a consensus, to move to table whatever motion was on the floor.

A Mrs. Warfield, a Negro woman from Rochester, rose to suggest that she lead a delegation to the Black Caucus, wherever it was currently being held, to express understanding of whatever its demands might currently be.

Someone denounced this proposal as out of order, but the chairman disagreed. "This body is free to be as parliamentary as it likes," he said.

"Perhaps we could use the old Steering Committee as adviser to the new Steering Committee," a delegate proposed, referring to the motion for more Negro representation on the Steering Committee.

"What is the criterion for being black?" someone asked. Since one of the delegates in the Black Caucus was Miss Grace Suzuki, this was not an altogether unreasonable question.

"It won't hurt the convention to send a delegation," Mrs. Warfield said, rather impatiently. "I'll be standing here, if anyone wants to approach me."

"I'll tell you who's black," another speaker began. "If you were with us in Detroit, if you were with us in Newark, and Watts, and Cincinnati . . ."

Mrs. Warfield began to lead her delegation—ten or eleven whites and four Negroes—out of the room.

The motion was put to a vote. "What will mean an aye vote and what will mean a no vote?" someone shouted. There was no answer.

The motion passed.

Someone proposed that the plenary adjourn until the Black Caucus had given its response to Mrs. Warfield, but the Chair ruled him out of order and shut off his microphone.

A delegate from Indiana rose to deplore the enlargement of the Steering Committee.

"You are debating a motion that has already passed—is that correct?" the chairman asked.

"That is correct," the delegate replied.

Mrs. Warfield's delegation never found the Black Caucus—or, rather, Mrs. Warfield left her delegation behind while she sought out all rooms that happened to have Negroes in them. "Don't discuss among yourselves," she said as she left. "There will only be so much confusion." The members of the delegation stayed on a staircase, adjuring one another not to talk, for fear of government agencies and the press. Mrs. Warfield returned to them briefly, to announce that she would continue her search. "Go back to the convention floor," she said. "Remember who you are—the committee to bring a black structure into this convention." Barry Jones, a Negro who had actually participated in the Black Caucus, kept repeating that the caucus had disbanded earlier in the day. The whites ignored him. "Darling, not in the presence of the press," a white woman said. Mr. Jones gave up.

Friday afternoon, in what had been described in the convention program as "a panel discussion of perspectives," a number of people delivered speeches. In the middle of a discourse by Manhattan Councilman Weiss, who argued, not altogether tastefully, that the regular Democratic Party might still give dissidents "a couple of shots at Lyndon Johnson—speaking figuratively, of course," Floyd McKissick, of CORE, preceded by five Negroes in a flying wedge, walked down an empty aisle to the platform. By the time Weiss had finished speaking, all the chairs on the platform were occupied, and he unceremoniously climbed off. McKissick, standing between two impassive, bearded, gum-chewing Negroes in fezzes and khaki jackets (one of whom performed a sort of ballet with his hands while McKissick was speaking), began his speech.

In the two years since the Mississippi March and the advent of the Black Power slogan, McKissick has tried to remain in touch with radicals and liberals alike, keeping his public utterances wild and his private influence moderate. It is a strange course to take, and the effort has told on him. His rhetoric veers back and forth from center to extreme. His head bobs and his voice climbs octaves. He blinks continuously. In describing the destruction wrought by Molotov cocktails, his words to the white man were "Hell, man. You made this problem. You clean it up." He spoke of "the twin brothers, capitalism and racism," and he referred to all Negroes who had risen to positions of national influence not as "blacks" but, contemptuously, as "Negroes." Then he remarked that no good could come to the black people from the New Politics Convention (he subsequently withdrew CORE from the Conference entirely), and invited all whites to attend the Black People's Convention that night instead. (Later, apparently under pressure from members of the Black Caucus, he revoked the invitation.) Preceded by the flying wedge, he left.

Robert Scheer then made a speech urging that the convention address itself to "the vicious nightmare" (boredom, wife hatred, alienation) of life in white America. Like many radicals, he managed to refer to the unarguable proposition that material affluence has not brought complete happiness, and to make the reference itself sound like an alternative offer. He seemed to imply that a revolution of the prosperous was imminent. Regarded by many as the Bobby Kennedy of the New Left (since the New Left thinks it bitterly opposes the real Bobby Kennedy), he was given a standing ovation. Another white radical, Robert Cook, formerly of the Yale S.D.S., now of the New Haven AIM (American Independent Movement), argued that whites should support Negro riots by diverting police to other areas during the looting and sniping in the ghetto. He was applauded also.

That night, the White Revolutionary Caucus (which consisted mainly of pale, thin, bespectacled women and pale, torpid men, making plans for guerrilla warfare) barred Negroes from its meeting; the White Radical Caucus (which consisted mainly of members of S.D.S., Vietnam Summer, and other local-project organizations) plotted to sway the convention from a national ticket, in order to use the Conference mainly as a servicing facility for the local organizers; and the Black Caucus—despite a last-minute plea from McKissick, who made a brief appearance there —voted to submit its thirteen proposals, along with an ultimatum stating that if they were not passed by noon of the following day the Black Caucus would leave the convention. All through the night, in an orgy of confession about their childhood feelings toward Negroes, the whites on the Steering Committee considered the ultimatum. Ivanhoe Donaldson, a Negro member of S.N.C.C., argued that since the blacks at the convention were the only radicals really "in motion," no real white radicals should balk at the letter of their demands. There was a great deal of soul-searching by whites. ("I have thirty years of working for civil rights," a white liberal said. "At least, nobody can take that away from me." Whereupon, with some dime-store analysis of his motives, they took it away from him.) Martin Peretz walked out. The steering Committee voted to submit the ultimatum to a "special plenary," to be called the following morning, and by dawn most of its members were ready to pronounce themselves "radicalized."

Casady announced to a crowded Grand Ballroom on Saturday morning that a session's declaring itself a plenary did not make it so and that he could not participate in an extra-legal plenary. Then he too walked out. (His walkout, with Peretz's of the preceding night, initiated a kind of daily ritual; the few responsible whites at the convention often found themselves walking out, only to walk right back in, and out again.) The front center section of the plenary was roped off and reserved for members of the Black Caucus, creating the impression that if only someone had thought to rope off the back of the buses in Birmingham and shout "Black Power!" the civil-rights movement would never have been necessary. Gary Weissman, who again presided, let the gathering "formally, duly convene itself as a plenary," and thereafter granted what he called "the indulgence of the Chair" to all deviations from parliamentary procedure that were favorable to the ultimatum. A woman who pointed out that one of the resolutions endorsed "wars of liberation," though many at the convention were pacifists, was ruled out of order. Several members of the Steering Committee, in the first of what became a series of conspiratorial jags, spoke in favor of accepting the ultimatum. The white radicals argued that the thirteen proposals should be accepted, regardless of their content, which was pronounced "irrelevant." (White radicals were constantly consigning matters, and people, of substance to some limbo of irrelevance.) Sidney Lens, representing the Labor Caucus, favoured "not proposing to split words or commas or periods." Everyone seemed determined to foster a black illusion that the only whites interested in political cooperation were those who would accept terms of complete capitulation. Robert Scheer, who got up to make a motion to go the "Zionist imperialism" resolution one better, was inadvertently shouted down. In a heated interchange with the chairman, Charles Samson, who at that point was spokesman for the Black Caucus, denied Scheer's right to speak at all. "All of a sudden this person pops up," Samson said, pointing at Scheer in absolute outrage, "and he wants to make an amendment." Several Negroes who wished to speak against the adoption of the proposals were hustled from the room by enforcers from the Black Caucus, and threatened and silenced outside. One of the enforcers who ushered several Negroes out was an African Nationalist from California who was rumored to be the United Nations Ambassador from Tanzania. The ultimatum was accepted, three to one, and the plenary closed after the chairman proposed, and declared adopted by acclamation, a resolution to send a congratulatory telegram to Ho Chi Minh on the occasion of the twenty-second anniversary of Vietnamese independence.

That afternoon, the White Radical Caucus was troubled. Its coup against a third ticket and in favor of local organizing had never got off the ground, and, as one member after another pointed out, the Israel resolution would scare off liberal money, and the bad press that the morning's developments would receive might scare off everyone else. No one mentioned the possibility that the resolutions might be substantively wrong—only the possibility that they might alienate support. Several members of the caucus proposed that the white local organizers withdraw from the convention and form an organization of their own. Todd Gitlin pointed out that "the convention might still rise from its ash," that, in any case, most members of the White Radical Caucus had voted for the resolutions, and that it might be worthwhile staying around to "neutralize" the convention. Eric Mann, a white organizer from Newark, and one of the few radicals present who never cast a disingenuous vote, suggested that the organizers remain at the convention to paralyze it by keeping the others from endorsing a national ticket and "from doing all the screwy things they want to do."

Saturday evening, the plenary voted down the proposal to form a permanent third party. Again, a delegate proposed that the plenary adjourn until the Black Caucus, which had again withdrawn into itself, was present, but his proposal was not accepted. The Black Caucus itself was in a state of shock. The advocates of withdrawal from the convention, who had rammed the thirteen proposals through the caucus in the first place, had been certain that the plenary would turn the proposals down, leaving the blacks with an excuse to move to the Black People's Convention on the other side of town. Now they walked out anyway, leaving the Black Caucus to the moderates. Claude Lightfoot, of the Communist Party (rated as moderate by the radical left), and several members of the Du Bois Clubs, also Communist, soon took over, to give the Black Caucus some direction.

The White Radical Caucus, meanwhile, was in session on another floor, still plotting whether to sway the convention from the idea of putting up even a temporary third ticket or to leave the convention. Theodore Steege, a white member of the Ann Arbor S.D.S., announced that the Black Caucus had come to a new conclusion: Since the white delegates had been willing to accept the Black Caucus ultimatum, the Black Caucus knew that it was not dealing with real radicals; it would therefore either withdraw from the convention or consider supporting a third-ticket proposal and withdrawing support from the local organizers. The only Negro present—who later turned out not to have been a participant in the convention at all—shouted from the back of the room that this information was false. His word was accepted. A delegate from the Third Ticket Caucus appeared before the White Radical Caucus to offer what came to be known as the California Compromise. The California people, mainly the staff of *Ramparts*, wanted to be free to put up a ticket of their own, and the proposed compromise was for all states to be free to put up local and national third tickets if they liked, but for the convention to go on record as mainly supporting non-electoral organizing. The White Radical Caucus adopted the California Compromise.

The delegates at Saturday night's plenary, however, did not understand the California Compromise. In fact, most of them had never heard of it. A little old woman got up to say that she never liked to make an important decision without "sleeping and praying," that she disapproved of all the "intrigue," and that she hoped no vote would be taken before morning. She was applauded. A hippie wearing a headband and a card reading "Free"—one of two hippies who showed up at the convention—tried to speak and was denied the microphone. Before the California Compromise could be introduced, a vote was taken and the third ticket was defeated by two votes. A Negro appeared and announced that the Black Caucus was once again being excluded from the decision-making process and that it would announce the method of its participation in the morning. A motion to postpone all decisions until then was defeated. Delegates from the White Radical Caucus and the Third Ticket Caucus agreed privately to reintroduce the California Compromise the following day.

Sunday afternoon, Rap Brown was scheduled to speak to the plenary, but, at the insistence of James Forman, who was once the executive secretary of S.N.C.C. and is now its international-affairs director, he agreed to speak to the Black Caucus instead. Forman, however, addressed the plenary session—originally announced as a Black Liberation Panel—for several hours, in the course of which he "passed" whatever resolutions he chose (although it was not a voting plenary); denied the microphone to anyone else; declared himself "dictator" at one point and then, when Peretz and some other whites at last walked out, dismissed the whole thing, rather unconvincingly, as a joke; and made a proposal that both calumnied the genuine plight of the poor and may puzzle genuine revolutionaries in other countries for years to come. As an act of revolution, he suggested a boycott of 1968 General Motors cars. He was given several standing ovations, and by the end of his harangue most people present agreed with the amphetamine radicals that although he might not have said anything either true or important, he had "really turned them on." (Bertram Garskof declared himself honored, at this point, to be part of "the white tail on the real movement.")

In the late afternoon, before the evening plenary, the Black Caucus made its new demands known: the plenary was to be regarded as merely another committee of the convention, and the Black Caucus was to be granted fifty per cent of the total convention vote. The White Radicals, who had been thinking of nothing but their conspiratorial compromise, were bewildered. Only one of them, in their caucus, spoke against the new demands. "I know it's all irrelevant and meaningless," David Simpson, of the University of Georgia S.D.S., said. "I'm just not going to vote for it, because it's such a sick thing. I just don't want to be part of such a sick thing."

In the California group, Simon Casady said to Warren Hinckle, executive editor of *Ramparts,* "I guess what they're asking is to let them hold our wallet, and we might as well let them."

"Especially since there's nothing in it," Hinckle said.

At the Third Party Caucus, rhetoric had lapsed into the style of another age. "We have preserved the unity of this convention," a delegate of the Socialist Workers Party was saying, "to present an alternative to the American people." "Hear! Hear!" the delegates replied.

At that evening's plenary, where the Black Caucus demand for half the convention's vote was introduced, Communist Party and Du Bois Club members rose one after another to endorse "our black brothers'" position. What had happened, it turned out, was that while the white radicals were planning their local-organizing coup, and then settling for the California Compromise, the Communist Party and the Du Bois Clubs had temporarily, for whatever it might be worth to them, taken over the Black Caucus, and, through it, the entire convention—an achievement roughly comparable to embezzling a sieveful of smog. By inducing the Black Caucus to make the demand at all, the Communists had turned blacks against whites: if the white radicals voted for it, they lost their power over any further decisions of the New Politics (including the power to paralyze a third ticket); if against, they lost Negro cooperation. "Radicalized," they voted for. ("Masochistic fascists," the Reverend James Bevel, a Negro veteran of innumerable civil-rights campaigns, called them later on.) In the plenary, any Negro who walked up to a microphone to speak—even *for* the new demand —was approached by two tall young members of the Black Caucus and persuaded to sit down again. The demand was accepted, and a pink card representing half the convention's votes was given to Carlos Russell, a poverty worker from Brooklyn, who was now the Black Caucus chairman.

From this moment on, the Black Caucus showed itself to be more intelligent, more sensible, and more independent than any other group at the convention, and than the convention as a whole. To begin with, after a unity speech by Russell, the Black Caucus adjourned the plenary. Then, as white petitioners from the White Radical Caucus, the Third Ticket Caucus, the newly formed Israel Caucus, and even the pre-convention Resolutions Committee and the Progressive Labor Party cooled their heels in an anteroom, and delegates from SANE and Women Strike for Peace (who had either abstained or voted for) wandered about in the ranks of the "radicalized," the Black Caucus—in a surge of good feeling—let any Negro in who cared to come. As a result, the Black Caucus may have had the first genuine discussion of the entire convention. When William Higgs, a white associate of the radical National Lawyers Guild, who was out in the corridor, cast about in his mind for the name of some Negro he might know inside the caucus, and finally succeeded in summoning one —a woman delegate from the Mississippi Freedom Democratic Party—he failed to persuade her that a national third ticket would really help her much in Mississippi. ("I see what you mean, Bill," she said when she came out into the hall, "but I can't help thinking I need all the energy I got for the local issues.") And Steve Newman, of the Progressive Labor Party, who now threw in his lot with the local organizers, and against the conservative, third-ticket-strategy Communists (since Maoists believe in revolution by non-electoral means), never got a chance to talk to anyone at all. By the time the plenary reconvened, at midnight, the Black Caucus had endorsed a proposal by the Communist Party's Claude Lightfoot: local organizing, with a third-ticket decision to be deferred. But, in another surge of fellow-feeling, the spokesman for the Black Caucus—having heard the

White Radical Caucus's point of view through an intermediary, Ivanhoe Donaldson—phrased his proposal as though it were the California Compromise. No one protested. Everyone was baffled. And it passed.

Monday morning, Arthur Waskow, of the Institute for Policy Studies and of the Steering Committee, tried to dissuade a woman from the Women's Rights Caucus from introducing a proposal that women be granted fifty-one per cent of the vote at the plenary. "You're not thinking politically," he said. "It will sound like a joke. A parody. I think you're completely insensitive to the politics of this convention." The White Radical Caucus was in session once again. Eric Mann said he thought that they would have to reckon with the possibility that most of the money except the Communist Party money would now withdraw from the Conference but that there was no point in being too fussy about where money for local organizing was coming from. In the two half-black, half-white committees—one for organizing, one for the third ticket—that would be set up in that afternoon's plenary, he went on, Scheer's people could be counted on to see to it that the Communist Party did not run away with the third ticket. And the white half of the local organizers could be turned into a white S.N.C.C.

Then the plotting began again, in the intimate, nearly inaudible voices that are part of the white-radical mystique: "people already in motion," "implement specific programs at the local level," "relate," "in that bag," "where they're at," "doing their thing," "power structure," "coalesce with," "crystal-clear," "relevant," "beautiful." It seemed that some awful rhetorical cycle was coming to a close. A radical movement born out of a corruption of the vocabulary of civil rights—preempting the terms that belonged to a truly oppressed minority and applying them to the situation of some bored children committed to choosing what intellectual morsels they liked from the buffet of life at a middle-class educational institution in California—now luxuriated in the cool political vocabulary, while the urban civil-rights movement, having nearly abandoned its access to the power structure, thrashed about in local paroxysms of self-destruction. Both had become so simplistically opposed to order of any kind that society may become simplistic and repressive in dealing with them. There just may be no romance in moving forward at the pace that keeping two ideas in one's head at the same time implies; at least, there have been no heroes of the radical center yet. But the New Politics, black and white, seems to have turned from a political or moral force into an incendiary spectacle, a sterile, mindless, violence-enamoured form of play. In the final plenary, the Black Caucus, in addition to reversing its Israel resolution, managed to pass a few resolutions opposing Vietnam and the draft, and to appoint the two committees to recommend things for the New Politics—if there should be any—to do in the future.